How Children Learn
to Learn Language

How Children Learn to Learn Language

LORRAINE McCUNE

OXFORD
UNIVERSITY PRESS
2008

OXFORD
UNIVERSITY PRESS

Oxford University Press, Inc., publishes works that further
Oxford University's objective of excellence
in research, scholarship, and education.

Oxford   New York
Auckland   Cape Town   Dar es Salaam   Hong Kong   Karachi
Kuala Lumpur   Madrid   Melbourne   Mexico City   Nairobi
New Delhi   Shanghai   Taipei   Toronto

With offices in
Argentina   Austria   Brazil   Chile   Czech Republic   France   Greece
Guatemala   Hungary   Italy   Japan   Poland   Portugal   Singapore
South Korea   Switzerland   Thailand   Turkey   Ukraine   Vietnam

Published by Oxford University Press, Inc.
198 Madison Avenue, New York, New York 10016

www.oup.com

Oxford is a registered trademark of Oxford University Press

Library of Congress Cataloging-in-Publication Data
McCune, Lorraine.
How children learn to learn language / Lorraine McCune.
p. cm.
Includes bibliographical references.
ISBN 978-0-19-517787-9
1. Language acquisition.
I. Title.
P118.M3144 2007
401.93—dc22

3 5 7 9 8 6 4 2
Printed in the United States of America
on acid-free paper

In loving memory of my brother,
Brian Patrick Maloney,
humanist and writer.
His early language inspired my interest.
His life continues to inspire mine.

Acknowledgments

I owe great thanks to Marilyn Vihman, with whom I collaborated closely in developing our understanding of the transition into language. Joint papers published in 1994, 1996, and 2001 were the product of long-term theoretical discussions that took on a hermeneutical flavor as we recognized the difficulties of defining what we meant by *word* and what were the best ways to measure aspects of children's emerging language and the behaviors that contributed to that emergence. Without her deep understanding of child phonology and children's ways of producing and perceiving the sounds of language and her wonderful skill in conceptualizing issues of importance the findings presented here could not have been achieved.

I am also indebted to the many reviewers who offered their help throughout the publication process but most specifically to Adele Abrahamsen, who read the completed manuscript in draft form and understood everything I was trying to convey. Her understanding and detailed advice on how to say it all in the best possible way improved the quality of the manuscript enormously. Her deep knowledge of linguistics, language development, dynamic systems theory, and manual as well as vocal means of communication broadened my perspective considerably. My editor, Catharine Carlin, was a continuing guide and source of support. Thanks are due to Stefano Imbert for creative work on the figures.

I had the advantage, early in my career, of studying with Lois Bloom in her seminar group. While I cannot claim the honor of being one of her own Teacher's College students, the entire book reflects the perspective she engendered and the influence of her thinking and her results on my own development as a student of child language.

Dr. Jane Beasley Raph, my dissertation advisor, now retired from the Rutgers Graduate School of Education, provided the nurturing opportunity for me to develop my own research style, and her efforts are still reflected in this manuscript, written many years later.

My husband, parents, children, and grandchildren never admitted to being tired of hearing that I was "almost finished" with my book and maintained their faith that something good would eventually emerge.

Contents

How Children Learn
to Learn Language

1

A Perspective

This book is about how children become language learners, progressing from wordlessness to their first word combinations. Children come to express word meanings they have learned from adults. But what is the source of a child's ability to experience internal meaning and express such meaning with language? MacNamara (1982) proposed that children's private meaningful experience might form the foundation for the development of linguistic reference but found no mechanism for this transition and so assumed that referring is innate. In this book I propose such a mechanism and provide initial data in support of it. The theory of language acquisition presented here emerged against the backdrop of broader developmental theories and, more specifically, from careful naturalistic observation of children as they interact with their parents. My most prominent influences have been Werner (Werner & Kaplan, 1963/1984), Piaget (1962), Thelen (1989) and, more recently, Johnson (1987). Werner and Kaplan's (1963) *Symbol Formation* is still prominently cited in developmental publications (e.g., Nalmy, 2005) but rarely forms the substantive basis for investigation. Glick (1992) described Werner's thought as radically ahead of his time and idiosyncratic in vocabulary; hence his work has been unrecognized in modern developmental psychology.

Piaget provides the counterpoint rather than the foundation in many contemporary developmental studies, although his basic approach remains the most prominent and effective framework for developmental questions of cognition. Thelen's dynamic systems approach continues to expand in influence, but her radical antirepresentational stance is not often acknowledged (e.g., Thelen & Smith, 1994, pp. 331–38). Johnson's view of the emergence of meaning through schematic processes has gained continued prominence due to adaptation by Mandler (e.g., 2004) but his deep views regarding "the central role of imagination in all meaning, understanding, and reasoning" (Johnson, 1987, p. ix) and the basis of meaning as grounded in embodiment (ongoing bodily experience as an early and continuing influence on thought) have not been integrated with mainstream developmental or cognitive science. In addressing children's learning to learn language, I call upon the interacting influence of these theories.

Imagination might be considered a unifying theme of my theoretical framework; not imagination as flights of fancy but as the function of mind that can link the present to the past and to the counterfactual. Piaget emphasized the internal logic of cognition; but—for the child to move from a logic of action to a logic of thought—he recognized the developmental task of internalizing meaning and action. Levels of representational play, first observed in his own children, proved to be guideposts to this critical development. In my work I consider "mental representation" as the description of a conscious state that includes the potential of mentally experiencing non-present reality. Sartre (1948) offered the example of viewing the portrait of a friend to evoke thoughts of the friend (an imaginal experience involving mental representation) in contrast with viewing the portrait for its pictorial values (e.g., color, symmetry—a perceptual experience). In the representational mode the subject establishes a relationship between one element (in this case the portrait) and another (thoughts of the absent friend). So the former comes to symbolize the latter. I consider mental representation as a developmental phenomenon, which is not available immediately to infants (Piaget, 1962; Werner & Kaplan, 1963).

Following Searle (1992), I consider children's language and other behaviors as aspects of their ongoing conscious experience. In order to consider how children might come to the realization that their vocalizations can express their internal experience as symbol to symbolized, it is essential to consider what that internal experience might be like, and to seek evidence in their behavior for developmental changes in the quality of that experience. In *The transition from infancy to language,* Bloom (1993) introduced the idea of *intentionality* from philosophy to the field of child language, where it refers to a focused mental state, asserting the necessity for considering the mental states of infants. By her definition, "*Consciousness* is the wakeful state of mind for alert attention and awareness; it consists of ordinary thinking that determines ordinary activity in ordinary events." (p. 18, italics in the original). Her position, more fully presented in Bloom & Tinker (2001) is that "What a child has in mind—the child's intentional state—at any particular moment of time—is expressed by the child's actions and interactions and interpreted from others' expressions, and it is these acts of expression and interpretation that determine development." (p. 5).

Searle (1992) detailed an approach to variation in the qualities of consciousness applicable to analyzing developmental change in children's activities. Every conscious state has a focus experienced in relation to peripheral aspects, against a background of knowledge that is not conscious at that moment, and a feeling tone. To take an example concerning children's play, an eight-month-old who encounters a toy comb and a nesting cup, one after the other, among a set of toys is likely to submit both to the same examination strategies. The first strategy is likely to be mouthing; then holding the object for careful visual examination, turning and shifting it from hand to hand, before mouthing again. Comb and cup are treated similarly. In each case the child's focus is on exploratory activities, while specific characteristics of the object may be experienced peripherally. By twelve months it is more likely that the comb, after a quick look, will be briefly passed over the child's hair, then set aside; the nesting cup, perhaps examined by inserting a hand into the concave space, then brought quickly to the lips, as if for drinking, then also set aside. In this latter case the focus is on properties and meaning of the specific object, with action subordinated to that meaning. A pleasurable affective tone might characterize both sorts of activities.

This example exposes the critical distinction between perceptual experience and the earliest mental representation that can be documented in play. The eight-month-old exemplifies perceptual experience. Nothing in her behavior suggests a mental focus going beyond the present. The twelve-month-old's treatment of comb and cup as previously experienced meaningful objects provides evidence of her linking this present encounter with the past, beginning to experience a consciousness beyond the here-and-now, moving toward *mental representation.* This approach to analysis aids understanding of children's meaningful experiences as these change with development.

The term *mental representation* or *representation* in psychology is currently applied more commonly to elements presumed to exist in the physiology of the brain or to characterize aspects of its function, under the assumed view that the mind is, at least by analogy, a computer program. Thelen and Smith (2005) consider this view representation in "the strong traditional sense ... [e.g.,] Newell, Shaw, and Simon's (1958) physical symbol system: internally represented propositions that operate as symbols (with a syntax and a semantics) *within* a computational system" (p. 206). Rejecting this view, they characterize less rigid relationships between recurrent internal events and behavior, as "representation-like," asserting that any theory of cognition recognizes some such regularity between recurrent internal events and behavior. Mental representation defined in this book as an intentional state or mode of conscious experience must be distinguished from representation defined as a neurological substrate of experience.

I agree with Thelen and Smith (2005) that the "representation-like" neurological processes underlying all behaviors, including conscious experiences of perception and mental representation, will need to be identified. But the task of defining relevant behavioral phenomena and their interrelationships in development can be addressed with minimal attention to this biological problem. We know that children must have biologically defined mental processes to support what we see them do, but we do not know what those processes are. Our major obligation is to produce developmental and behavioral proposals that are consonant with brain processes as they are known thus far. In *Symbol Formation,* Werner and Kaplan trace children's co-construction of word and meaning from earlier presymbolic processes, such that words come to mentally represent meanings as symbol to symbolized. Such representation is apparent in every occurrence of word use, but the nature of the underlying biological substrate is not specified.

Grounded in a strong theoretical background, I have nonetheless taken an inductive approach to the transition to language. That is, believing that children's frequent and consistent behaviors must be meaningful, I have sought to discover the significance of what children actually do as they learn to produce language. While my earlier work had emphasized the development of mental representation as observed in a succession of symbolic play levels (e.g., McCune, 1995), careful observational approaches to children's vocalizations led me to recognize additional pivotal phenomena that, while previously observed, had not been fully appreciated as significant. Children at the threshold of speech tend frequently to grunt as they attempt to communicate (McCune, Vihman, Roug-Hellichius, Bordenave, & Gogate, 1996), and children who will become early talkers tend to produce the same consonant sounds month after month before speaking (McCune & Vihman, 2001). Some children additionally show a range of variegated babbling patterns, while others succeed with only a couple of well-practiced sounds, the specific frequently used sounds varying somewhat from child to child.

In addition to names for things children's single word expressions include words expressing the meanings of movement and change. These "relational words," well-known at least since Bloom's (1973) case study of her daughter's single word language, have not been accorded their deserved importance in the process of child language acquisition. I have discovered that meanings expressed in first sentences can be traced to meanings of these single words (McCune, 2006). These words express experience of space, time, and movement interpreted through the logic of sensorimotor action and understanding (Piaget, 1954). Johnson's (1987) exposition regarding the derivation of many linguistic meanings from bodily experience, both directly and by analogy, prefigures the sorts of meanings underlying these single words. Such words address dynamic aspects of events in the environment and form the foundation for early sentences (e.g., *down* in response to the effects of gravitational force on self and objects; out in relation to efforts to remove objects from containers). Analyzing the use of such words in relation to Talmy's (e.g., 1975; 2000) motion event semantics highlighted critical links between children's prelinguistic cognition, their first single-word predicates, and their first sentences (McCune, 2006).

In this volume I take up two major themes: First, language does not stand alone as the crowning achievement of infancy. Rather, other equally complex achievements are ongoing and contribute to linguistic development. Second, a set of precursor achievements organized from a dynamic systems perspective can successfully predict, for individual children, the onset of referential word use. The possibility for such prediction removes some of the mystery from the development of language and restores linguistic ability to the roster of skills acquired through cognitive and behavioral effort in a sociocultural context. In this analysis I have relied upon the "self-organizing" approach characterizing dynamic systems views of development (Thelen, 1989), more recently described as follows: "By self-organization we mean that *pattern and order emerge from the interactions of the components of a complex system without explicit instructions,* either in the organism itself or from the environment" (Thelen & Smith, 2006, p. 259; italics in the original). The emphasis in this book is on how a previously nonexistent ability can be derived from earlier and simpler behavioral experiences. Once children begin to produce a substantial number of words, the first critical transition—the transition that is the focus of my work—has already occurred. In this book, I propose a theoretical and empirical account of how this first transition is made and begin to look ahead through longitudinal data to what follows. When children begin to speak, words occur only one at a time. Next, children go through a period dominated by two-word utterances. Each of these periods and the transitions between them can last from a few weeks to several months. Processes that occur during these periods and transitions are crucial to understanding later developments.

When the development of language is studied from its earliest roots in individual children, it becomes clear that language is not itself an instinct but a product of our human heritage and the work of infants and the adults who care for them. From birth, infants are directed toward experiencing and understanding the environment. Instinctual behaviors as strong as those directing geese to follow their mothers impel human infants to respond in predictable ways to physical closeness, touch, visual and auditory experiences—tendencies that guarantee children's initial direction on the path toward human communication, knowledge, and language. Patterns of mutual communication with caregivers and rhythmic regularities of everyday life emerge within the first few weeks to support the development of the first human relationships, which are so crucial to language. In the early months, crying gradually becomes only one of the variety of vocalizations expressive of infants' feelings and attitudes, mirrored by parental responses. Meanwhile, infants' interest in moving objects, such as leaves stirred by a breeze or a crib mobile, and in human faces and voices, provide early evidence of attention, which will eventually contribute to learning and language.

Indeed, from the moment of conception, our nature as humans renders the development of language skills virtually inevitable. Our journey into language begins even before our first breath; in the womb, the fetus becomes familiar with the sound and cadence of the mother's voice. Even before hearing develops, the human brain is inexorably organizing to make language possible. Language is a multifaceted outcome of infancy that emerges in the broader interactive sweep of biological, neurological, cognitive, and social developments.

Babies' ability to sit upright and then to crawl about and explore the world with their hands, mouths, and eyes accelerates their acquisition of knowledge. Greater control of movement and stability of posture also affect vocalization, so that rhythmic vowel and consonant sounds emerge in the second half of the first year. This regularity of making sounds is the beginning of babbling. As babies meet resistance to some goals and so extend greater effort to accomplish them, they grunt with the effort, demonstrating a critical underlying physiological process. The grunt used communicatively signals babies' readiness for rapid word learning; as we share it with other primates, it may also be a clue to the evolutionary origins of language.

The idea that language acquisition is a behavioral phenomenon, or acquired through principles of learning, was scrapped during the 1960s in favor of the idea that language is innate, or programmed in the genes. The genetic proposal may have appeared to be more plausible because researchers believed they completely understood the principles of learning and had found them inadequate for explaining language aquisition. At the same time, the operation of genes was a mystery, and this mystery sustained the hope that its solution might eventually lead to an account of how language is acquired. Since the acquisition of language could not be derived from established principles of learning, perhaps researchers were more comfortable attributing it to the unknown, somewhat magical potential of genes. As Braine (1994) recognized, and Culicover and Jackendoff (2005) reiterate, the problem with this approach is that any appeal to innateness creates an obligation to explain the presumed genetic mechanism in detail. A dynamic systems view avoids the difficult dichotomy of innateness versus learning by maintaining a respect for the unknown but filling in the elements of the developmental system that can be demonstrated behaviorally. In this way, appeals to innateness are reduced, at least to the extent that behavioral and cognitive principles can explain development.

Werner and Kaplan (1963) proposed that objects, people, and events in the world are "expressive" in ways that the human senses and mind can perceive. *Dynamic schematizing* is the term they give to the child's bodily and mental responsiveness to the expressivity of objects, leading eventually to the capacity for symbolic representation of meanings. This approach exemplifies "emergent cognition," or the development of a more complex cognitive ability through the exercise of earlier, simpler processes. Objects participate in activities, and some of their dynamic quality is due to such participation. In Chapter 2, I provide examples, including one of the child's reaction to a rocking chair: the sense of motion and meaning that emerge from participation in interactions involving the rocking chair, along with accompanying maternal language, lead to development of applicable word meanings. Werner and Kaplan focused on symbol formation both as a major transition of infancy, the transition to mental representation, and as a real time process continuing throughout life in human transaction with the environment. This volume provides evidence in support of their theoretical views regarding infants' transition into language.

Piaget (1954, 1962) proposed a mechanism of adaptation involving two complementary processes, assimilation and accommodation, as underlying all cognition. This cognitive mechanism is proposed as very general, applicable both for the 6-month-old learning action schemes, such as how to reach directly to obtain an object, and, for the 7-year-old, how to recognize the equivalence of the numbers of items in two rows, even when one row is spread to a great distance. This assimilation/accommodation process has as its major purpose the building of a cognitive capacity allowing ever more complex understanding as the child develops.

This process occurs in real time and a "cognitive capacity" need not be considered as an internal computational procedure such as those described in modern cognitive science. Rather, for Piaget, cognition accompanies and guides action in ways that remain opaque. At the sensorimotor level Piaget's examples always involve changes in behavioral reactions: exercise of various "action schemes" comprising perceptual and motor skills. Later changes in children's cognition are identified by their ability to demonstrate understanding by language or action. The perceptual and motor skills of the sensorimotor period culminate in a "logic of action" grounded in the potential reversibility of many actions in space and time.

Like Werner and Kaplan, Piaget relies on the child's bodily reactions to the environment, in particular imitative actions, as the initial means for the transition to mental representation. Some of these reactions, as recognized by both theories, occur in playing at observed activities out of context—that is, pretending. Symbolic schemes, analogous to sensorimotor schemes, are the organizing elements of these representational processes. Sensorimotor schemes and later symbolic schemes are similar to the "image schemas" described by Johnson (1987) as organizers of meaning. In fact, Johnson acknowledges the profound influence of his son's activities on his own thinking, as the child "grew to age two." These activities constantly reminded his father "of the obvious centrality of our embodiment in the constitution of our world and of all its possibilities for meaning" (p. xviii). Piaget and Johnson were similar in using attentive observation of their own children's development as a source for theoretical insight. The notion of "dynamic schematizing" posed by Werner and Kaplan draws together these apparently somewhat disparate approaches.

The terms "scheme" and "schema," like "representation" have been variously applied in psychology. Piaget's use of these terms is to specify a process, rather than to identify specific mental content. In contemporary schema theory a scheme is understood to be an internal representation in the strong sense mentioned earlier. I relate Johnson's (1987) use of the term "image schema" to the Piagetian sense, although Mandler (1988, 1992, 2004) seems to interpret image schemas as stable internal elements. Despite the vexed history of various terms, there is no alternative to their use, and care must be taken in interpretation.

Domain-specific theories can describe variables that contribute to development, such as cognition, neurological organization, and social and emotional processes. Because all of these diverse variables contribute to the development of language, a broader, less domain-specific theory is needed to describe their interaction. A dynamic systems theory is a metatheory, a theory of theories, as well as an explicit theory of how change can occur with development. As a metatheory, dynamic systems theory (Thelen, 1989; Thelen & Smith, 1994, 2006) provides a framework for a number of variables, each with its own trajectory, which, in their interaction, contribute both to the production of individual behavioral actions and to the shift from one level of development to another.

Sameroff (1983, 1989) and others (e.g., Gershkoff-Stowe, 2005; Gunnar & Thelen, 1989; Thelen & Smith, 1994) have similarly proposed that systems theory provides an appropriate metatheory for elucidating a broad range of developmental variables. Esther Thelen and colleagues were the first to apply dynamic systems theory broadly to developmental variables. While I will apply this theory primarily to describe the interaction of variables in a holistic developmental transition, this same approach is useful in studying microgenetic activities (e.g., potentially underlying neurological activities as these become known). Thelen argued that developmental patterns arise through the same process as related individual acts and that such acts are elements in the establishing of such patterns. For example, the same synergistic principles of organization that might explain how a child produces a word at a given time can also explain how the child's overall system develops from prelanguage to the capacity to produce words (Thelen, 1989, p. 81).

Dynamic systems theory thus allows us to describe both how babies attain major language milestones over time and how they produce distinct, individual communicative acts in real time. In a dynamic systems view, organization results from the behavior of a number of interacting variables, organismic and environmental, all viewed across multiple time scales, including, for example, both individual acts and developmental change occurring over time. The behavior of a moment, dynamically produced, contributes to the system developed over months and years. In development, the language system organizes itself over time from the effects of a countless number of individual communicative and other prelanguage acts. In describing Werner's view of development, Glick (1992) articulates a similar vision:

> If the developmental unit is defined by moments of linkage between organismic functions and environments....The fundamental unit becomes the moment that is codefined by an existing organismic level of interfunctional development and by an environmental medium within which and with respect to which the organism is organized. (pp. 564–65)

At any given moment, the entire biological system of an organism exhibits certain properties that interact with the environment to bring about a given developmental sequence or behavioral event. Both Thelen and Werner would expect variation in the environment to contribute to behavioral and developmental variation.

In order to use a dynamic systems perspective to investigate how infants acquire language, language acquisition must be considered a series of phases defined by dominant behavior patterns during each phase, termed "preferred states" of the system—that is, behaviors typical of a given developmental phase. We can then examine the variables that contribute to maintaining the preferred state and investigate which developmental and environmental changes would make it possible for the infant to shift to the next developmental phase. Preferred states can be defined with varying degrees of specificity: We might consider vocal phases such as crying, followed by babbling, followed by prelinguistic communication, followed by single words, followed by word combinations. While such phases can be identified clearly, once the child has made a phase transition, the paths of transition from one phase to the next are not distinct and behavior apparently characteristic of an earlier or later phase may sporadically occur (e.g., see Gershkoff-Stowe & Thelen, 2004, regarding U-shaped development). In this volume, I am primarily interested in the transition from a period of implicit and indefinite communication, where parents construct meanings from their interaction with their infants, to the period where children express meanings with an expanding repertoire of referential words that can be understood in the larger language community. The transition from this phase of frequent single words to the period where children begin to create their first sentences is touched upon in this volume, but neither theory nor data as yet allow prediction of this second transition.

Related to the identification of phase transitions is the critical methodological question of identifying what should count as a word in a study of language onset. Werner and Kaplan describe the emergence of meaning from prespeech sounds, significant between parent and child, to words with rough equivalence to those of adults, but they do not specify an identifiable moment that marks the first word. Parents, the closest sources of evidence, vary in how they define baby words. Do *mama* and *dada* qualify, even if the baby doesn't seem to know what they mean? To be an actual word, must it sound exactly like the adult rendition? How many times must a word be used before one is sure it is really a word? Language researchers struggle with these same questions. Therefore, from all points of view, the first entry into language is a complex topic that requires careful consideration. One difficulty is that in children who will be equally language-competent by age 3, development of a speaking vocabulary of approximately 50 words may occur as early as 14 months or later than 2 years. Is it possible to determine why children learn language when they do, and so to predict when significant language-learning milestones will occur? There are a number of underlying internal events, observable external skills, and environmental supports that can make it possible to predict when a child will begin to speak and make certain early transitions in language development, as this book will show.

Two developmental approaches to examining extralinguistic influences on language transitions emerged during the 1970s and 1980s. Both involve the search for homology and theoretical analysis of the similarity between linguistic and nonlinguistic behavior. Homology is defined by structural similarity of behaviors across domains, where transition in one domain can be predicted from observations in the other. Both also proceed by first identifying theoretically homologous domains and then evaluating the statistical relationship between them. One approach that demonstrated a variety of critical relationships was that of Bates and colleagues (e.g., Bates, Benigni, Bretherton, Camaioni, & Volterra, 1979). They used correlation analysis of behavioral frequencies and rates of development across time to examine relationships for groups of children between language and other variables in theoretically homologous cognitive and communicative domains.

I developed the other approach, a cognitive-prerequisites model within a dynamic systems framework (1992). First, I analyzed the structure of language and a nonlinguistic ability (representational play) to determine levels of accomplishment that appeared homologous—that is structurally the same— in both domains. I then examined the profiles of individual children's development to evaluate how often homologous shifts of interest occurred close in time across the linguistic and nonlinguistic milestones. To accomplish this, the individual child must be the unit of analysis, rather than groups of children, because group results tend to mask critical relationships exhibited by individuals.

The initial goal of my research was to assess the extent to which mental representation, assessed through play, could predict language transitions (McCune-Nicolich, 1981a). I chose representational play as the nonlinguistic measure because such play is the primary cognitive predictor of language change during the transition period. Among the underlying skills that representational play shares with referential word use are the capacity for mental representation and an internal sense of meaning. For example, when a child feeds a doll with a spoon, he expresses some knowledge of what spoons and eating mean and "represents" that meaning by play action, outside the usual context of eating and feeding. This is similar to word meaning (Bates et al., 1979). But I did not propose that representational play ability causes language change. Rather, such play is a nonlinguistic measure of the capacity for mental representation, a process that affects both play and language. Language and representational play both require the capacity to symbolize, but they differ in other components required for successful performance.

In my research, the majority of children displayed accomplishments in representational play either at the same time as or before displaying the theoretically homologous accomplishments in language, although a lag of weeks or months might intervene between them (McCune, 1995). Thus, homologous capacities for nonlinguistic mental representation tend to be available by the time of the two language transitions that are of interest to me—from prelinguistic communication to frequent single-word use and then to first sentences. However, a minority of children showed extensive delays between their nonlinguistic and linguistic achievements. This pattern demonstrates that although mental representation is a necessary prerequisite for language transitions, it is not in itself sufficient to fuel such changes. Additional developments beyond growth in mental representation must also be necessary.

Analysis of the range of additional component skills required for language and those required for representational play allowed me to compare language and play and identify skills needed for successful language transitions in addition to mental representation as assessed in play. The developmental trajectory of the specific skills hypothesized to affect language could then be evaluated within a dynamic systems framework. To determine the contributions of these skills, I evaluated developments within each skill domain in relation to the language phase shifts of interest.

Language requires knowledge of the specific meanings and sound shapes of some words and the capacity to produce them either by voice or by sign, as well as the recognition that a sound or sign can represent an internal state. Phonetic ability seemed, from observation, to distinguish children who made the transitions in representational play and language closer in time from those who made them further apart. Collaborative findings with Marilyn Vihman have now demonstrated the specific nature of this relationship (McCune & Vihman, 2001). In the course of phonetic analyses, we also discovered critical behavioral evidence of both the importance of children's learning about sound/meaning links and the way in which this realization might be accomplished (McCune et al., 1996).

Although my research finds play transitions often preceding language transitions, this is not necessarily the case with homologous variables. For example, children with some disabilities tend to express representational meanings in language prior to expressing homologous levels in pretend play. Representational play requires the motor capacity for expressing these meanings. For children with motor disabilities, lack of fine motor control limits play with small objects, even if mental representation is well advanced; but an intact oral motor system may allow language. Similarly, children with visual impairments may pass language milestones first, as they lack opportunities to see the objects employed in play as well as opportunities to observe the real activities often reproduced in children's earliest representational play acts; however, they can hear language from their parents and learn meanings in nonvisual ways.

The use of a dynamic systems approach allowed me to predict the transition to referential words more precisely than I had by using only a single cognitive variable. Unlike a pure prerequisites approach, prediction in dynamic systems does not specify an order in which presumed underlying skills are acquired. Rather, a shift from one preferred phase of behavior to another in a given domain occurs when the last element required for the phase shift, termed a "control parameter," becomes available. I have identified a set of four measurable underlying skills which, when all reach their critical level, are followed by a child's shift to spoken referential language. In other words, having each of these skills is necessary to the transition, but only having all skills in place is sufficient for the transition. However, each of these skills is also a dynamic and developing variable. As each changes and evolves in its functioning, it interacts with the others and with maturational factors, leading to variability in language expression across the first years of life. These skills are:

1. Mental representation, shown in representational play
2. Control of the oral motor apparatus
3. Recognition that a vocal production can express an internal state or meaning
4. The capacity for communication with a social partner

These same skills are implicated in *producing* a particular instance of a given referential word. From a dynamic systems perspective, the expression of a word is assembled from variables specific to the organism and immediate context when a given word is produced. Each instance of referential word production reflects the interaction of conscious states of the speaker and conversational partner, the condition of the vocal apparatus, contextual elements of interest, and underlying variables such as the child's neurological and brain function and the characteristics of the language in use. For this to happen successfully, both the child's internal systems and the external variables must be aligned.

The children I have studied were all learning vocal language. I assume that, for children learning a sign language, the capacity to form meaningful symbols manually would require analogous control of bodily systems capable of producing sign rather than control of the oral motor apparatus.

The plan of the book is as follows. Chapters 2 through 5 explain my approach to defining early language and the social and cognitive processes that provide the background for the effects of specific variables and their interaction, as described in Chapters 6 to 9. Language as a symbolic ability emerges in the context of human relationships with caring adults who provide an accessible language model (Werner & Kaplan, 1963), as demonstrated in Chapter 2. The processes of developing a meaningful sense of the world and symbolic means of reference depend upon the guiding interaction of adults who engage with the infant in defining meanings that, at first, require the mutuality of their relationship for interpretation. Cognitive and social processes are proposed to demonstrate the feasibility of this position. Chapter 3 then addresses characteristics of the single-word period, including definitions applied in this book and some areas of current controversy in lexical development. Predicting the onset of referential words requires careful definition of referential language. This chapter includes an initial presentation of data that will be analyzed in support of my theoretical proposals throughout the book.

Chapter 4 elaborates the cognitive bases of language transitions, including studies of infant "category formation" (e.g., Rakison & Oakes, 2003), the logic of action characterizing infant problem solving, and the earliest evidence of the mental representation of objects). Chapter 5 links specific elements of cognition with the expression of dynamic event meanings in language, based on Talmy's (1975, 1983, 2000) semantic approach.

In Chapter 6 I evaluate developments in representational play (Piaget, 1952, 1954, 1962) as control parameters for sequential phase shifts in language. Chapter 7 addresses the contribution of phonetic development and establishes control parameters in this domain for language transitions. Chapter 8 evaluates the contribution of prelinguistic communication and the recognition of sound/meaning correspondence, emphasizing the importance of communicative grunts. Finally, Chapter 9 presents a dynamic systems analysis of the variables contributing to the transition to reference, integrating material from the previous chapters.

2

Primary Relationships and the Symbol Situation

It seems mysterious how a baby, so primitive in early movements and vocalizations, so incapable of entertaining and expressing meanings other than discomfort and satisfaction, should come to produce and understand language regarding myriad complex matters. But language has its origin in the microcosm of adult–child communication, where simple, locally shared meaning provides a bridge to the larger linguistic community. Fathers and other special caregivers may provide primary care and language interaction as well as mothers. In this chapter I often use the word mother as a matter of both convenience and history, citing previous authors, but also because mothers still often serve this primary role.

Vygotsky attributed the capacity for internal thought to the organizing aspects of language: "Language arises initially as a means of communication between the child and the people in his environment," only later taking on internal mental functions (1935/1978, p. 89). This "arising" appears so automatic that some have assumed language to emerge through simple biological growth, with minimal influence from learning. As language development was examined more closely, broken into components and steps, and studied comparatively across different native languages, the complexity of the learning processes became more evident, but the mystery remains. How can someone initially unaware of even the possibility of linguistic communication become a competent language user? The solution to this mystery depends on an understanding of the nature of human language. What is its basis? What critical shifts in the internal life of the baby are needed to allow language to come about?

In this chapter I discuss the nature of what children entering language must learn and the role of relationships with caregivers in this transition. I do not believe that a single definition can encompass the reality of language from its developmental emergence to its full flowering. At the very simple place where language can first be recognized, I would define language as a *system of symbolic representation that serves communicative goals*. This is a minimalist definition, leaving modality open—sign or speech—but sufficient for our present purposes. I assume that the human infant develops holistically, as a total organism in a social and physical environment that forms the highly influential context for that development. Humans, to a greater extent than other animals, are directed toward knowledge, understanding, and reflection upon their world. The demands of survival in the wild prompt other animals to utilize the environment for basic needs rather than to reflect upon its elements as a source of meaning, as humans do. In contrast with other young animals, human infants more strongly seek interesting events and novelty from soon after birth. By as early as 3 or 4 months of age, a human baby may cry from boredom because nothing interesting is happening! Thus perceptual experience is a robust contributor to implicit learning, fueled by the human infant's continuing interest in novelty.

Yet much environmental knowledge comes arduously to the infant through the development of an interior mental understanding of the physical and social world; this is facilitated by a close reciprocal relationship with one or more special caregivers, among whom the mother is often primary. One might argue that not all infants enjoy such a relationship, yet virtually all biologically intact infants do acquire a language. There is evidence for variation in the kinds of infant–adult relationships leading to language as an outcome (e.g., Rogoff, Mistry, Gongcu, & Mosier, 1993; Schieffelin, 1990; Schieffelin & Ochs, 1998), but children raised in isolation do not become competent language users.

Gradually, during the first 2 years of life, the child becomes capable of internal mental representation, allowing an understanding that goes beyond immediate perception yet remains integrated with the external world. The ambient language (or languages) of the child's environment provide the primary mode for communicative competence, which emerges in the broader context of perceptual and motor experience. Every language event, as part of a system of symbolic representation serving communicative goals, involves a "symbol situation" that includes an addressor and an addressee, a symbolic vehicle (word or sign), and a meaning (Werner & Kaplan, 1963, p. 40 et seq.). The symbolic vehicle becomes the means of communicating meaning between addressor and addressee. These components only gradually become distinct as the child develops from a sense of assuming shared consciousness with mother to creating messages to engage her.

Language Development in the Context of Relationship

If we assume that the development of language includes a process of internal symbolic development that is inherently social, we can then consider the baby as at first experiencing the world through perceptual processes and movements and only later symbolically—a transition that can occur only with the help of a social partner. From birth, the child is physically separate from the mother, and both exist in a world of objects. Mother and child interact directly through holding and being held, mutual gaze, and caregiving routines. In modern western culture they also interact indirectly through objects, such as baby bottles, pacifiers, diapers, and toys. Lieven (1994) finds wide variety in the social situations leading to successful language acquisition cross-culturally. Yet some aspects of infancy are universal. As a mother carries her child about in any culture, the child experiences visual scenes of people and things, in motion or at rest, passing behind or in front of one another.

Many theorists, myself included, believe that initially the child has little sense of self as distinct from the nonself, little ability to recognize the mother as separate and things as "out there." As Winnicott expresses it: "From the baby's point of view there is nothing else but the baby, and therefore the mother is, at first, a part of the baby" (1966/87, p. 11). Through close and evolving relationships, across societies, mothers and other early caregivers become the essential means for babies to develop the capacity for symbolic representation and language. Mahler, Pine, and Bergman (1975) proposed that between birth and 2 or 3 months of age, the ministrations of a caregiver gradually woo the infant into the symbiotic relationship of mutuality that will form the basis for later differentiation and symbolic development. That is, the infant becomes aware of the caregiver as an adjunct partner to the self, physically separate but psychologically integrated. Werner and Kaplan (1963/1984) described the parent–infant relationship as a "primordial sharing situation" that begins with the infant's lack of differentiation from mother and the world of objects and other people.

Of course this initial "egocentrism" or "adualism" rapidly declines with experience (Figure 2–1). For example, it feels different to touch one's own skin versus being touched by another, and this is immediately perceivable by the infant. Try clasping your two hands, then take and hold the hand of someone else. The difference in perception is obvious. Rochat and Hespos (1997) compared newborn infants' rooting response when touched on the cheek by the experimenter's finger with their response to random touches on the cheek

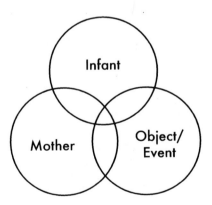

Figure 2–1. The infant/mother/object relationship. The three intersecting circles represent the child's experience of the world as including self, other, and the objects/events involving self and other. Initially there is little differentiation among these components of the infant's perceptual experience. Gradually the three components differentiate, so that the child experiences them as separate and interrelated. [Adapted from Werner and Kaplan (1963/1984), Figure 3.2, p. 42, with permission.]

by their own hands. The infants so tested showed their discrimination by producing more head turns and rooting responses to the adult finger than to touch by their own hands.

For an infant, variety in the experience of touch—in holding experiences with mother, father, and others and of lying untouched on a surface—contributes to a growing sense of physical separateness. Scheiffelin and Ochs (1998) found that the Kaluli, an aboriginal tribe of New Guinea, carry their babies almost constantly, allowing them to nurse on demand. Similarly, infants of the Efe foragers of Zaire spend "less than 1% of their time in the absence of a companion" through 5 months of age, as they "are rarely put down on the ground," spending much of their time carried by a caregiver (Tronick, Morelli, & Ivey, 1992). In comparison with infants in contemporary western culture, infants in both of these cultures experience minimal physical separation in the early months: a Kaluli mother will even place the baby against her when she is seated working with her hands. Infants across all cultures have some control over their head and limb movements, while objects and people in the environment come and go without the infant's control. Therefore from the earliest days of life, the infant begins to experience aspects of separation and differentiation from the environment.

However, it is not until 3 or 4 months of age that the infant is able to hold his head upright when at mother's shoulder and look into her eyes; not until 6 months that the infant's control of attention allows shifting of gaze from mother to objects out there, and back to her face. Finally, it is often not until 9 months or more that the baby can crawl away from mother then turn and look back. Consequently the child develops a sense of the separation between self and caregiver only slowly, but these milestones offer increasingly strong evidence to the infant of physical separateness from mother. The early physical closeness is mirrored by a pervasive psychological closeness. The infant's gradual understanding of separateness from mother remains a challenge throughout the early years. In fact, throughout life, issues of closeness and separateness remain critical features of human experience.

The essential implication for language development is that without a sense of separateness from others, communication remains implicit and mutual understanding expected. With no sense of separation, there would be no perceived need for a medium of communication and no motive for special communicative behaviors or language. Therefore changes within the parent–child relationship—in particular, the gradual recognition of separateness by the infant—strongly affect the course of language learning. The intention to communicate that underlies language originates in the knowledge that "the other" is separate from the self.

The understanding of others' viewpoints as different from one's own is a gradual, at first implicit aspect of the process of individuation and dawning representational development. The infant's following of mother's gaze as early as 6 months of age is an implicit acknowledgement that someone else's focus may indicate something interesting. Later, gradual changes in the child's pretend play with parents and peers demonstrate seamless growth toward an understanding of others' distinct conscious attitudes (McCune, 1993; see also Chapter 6).

Shared Meaning Prior to Language

It is on this basis of mutually recognized focus on the same phenomena, that the child can effectively develop internal meanings similar to those that adults experience when they use the words of a language. To learn a language, a baby must first have a sense of shared meaning with others that is nonlinguistic and that begins within a framework of physical and emotional closeness. At the same time, an emerging sense of separateness is an early foundation for this development. Sometime in the second half of the first year of life, infants begin to protest vigorously when passed by the mother to someone else or when the mother leaves the room, moving out of visual contact. Even earlier, parents may realize that a familiar caregiver can soothe the crying infant, while a less familiar relative, no matter how loving, may not be able to do so. Some parents notice that the older baby fusses when they are "out of range"—perhaps a few yards away for some infants or out of the room for others. These effects follow from the sense of familiarity and comfort that is part of the parent–infant system and gradually develops over the first few weeks of life. Baby and caregiver will learn, as the baby gradually feels more separate, how to continue the sense of comfort, previously achieved through the illusion of both physical and psychological unity, by symbolic means alone.

Efe infants, while in continual contact with others in the early months of life, spend only about 50% of that time with their mothers, remaining contentedly with other adult or child members of the community of 20 or so adults who form the extended family settlement typical of this forest-dwelling group (Tronick et al., 1992). This demonstrates shared care as a successful variant in human culture and raises the question of how this infant experience influences the sense of self-mother-object—in contrast with western culture, with its emphasis on individual mother–child attachment.

In an early and insightful paper, the psychoanalyst Ernst Schactel (1954, p. 318) suggested that both affective needs and "a distinctly human capacity for object interest" provide the means for the development of consciousness of self and other in an objective world. "Focal attention is the tool, the distinctly human equipment, by which the capacity for object interest can be realized." Repeated acts of focal attention provide the experiential means leading toward representational consciousness, with focal attention in interaction with a trusted adult being the most powerful vehicle for the infant's developing consciousness. Each act of focal attention differs slightly from the last, even if the same stimulus is focused. What is seen in one focused look may be gone in the next yet retrievable by a third fixation. This controlled "absence from view" provides an experiential precursor to mental representation. The contrast in perceptual experience between one act of focal attention and the next contributes to the child's sense of temporal continuity between the present and the immediate past.

Prior to the capacity for focal attention, emerging at about 6 months of age, perceptual experience is merely reactive to the forms and properties of stimuli, limited to objects and people in view and limited to perceptual attention. Later, children engage in representational attention, which is characteristic, for example, of pretend play.

The first object of early reactive attention is the mother's face, which is explored visually from birth and manually beginning with the child's capacity for directed reaching at about 4 months of age. An infant's waking hours are ideally spent with one or more caregivers who observe and interpret the infant's experience through facial and vocal expression. Ongoing observation of the infant by a caregiver yields an intuitive sense of the infant's readiness to explore and the focus of her interest. This common history and resultant subtle aspects of mutual perceptual understanding promote the likelihood of shared focal attention as the infant begins to explore objects manually and to focus on other members of the social group.

Richman, Miller, and Levine (1992) found holding, touching, and looking to be prominent maternal responses to 4-month-old infants by both Gusii mothers with only 2 or 3 years of schooling (members of a highland agricultural community in Kenya, East Africa) and Boston mothers who had completed high school. By the time their infants were 10 months old, the Boston mothers had a greater tendency to look at and talk to their infants, while for the Gusii holding and touching remained prominent, with talking a less frequent response. Attunement to infants can occur in modalities varying by culture.

In the early period, caregivers may not realize that they are doing anything specific in comforting the baby; but a bodily knowledge develops between infants and caregivers that is itself a comfort. By 6 to 9 months in modern industrialized societies, the caregiver is becoming the infant's interpreter of the broader world of objects. If mother touches an object, infant will look. If mother offers an object, infant will reach. These are highly charged interactions that, by their frequent repetition and familiarity, reduce the complexity of the world the infant encounters and invest various experiences with meaning, which is shared with the mother. These occasions provide a context for the development of shared representations or internal meanings that will follow.

No doubt related to attachment with their infants (Ainsworth, 1964; Bowlby, 1969) it is in the nature of human parenting (provided by parents or others) to monitor the infant's focus of attention and affective reactions and let the baby know that we understand. This caregiver skill was best described by Daniel Stern (1985) and given the name "affect attunement." When the baby cries, we feel hispain and are greatly impelled to provide relief. When the baby shows interest and excitement, bouncing with joy, we may reflect his experience by accompanying each bounce with a joyful sound. Stern has observed parents attuning to their babies' feelings by matching the baby's reaction in intensity, rhythm, and duration. Such attunements have the essential quality of shared affective meaning that allows the infant to experience a unity with the parent that is psychological, occurring in the context of physical separation but in visual and auditory contact. These attunements exemplify the dynamic expressive qualities emphasized by Werner and Kaplan as critical to symbol formation. By 6 to 9 months of age, for many healthy infant–caregiver pairs, this system is firmly in place. By this age as well, infants are launched on the path to establishing attachment to their parents. Around this same period of time, they begin to spend more time at a distance from parents by their own volition and under their own steam. They begin creeping on all fours and within some number of months will walk and run.

For many babies there is a period after they are "up and running" at age 1 or 1½ years when they look back only occasionally to check on the mother, and may often expect her to run after and retrieve them before the distance between them becomes too great. (This is termed the "practicing period": Mahler, et al., 1975.) It may be that the contrast between the earlier period of close interaction and this later period of motoric activity and occasional distance strengthens the child's recognition of physical separateness from parents, opening the door to an uncomfortable sense of psychological separation that can be bridged only by the more conscious sense of shared internal understanding that comes with purposeful communication. At the height of this intense period of exploration, children typically express the need to include the mother in their expanding sphere of knowledge by bringing her objects, often multiple objects, offered to her hand or dumped in her lap.

The internal aspect of unity versus separateness is more complex than the physical. In affect attunement, parents naturally match the psychological state they impute to their infant based on observation. When this succeeds, the infant has the gratifying experience of feeling completely understood by another. . Gradually the child comes to experience this as a contrast from the alternative possibility of lack of understanding. When the active baby begins "getting into things" and hears a stern "no" as he is physically removed from such interesting items as wall plugs and hot stoves, he receives evidence of separateness and, in fact, of conflict. Eventually the baby learns to use parental reactions as a guide to her own. When faced with alarming or ambiguous situations, the baby who has begun crawling about acknowledges psychological separateness and the potential for communication by looking to parents and monitoring their facial and vocal reactions. If parents smile and vocalize encouragement, young children are more likely to explore; if parents project fear, their babies are likely to cry or cling. Joseph Campos has termed this child attunement to parental reactions "social referencing"(Campos & Sternberg, 1981). During this same period between 9 months and 2 years or so, as parents attune to children and children monitor parental reactions, the child develops symbolic ability and language on the basis of this mutuality of understanding.

Development of Joint Attention: A Special Context for Language Learning

During the early months of life, infants' attention to both objects and people is obligatory. The perceived stimulus is fixated visually until processing is complete. It is because of this tendency that experimental work demonstrates—once processing of familiar stimuli is complete—a preference for novelty in visual displays. Similarly, the infant's social attention to the mother's face comes in bouts interspersed with looks away, despite the continued availability of the mother's face. While infant looks to mother are influenced by maternal vocal behavior, facial movement, and touch, it seems that in the early months attention to mother's face is similar to looks at other displays (Ruff & Rothbart, 1996). By 6 months of age, children begin to gain some control over attentional processes; during the next year, they develop greater flexibility in selective attention.

In particular, between 6 months and 2 years of age, infants become more adept at attending to mothers through social referencing: 6 to 9-month-olds are as likely to look to mother's body as her face, while 14 to 22-month-olds look more frequently to mother than do younger children and almost exclusively toward her face (Walden & Ogan, 1988). Sorce, Emde, Campos, and Klinnert, (1985) found that by 12 to 14 months of age, children use the information from social referencing to decide whether to crawl across a visual cliff (apparent drop-off) and to avoid toys that mothers viewed and commented upon with disgust (Hornik, Risenhoover, & Gunnar, 1987). Affect attunement on the part of parents and social referencing of parents by infants form a mutually reinforcing system that functions fully by 1 year of age, providing the affective background for symbolic communication using language.

Tomasello (2003) regards the "joint attention frame" as an essential cornerstone of language acquisition (p. 21). During the second year, children's opportunities to learn language are supported by joint attention with parents. In an early study, Rocissano and Yatchmink (1983) found that preterm toddlers of parents who tended to follow their infants' attentional focus in play, talking about toys the infants attended, showed more advanced language than children of parents who tended to redirect their children's focus. Ahktar (2005) reports that "from a young age children are quite good at tuning in to the attentional focus of others" (p. 165), suggesting that special effort may not be needed to insure joint focus.

As the child becomes aware of separateness, the availability of a powerful caring "other" provides protection from a sense of despair and isolation. In the context of being with the mother or another special caregiver, infants take a calm and studied interest in the world around them. Mutual gazing at or touching of objects of interest invests the objects themselves with significance for the child because of the inclusion of the object in the primordial sharing situation.

The capacity for joint attention develops in the same time period as children's social referencing looks to parents. Infants tend to follow parents' line of regard to a single object in view by 6 months of age (Butterworth & Jarrett, 1991) and are able to selectively follow the direction of another's gaze by 12 months (Morissette, Ricard, & Gouin-Decarie, 1992). Corkum and Moore (1998), in a training study, demonstrated that 6-month-old infants could be trained to follow maternal head turns signaling an interesting event (noisy toy), but only if the toy's location matched the direction of maternal head turns. Children who were rewarded by a toy located in the direction *opposite* to the maternal gaze direction still increased responses *following* maternal head turns in the test trials. The children failed to learn a reinforced operant response that involved looking in a direction opposite that of mother and instead used the learning situation where they were exposed to frequent maternal head turns as a springboard to earlier acquisition of the "natural" (unreinforced) gaze-following response.

Maternal pointing enhances children's following of parents' attentional focus. Butterworth and Jarrett (1991) found that by 6 months of age, infants followed a maternal point and gaze as long as the target was within 10 degrees of midline, while only infants older than 10 months followed to more divergent targets. Between 14 and 18 months, a period of rapid language learning, children not only follow points to objects of interest but also monitor both adult gaze behavior and the object located, a strategy that should clearly enhance language learning (Blake, McConnell, Horton, & Benson, 1992). Adult vocalization and naming further increase children's tendency to follow parental gaze and point (Baldwin, 1991; Baldwin & Markman, 1989; Leung & Reingold, 1981). See Tomasello (2003, pp. 65–68) for a summary of findings regarding joint attention and language.

Varied forms of Interaction Can Support Language Development

Not all societies provide the same forms of interaction between caregivers and infants—that is, those described as ideal in the language acquisition literature, which is based primarily on industrialized western culture. Even in twenty-first-century America, as in many other highly developed societies, nonmaternal care is a significant aspect of infant development. How does a theory of language acquisition founded on close mutual understanding between infant and caregiver account for the successful language acquisition of children experiencing multiple caregivers and/or group care for a significant portion of their daily lives? The relationship between quality of maternal caregiving and child language development is relevant here. Reviewing a large number of studies available at the time, when primary maternal care was typical in the United States, Snyder, Bates, and Bretherton (1981) found that variation in the quality of social interaction between parent and child failed to show substantial correlation with children's language acquisition. This leads to the conclusion that social interaction with a caring adult is a threshold variable. That is, given "enough" appropriate social interaction, rate of language acquisition is not related to further gradations of social interaction quality, no doubt because so many additional variables contribute to language acquisition. It is also the case that children referred for neglect tend to show greater delays in language acquisition than those referred for abuse (Culp, Watkins, Lawrence, Letts, et al., 1991). Where neglect is likely to be pervasive, potentially eliminating social interaction, abuse is likely to be sporadic, interspersed with opportunities for social interaction. These findings do not diminish the importance of adult care but point to the resilience of language acquisition.

For the processes of mutuality described here as critically important to the child's initiation into language, a close relationship with a caring adult, someone invested in mutual understanding with the baby, is clearly needed. However, both parents and possibly additional caregivers can contribute to this process through their close understanding of and attunement to the child. In most cases, even where children experience child care apart from their parents, several hours in the evening as well as weekend time are spent with parents. The fact that children develop language appropriately and thrive in situations of high-quality child care suggests that this pattern meets the threshold needs for parent–child social interaction. Within the child-care situation, where staff are stable, relationships between the children and adults in the center can also provide the kind of mutuality and support for symbolic and language development described here. This is reminiscent of the Efe, where shared care is the norm in small communities of 20 or so adults and children, many sharing biological as well as social relationships (Tronick et al., 1992).

Schieffelin and Ochs (1998) describe the Kaluli initiation into language as different in some ways from the experience in western societies—that upon which most of our literature is based. In her extensive participant-observer fieldwork, Schiefflin (1990) observed little face-to-face interaction or mutual eye gaze between mothers and infants, in keeping with the cultural practice among adults. Until a baby is 4 to 6 months of age, mothers arrange triadic interactions where the baby is held facing outward and the mothers orchestrate pretend conversations with older siblings, creating "a high-pitched nasalized voice for the baby" but otherwise making no adjustments to the well-formedness of their remarks (p. 55). The goal seems to be promoting the relationship between the children, and the conversations do not follow infant initiatives. This contrasts with the emphasis on shared interaction with mother and objects following the child's interest that is often proposed as optimal for language acquisition. However, these children are successful language learners, demonstrating the variability of social context effective for learning a language. (The "high-pitched" quality is notable for a similarity to western society's "infant-directed speech" or "motherese"). The Kaluli pretend conversations also promote a sense of unity between mother and child, although in a different way; and other individuals rather than objects seem to be the more important joint focus. Perhaps valuing of and interest in siblings takes the place, for Kaluli infants, of object interest. Indeed, older siblings' interest in babies seems to be reciprocated by the babies across societies.

By 9 to 12 months of age, with the coming of a greater differentiation of self from caregiver, the baby will point excitedly at objects of mutual interest, perhaps vocalizing as well. Pointing to "things out there" is a good demonstration of the young child's understanding of objects as separate from self. When babies point, parents are impelled to name, so a situation arises that favors language. However, this learning paradigm emerges from a broad supportive background. This is also a period of rapid motor development, leading to more distant interactions between mother and child and a greater need for explicit symbolic communication.

In the alternative Kaluli developmental story, babies have a different early experience of language. "They are greeted by a variety of names (proper names, kinterms, affective and relationship terms) and receive a limited set of both negative and positive imperatives," including "firm one-liners" requiring a compliant rather than a verbal response (e.g., not to touch some item) (Schieffelin & Ochs 1998, p. 56). Adults also repeat the vocalizations of 12 to 16-month-old infants back to them, thus shaping these toward person names or kinterms but not particularly expecting the babies to repeat these vocalizations. The one type of occasion where Schieffelin observed mothers expressing infants' intentions with language was that "when the toddler shrieks in distress at the assaults of an older child, mothers will interpret the toddler's shriek with language, saying 'I am unwilling' (using a quotative particle [a linguistic device] referring to the toddler's shriek)" (p. 56).

Rather than talking *to* the baby, Schieffelin found that Kaluli adults tend to talk *about* the baby's activities, often prefacing their remarks with the infant's name or kinterm, which might tend to call the child's attention to language. So as they begin to walk and play, the infants have plenty of experience with language accompanying and matching their activities, although not necessarily in dyadic conversation. Once the children show that they know how to speak (and this requires that they know the words for both "mother" and "breast"), mothers begin showing their children how to speak by presenting model utterances in dialogic frames and requiring the baby to repeat what was said. Within this culture the child is taught the "social uses of assertive language (teasing, shaming, requesting, challenging, reporting" p. 57). However, neither object labeling nor object requesting is a part of this instructional system. Adults neither expand child utterances into complete sentences nor try to guess what the children have in mind. Saying what another, even a child, thinks is "a cultural dispreference" for the Kaluli (p. 55). Rather, parents use clarification requests (similar to "huh?" or "what?") to encourage clearer expression from the child (p. 59).

In comparing Boston mothers' interaction with their infants with that of Gusii mothers, Richman et al. suggest:

> Furthermore, the more frequent talking and looking of the Boston mothers in response to infant vocalization at both ages [4 and 10 months] suggest that they are treating the baby's babbling as incipient speech, thus creating the "proto-conversations" that have been described elsewhere for American white middle class mother-infant interaction (Ochs & Schieffelin, 1984; Richman et al., 1992, p. 617).

In contrast, these researchers understood the Gusii mothers as intending to protect their infants, their role as comforting distress rather than playing with them, educating them, or engaging them in conversation. Emotional excitement is meant to be avoided rather than encouraged in Gusii culture, and there is a "specific prescription of emotional restraint for parents with their mature children" and less tendency for mutual gaze during adult conversation. These cultural views may affect mother-infant interaction. In addition, "older Gusii mothers tend to ridicule the idea of talking to children before they are capable of speech, which they estimate at about two years" (Richman, et al., 1992).

The observations of Schiefflin and Richman and colleagues require that we expand what has often been a limited cultural view of what sorts of interactions are needed to promote language, providing useful examples of variation. More work is needed within cultures where child-rearing variation suggests variation in the language-learning situation (Lieven, 1994). Even across industrialized societies (Argentina, France, Japan, the United States), there is variation in emotion-emphasizing versus informative language, apparently reflecting variation in cultural values (Bornstein et al., 1992; Fernald & Morikawa, 1993). It would be of great interest to learn whether variation in modes of successful transition to language vary cross-culturally and cross-linguistically.

The Formation of Symbolic Vehicle–Referent Relationships

The simple definition of language as a *system of symbolic representation* adopted here requires that children develop representational consciousness in order to participate in a language community. Piaget, in his infancy books (1952, 1954, 1962), describes the beginnings of cognitive development as limited to perceptual and motor experience and gradually yielding to the potential for mental representation. This transition is not abrupt. Rather, bodily experience over the course of the first year interacts with neurological maturation, bringing about a new form of consciousness. Thelen and Smith (1994) distinguish their view from Piagetian theory. Yet Piaget's analyses prefigure the "embodied cognition" (Johnson, 1987) favored by Thelen and

Smith. In their developmental interpretation of Johnson's approach, Thelen and Smith describe a process whereby infants' multiple repeated goal-directed actions in response to environmental opportunities yield generalized knowledge of the effects of those actions and of environmental contingencies. From a Piagetian (1962) perspective, this generalized knowledge leads to "expectations," conscious moments that "imagine" the effects of actions not yet taken, as well as sensorimotor schemes.

Werner and Kaplan (1963) similarly assumed that children derived symbolic meanings from perceptual and motor interactions in the context of social relationships. In order to address the development of symbolic relationships in terms more specifically related to language, they asked: How can a sound pattern, for example, which is so different in practical terms from an object to which it might refer, come to symbolize that object of reference? They were asking how bodily experience of the world could lead to the development of abstract meaning, where a seemingly arbitrary expression could mentally evoke an internal meaning related to real-world experience. Their organismic theory calls upon four factors that are often overlooked to solve this problem. First is the sensitivity of humans to the actual or potential expressiveness of objects, a sensitivity recognized by Gibson (1969) as the essential evolutionary tuning of species to environment. Second, they recognized properties of "dynamic expressiveness" (e.g., sounds and typical movements) apparent in otherwise dissimilar objects (e.g., the rocking motion of a rocking chair and other unstable objects; the common response of objects to gravity). Third, humans take a knowing or thoughtful approach to objects that can lead to the intention to use one item of experience (e.g., a motion or sound) as a symbolic vehicle to denote another. They call these creations of symbolic relationships "intentional acts of denotative reference." The fourth factor is the availability of processes that yield semantic correspondence; that is, the capacity to construct the symbolic vehicle (word or sign) so that its expressive meanings correspond to that of the referent (entity/event). These four factors are discussed below.

By this theory the child must creatively construct both meaning and form in relation to one another. Meaning has its basis in bodily experience. This includes motor action as well as the infant's perceptual experience of speech sounds of the ambient language and the sounds of her own babbling. The notion of correspondence in expressive meaning between word and referent could be interpreted to mean that there would be some continuing literal similarity between the two. Alternatively, the integrative internal neurological process of developing both meaning and form can be the continuing source of this nonarbitrary quality. Meaning and form remain linked through their common history of mutual neurological activation, although the external relationship between the spoken word and the objects or events to which it refers may appear arbitrary to the observer. As speakers we do not ordinarily experience a disconnection between the words we use and the meanings they express. Werner and Kaplan use the example of our lack of confusion in interpreting homonyms to suggest that although words may be similar in form, "differences in the schematizing processes underlying the superficially identical verbal forms" (p. 126) account for the ease in distinguishing them both, even in infancy, when limited production ability can lead to extensive homonymy (e.g., Vihman & Miller, 1988), as well as in adulthood. The following sections amplify the factors proposed by Werner and Kaplan.

Sensitivity to Expressiveness

Sensitivity to expressiveness is a human quality that allows the construction of symbolic meanings. Werner and Kaplan's use of the term expressiveness may seem obscure. I believe they sought to capture the idea that our interactions in the world of things always involves movement and often sound. These aspects of information are termed "expressive." Their idea is that humans are attuned to these dynamic and rather difficult-to-capture aspects of our commerce with the world. Expressiveness inheres both in objects (their rhythms and dynamic vectorial—i.e., directional) properties, and in the actions of human beings. Action on or with things—that is, sensorimotor play with objects—and perceptual activity provide the starting point for developing symbol/symbolized relationships, offering opportunities for the child to experience and react to the expressiveness of objects directly. Children's initial symbolic development is apparent in both the gestural and vocal modes, and the source of such representational effects is found in both acoustic and nonacoustic experiences. Rovee-Collier's extensive studies of infant memory in the age range of 8 weeks to 1 year (summarized in Rovee-Collier, 1995) demonstrate the child's sensitivity to the expressive movement of a visually experienced mobile and other toys that reward the child's action with interesting displays. In this work, the infants are first exposed to training sessions where, with one leg loosely attached to the mobile above the crib, they learn that the mobile responds with a characteristic jiggling pattern to the movements of the leg.

Initially, there was amazement in the research community that such young infants could learn this skill, eventually limiting movement to the attached leg and timing movement to keep the mobile in motion. However, if we consider the mobile as a dynamically expressive display and the infant's movement as a natural reaction to that display as well as the activity powering its movement, this simple behavioral sequence demonstrates the child's available sensitivity to the dynamic expressivity of objects. It is this underlying sensitivity that fuels learning and memory. The subsequent Rovee-Collier experiments demonstrating both memory and reactivation following "forgetting" showed the depth of children's learning of this behavior as well as the initial sensitivity of memory to context. In reactivation experiments, once the infant has "forgotten" the learned response to the mobile, the mobile is jiggled above the crib at the rate at which it moved at the end of the learning sequence and in the context in which the movement pattern was learned. Several hours or a day following the reactivation treatment, depending on age, the infant again demonstrates memory of the learned response through appropriate kicking action. It seems to be the linked dynamics and perceptual background of the learning situation that allows the infant's successful reactivated memory performance. These same processes are available for learning language.

The Transcendence of Expressive Qualities and the Knowing Attitude

The source for contemplation is the emergence of objects as slightly differentiated from the interpersonal matrix of mother and child. In their activities involving more than one object, children also demonstrate that individual objects are differentiated from one another and can be brought into relationship. From 6 months of age on, children show a knowing or thoughtful approach by their explorations of single objects and their arrangements and comparisons of multiple objects. They seek to learn about object properties rather than use the objects for some pragmatic goal. These activities yield information for the child about the "expressive qualities" or distinguishing characteristics of particular objects, including spatial and temporal aspects of motion.

As an "object of contemplation," one item can be visually and tactually compared to another. Perceptual similarities and common action potential (balls roll, sticks make a noise when banged) across groups of objects, as these characteristics are experienced in child action, serve sensorimotor processes in the child that are directed toward knowledge. The child's manipulation and arrangement of objects offer opportunities for contemplation of the similarities and distinctions among the objects as well as potential relationships between objects.

Johnson (1987) regards bodily experiences of containment as the source for literal extension to understanding physical relationships and later metaphoric extension (e.g., the exclusion of a potential bit of evidence from an argument). Gradual development of understanding of containment can be traced to early infancy. as summarized by Mandler (2004, p. 112). In research regarding children's play with objects where some objects afforded the possibility of containing others, Sinclair, Stambak, Lezine, Rayna, and Verba (1989) found that the children both explored the container/contents dimension of objects with hand and mouth and used their manual actions to create these relationships between pairs of objects. The sensorimotor actions of placing objects in containers and removing them by hand or by inversion and dumping become internalized, contributing to the child's basic understanding of "containment." These observations demonstrate children's active experimentation with the generalized potential of containment.

A social example of sensitivity to the expressiveness of objects is seen in children's reactions to the many musical and moving electronic toys they experience. My granddaughter, Brielle, at 12 months, would move her body in rhythm with such toys and occasionally use the characteristic motion of the toy as she looked, smiling, from the toy to an adult, using look and motion to draw the adult into a mutual contemplation of the situation.

Denotative Reference and Semantic Correspondence

Pointing, sometimes accompanied by vocalization, is recognized as the child's earliest form of denotative reference. The point does not symbolize a particular object or meaning but denotes it, identifying for a social partner that the object indicated should be their joint focus. Pointing and directing the body toward an object seem to be initially aspects of the child's pragmatic action with the surrounding milieu. One might think that these movements indicate a desire to hold or possess the object. In fact, research by Ruff (1982, 1984) has demonstrated that examining objects by touch with an extended index finger is a prominent exploration strategy, beginning as early as 6 months, well before, at 9 or 10 months of age, the child extends an index finger, locating objects at a distance by pointing. (This is the approximate age range when children develop the ability to follow maternal points to locations ever more divergent from midline.)

Directing attention and pointing to objects undergoes a shift of function, so that instead of manual exploration for self, the point comes to serve as an indicator that the object is separate from and located at a distance from the self. (See Bates, 1976, pp. 61–74.) The point then becomes a gesture of denotative reference: that is a communicative act serving to select and indicate an object in view. Indicative pointing is essentially different from grasping, because in grasping the child tries to incorporate the object into physical control; in pointing he seeks to establish mutual attention. In addition to such direct denotative reference, touching objects in a shared context with an adult, often involving looks between adult and object, or handing the object back and forth, has some of the referential aspects of pointing. Joint attention to siblings no doubt occurs in all societies and may be particularly effective in Kaluli society in promoting mutuality of focus for mother and infant.

Outward actions such as mimicking the movements of objects or indicative pointing necessarily entail underlying neurological activation. This activation brings about an internal relationship between the action pattern of the child and the external object involved, integrating visual and movement information (Pulvemuller, 2002). This is a partial step toward symbolizing internal meanings. The shift from outward actions and reactions with objects to internal mental understanding and reference is aided by the internalization of sensorimotor patterns. The neurological basis of internalization is not currently known. Internalization of object meaning can be understood as bringing disparate motoric actions and their neurological correlates under the umbrella of a more complete and integrated underlying structure, perhaps mediated by frontal lobe function (M. H. Johnson, 1997). This could be considered the transition from the sensorimotor scheme to "image schema" or early representational meaning (M. Johnson, 1987; Mandler, 2004). Werner and Kaplan suggest that when a child extends use of a given vocal form from a single habitual context to a range of situation, dominance of internal schematizing, as opposed to immediate reaction to environmental stimuli, is evident.

The recently discovered mirror neurons in Broca's area (and the monkey analogue), affecting both manual and oral behaviors, may support processes of integrating bodily dispositions with external stimuli (Iacaboni et al., 1999; McCune, 2002). In the initial research, specific "mirror" neurons in a monkey's brain were unexpectedly observed to fire when the monkey *observed* the researcher enacting a manual action the monkey had previously been trained to perform. The activated neurons were the same ones that fired when the monkey performed the same action itself. It thus seems to be the case that the "meanings" of some actions can be learned in a way that allows recognition of these actions when their performance is observed.

The child's learning of the meaning of spoons and eating provides a simple example. Grasping and mouthing of objects begins between 4 and 6 months, and children learn to use a spoon for self-feeding between the ages of 1 and 2 years (Connolly & Dagliesh, 1989). Through play, observation, and practice, the child learns to pick up a spoon, eventually in the correct orientation, and to sequence the actions of filling and food delivery. There are variations of movement and action in every eating action produced, but an internalized "spoon" motor pattern allowing such variation comes to guide self-feeding. It is of interest that between the ages of 1 and 2 years, even children who do not yet spoon-feed themselves indicate knowledge of the "meaning" of a spoon by pretending to eat; they feed dolls and play partners, showing the ability to use a motor pattern as a representational vehicle. Pretend feeding represents the real experience of feeding and eating. When the child encounters a spoon there is an internal response of understanding that at first elicits a characteristic motor pattern. Eventually this meaning is experienced separately from any action with the spoon. This is an internalized meaning.

This early simple "meaning" is provided by the ordinary actions that children use with spoons, so the semantic correspondence between the gesture simulating eating and the meaning "eating" are closely related. In fact, the action expressing the meaning overlaps with the real action. Learning to comprehend or produce the word *spoon* requires shaping of a phonetic form and a word meaning, establishing semantic correspondence between a word spoken by adults and an internal meaning for the child. This is a more complex accomplishment than expressing meaning by play action.

Shared Perceptual and Representational Meanings

The world in which Werner and Kaplan see infant and mother is partly an objective world and partly a world of their own making. Although the mother is a representative of the wider cultural world, where there is relative agreement on the meanings of language in relation to objects and events, she is also a partner in the infant's construction of a world of meanings that only gradually attains parity with that surrounding language. The initial lack of differentiation characterizing self/mother/object from the infant's point of view provides the basis for gradual entry into the world of independent objects and people from a vantage point of safety. Mothers' monitoring of infants naturally takes in the objects infants encounter in their explorations. Because objects participate in the infant–mother matrix, they can be approached with freedom from anxiety, a state most conducive to learning. The 6-month-old who turns her head to follow mother's gaze to an object experiences both the separation of self/mother/object and the mutuality of common gaze. This, as well as manual exploration of objects, beginning around the same age, demonstrates the earliest phase of infants' more reflective approach to the world around them. Meanings emerge between adult and child in relation to mutual contemplation of objects and later understanding of gestures and vocalizations.

Perceptual experience, termed "primary consciousness" Edelman (2000), is a conscious state that involves activity of the brain, not merely an object-to-eye phenomenon. Infants' perceptual understanding is supported by their initial tendencies, for example, following with gaze the moving portion of a visual display. Within the interpersonal framework of infant-world-mother, Werner and Kaplan (1963/1984) describe the young child as articulating objects in terms of available human abilities and in relation to human bio-psychological goals. The primary goals are knowledge of one's world and affective security within that world. Werner and Kaplan suggest that a specifically human approach to the world demands articulation of objects in relation to their meanings within a human framework, such that they can become a focus of internal contemplation in addition to being experienced in perception and action.

Perceptual processes have evolved in relation to environmental physical reality (Gibson, 1969). In a sense the meaning accorded to objects becomes a part of the human experience (Rosch, 1999). Xu, Carey, and Quint (2004) found that between 10 and 12 months of age, children come to recognize the meaningful character of real objects (sippy cup versus baby bottle), discriminating such objects as individuals in experimental situations where they fail to make this discrimination across objects differing only in size or color. The human significance of such objects no doubt enhances their perceptual distinctiveness.

Human commerce with the world involves handling and moving discrete objects, learning about them, and monitoring their movements—concerns that do not engage other animals to the same extent. Gibson (1969) has demonstrated the exquisite attunement of the infant perceptual system to relevant properties of the human world, termed "affordances"—properties that "afford" opportunities for human action and understanding. Infant perceptual abilities are applied to the objective world, guided by interaction with adults. In this way objects attain their unity, individuality, and special human usefulness and human meaning. It is apparent that object articulation should influence word learning. But is this a developmental process as described here or innately given? Golinkoff, Mervis, and Hirsch-Pasek (1994), for example, initially suggested "the whole object bias" as an innately given constraint on word learning; but where developmental processes can be articulated, it seems unnecessary to revert to innateness.

To exemplify human object articulation, culminating in the contemplation of a meaningful object, consider a somewhat extreme comparison. Caterpillars' commerce with the world requires that they consume appropriate vegetation as they encounter it. Thus the caterpillar uses the distinction between "road stuff" such as pavement or stones and "leaf stuff." The month-old infant sucks at the breast for nourishment and differently at the pacifier for soothing, distinguishing these objects from the surround and discriminating them. Later, the 18-month-old child picks up a leaf from the driveway, enjoys its color and shape, and uses it to mediate an interaction with mother; but unlike the caterpillar, the child will probably not taste it at that age.

At a higher phylogenetic level than the caterpillar, a groundhog goes snuffling over the lawn seeking edibles. These edibles form a core group for the groundhog, perhaps not as objects but as "stuff to be ingested"—distinct from other, perhaps visually similar materials. But the 18-month-old child may not even notice these items, critical to the survival of the groundhog, as the lawn is a background for activity rather than a focus. For each of these creatures the affordances of the world's objects are species-specific; hence human infants' need to articulate the relevant objects of their world. Furthermore, the child not only articulates objects as separate and significant entities but will come to contemplate, symbolize, and share their meanings.

Dynamic Schematizing

Given the reflective aspect of human cognition, understanding of objects will go beyond the mere utility motivating the groundhog's recognition of edibles. Humans readily note aspects of interest, develop preferences, and compare objects one to another by active cognitive processes. Children's perceptual sensitivities to the world of objects and people and relational movements in space set in motion what Werner and Kaplan term a "dynamic schematizing process." In this process children go beyond the articulation of real objects from the surround and come to represent meanings internally and mentally. Children's perceptual and motor sensitivity to objects, people, and movement in space leads them to express their initial understandings mimetically by movements and sounds related to their increasing understanding of the significance of objects and the events involving those objects, as in the "spoon" example above. Some relevant activity occurs without adult intervention, as a child may sway to music or imitate the bouncing movement of a jack-in-the-box or the sound of a ticking clock. Werner and Kaplan consider these bodily reactions to objective situations as the initial "taking in" and shaping of perceived reality toward internalized meanings. The child shows sensitivity to the dynamic expressive character of the object as in earlier examples.

Parents may also structure recurrent situations to include characteristic vocal and movement aspects that offer the child opportunities for bodily and vocal participation in perceptuomotor sequences that prompt dynamic schematizing and potential word learning. Bruner (1981, 1983) identified routines in the child's interactive life with a caregiver as the primary opportunities for beginning to learn language. For example, an adult rocking a child might accompany the rhythmic motion of the rocking chair with the words "rock-ie-rock," timing the sounds consistently with the chair's movement. It would not be unusual for a 9-month-old child with good babbling skill to begin expressing a similar sound while rocking with a parent.

Adults devise sounds to describe the vocalizations of animals and present these onomatopoetic forms to children when the animal (or its picture) is encountered. Werner and Kaplan consider such "mimetic" vehicles for expressing meaning as transitional to more "distant" and somewhat arbitrary relationships between word and meaning. It may be surprising to English speakers to realize that dogs worldwide do not say "woof-woof." For example, in Costa Rican Spanish, they say, "gwow-gwow"; in Japanese, wanwan; in Estonian, iauh-auh; and in French, ouah, ouah. The child's natural sensitivity to the expressive qualities of objects and events in the world allows and in fact impels him to express understanding of meanings by bodily action and sound. Werner and Kaplan provide examples of bilingual speakers who can differentially "hear" animal sounds through the medium of their two languages (pp. 102–3). Parents notice and capitalize on this, shaping child sounds and meanings into gradual synchrony with the ambient language. By 1 year of age, with the gradual development of representational play, children contribute actively to the shaping of meanings as they reenact details of interesting routines such as feeding, sleeping, and grooming with replicas as well as real objects, often displaying these activities to parents. The successful contribution of these experiences to children's transition to referential use of spoken words depends upon their capacity for mental representation, phonetic skill, and recognition of the potential for a sound to convey meaning.

The Symbol Situation: An Outgrowth of Relationship

The "symbol-situation" as Werner and Kaplan (1963) conceive it includes an addressor and an addressee, an object and a symbol (pp. 40–51). In infancy, where parent and child are considered as addressor and addressee, all components are initially only slightly differentiated (see Figure 2.1). This substantial fusion and slight differentiation allows the infant to be gradually initiated into a more mature symbol situation where all of the elements can now be quite "distant" from one another. The eventual result of this distancing process is a language whose elements seem arbitrary in their meaning, where such elements (words) can now be integrated directly in syntactic messages, and where these can be conveyed across literal distance between addressor and addressee, who may have no more direct contact with one another than a telephone link or the Internet.

The changing nature of mothers' and infants' interactions with objects demonstrates the distancing process. Even prior to children's understanding and expression of words, experience with adults includes referential activities. Mutual contemplation of objects in joint focused attention is the earliest form of mutual referential experience. Following mother's pointing finger to contemplate a selected object, an infant gives evidence of comprehending a referential communication. The point designates an object of interest but depends upon internal mutuality of addressor and addressee and the presence of the designated object for successful communication rather than specifying meaning by a more articulated signal (word or symbolic gesture). Mother and child take on roles of addressor and addressee, with an indicating gesture as the means of communication and a present object as the external and presumed internal mental focus of both participants. Similarly, the infant's earliest referential productions, well before words are produced, are likely to be extending an object for mother's examination or pointing to select an item for joint attention. These are presymbolic referential acts that do not convey symbolic referential meaning. However, they do show initial acknowledgment of mother's separate focus of attention and the need to engage her actively. Mothers take up these opportunities and address their children with words within this primordial sharing situation, setting in motion the process of mutual shaping by which adults and children create the next generation of speakers. For example, Tamis-Lemonda, Bornstein, and Baumwell (2001) found that at 9 months, mothers' affirmations and descriptions of children's focus or action predicted early language milestones, such as first words and beginning vocal imitation.

In Figure 2–2, Werner and Kaplan tried to capture the dynamic and changing aspect of relationships encompassed in the "symbol-situation."

Comparing Figure 2–2 with Figure 2–1, where infant, mother, and object were illustrated by intersecting circles, mother and child—now expressed more generally as "addressee" and "addressor"—show substantial differentiation while being integrated in the "symbol situation" through their mutual relationship with object and symbol. Both the "object" (usually considered as "something out there") and the "symbol" (usually considered to be the audible word or visible gesture) have an external form and an internal form. The internal forms must consist of neurological activation as well as conscious experience. While the concentric circles for object and symbol appear at opposite sides of the figure, the experience of these is simultaneous and serves to integrate the internal states of addressor and addressee. For communication to be

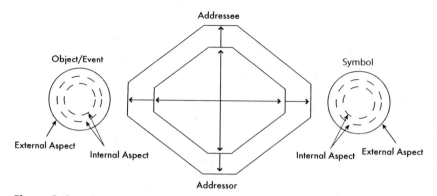

Figure 2–2. Relations among components of symbol situations. The central hexagonal figure represents the communicative situation. Here the components have substantially differentiated. Addressee and addressor, object/event, and symbol are portrayed at the edges of the hexagon, with the arrows suggesting their prior developmental history. Concentric circles identify the internal (broken lines) and external (solid line) aspects of the object/event and the vocal or manual form of the symbol that comes to represent it. Thus, the external form of the object/event (e.g., in the rocking=chair example) would include all sensory aspects (e.g., movement, visual aspect of the chair, feel of the surface of the chair, experience of mother's touch), while the internal aspect would include the neurological activation and the consciousness of the rocking=chair experience. The sound *rockie-rock* is the external aspect of the symbol or word, while the internal aspect encompasses the neurological and the conscious experiential aspects of producing and hearing the word. Objects and events attract the attention of addressor and addressee (e.g., mother and child). The components are integrated by the mutual consciousness of the participants. [Adapted from Werner and Kaplan, Figure 3.2, p. 42, with permission]

effective, both addressor and addressee must share significant aspects of such inner and outer forms.

In an example with minimal differentiation among the elements, when the parent rocks her child, intoning *"rock-ie-rock"* in a soothing voice, she may be herself in a conscious state fusing motion and the sense of her child in her arms, with the accompanying words forming an expression of this internal sense. The child who joins in producing this vocal expression shares much of the sensory and affective experience of the parent. The vocal form *rock-ie-rock* (termed a "symbolic vehicle") is a means for expressing the shared internal symbolic experience of the pair.

The dynamic schematizing process allows the child to use the motion of her own body and the sounds she hears, to engender both an internal meaning for the situation (the internal object) and an internal symbol (the specific production potential, or motor scheme, for the sound *rock-ie-rock*). The external "object" is the real event: being held and rocked; the external symbols are the child's and the parent's audible vocal productions. The child's vocalization may be only vaguely similar to that presented by the adult, as the child's own vocal repertoire is a strong factor in production (Vihman, 1996).

Although the child uses the opportunity for imitation, the vocalization is his own construction, based on internal processes such that meaning, internal aspects of sound, and their interrelationship are co-constructed by the child while closely reflecting outer experience. In this example there is very little differentiation between addressor and addressee, internal and external symbolic vehicle and object. The real event includes both a sense of self and other, a characteristic object and its motion. Initially this sound/word may occur only in the context of rocking with mother and be idiosyncratic enough in production to be incomprehensible outside that context.

The initial fusion of addressor with addressee, symbol with object, and gradual differentiation and eventual reintegration of these elements defines the process whereby the child can make the transition from presymbolic creature to representational individual and from nonlinguist to language user. The child's natural tendency (dynamic schematizing) to reflect experiences of reality mimetically sets him on a path where, with the guidance of an understanding adult, he can enter a language community. Continuing with the example above, the child's continual internal development and social experience may allow him, soon after expressing *rock-ie-rock* within the original situation, to be reminded of this internal meaning in more distant situations, such as moving the rocking chair with his hand or while rocking his body when someone else rocks in the chair. (This extension depends upon the availability and integration of additional skills.) The meaning, or internal mental "object" is not merely the chair but a sense of the entire experience, perhaps generated by an underlying image schematic process.

Johnson (1987) proposed the view that "in order for us to have meaningful connected experiences that we can comprehend and reason about, there must be a pattern and order to our actions, perceptions, and conceptions. *A schema is a recurrent pattern, shape, and regularity in or of these ongoing ordering activities.* These patterns emerge as meaningful structures for us chiefly at the level of bodily movements through space, our manipulation of objects, and our perceptual interactions" (1987; p. 29). Also, an image schema is "a dynamic pattern that functions somewhat like the abstract structure of an image, and thereby connects up a vast range of different experiences that manifest this same recurring structure" (1987, p. 2). Johnson's analyses comprise predominantly adult linguistic expressions and their source in bodily understanding. In support of this approach, such analyses can be traced to children's prelinguistic and early language experiences. In the "rockie-rock" example, image–schematic organization of the child's thinking promotes the extension of meaning from bodily experience to diverse situations, such as rocking a toy back and forth with accompanying vocalization.

Werner and Kaplan trace the gradual shift from personal image–schematic understanding to the acquisition of a word, which becomes integrated with the meanings of the ambient language. This process of learning how to learn words may be laborious at first. Over multiple instances of its occurrence, the representational approach to the world becomes as automatic as the earlier perceptual approach. As addressor, addressee, object, and symbolic vehicle(s) become more differentiated, a linear sequence of words can express the situation more fully (e.g., "Mommy rock me chair"). At their time of writing, the analysis of the emergence of representation and language proposed by Werner and Kaplan did not touch on underlying neurological processes. Yet such processes are essential to the psychological scenario they proposed. As more information regarding brain processes and neurological development becomes available, aspects of this theoretical proposal can be evaluated on neurological grounds.

In this chapter we have considered the nature and growth of the parent–child relationship as it sets the stage for the child's transition into language and, in some sense, defines the nature of that transition. In subsequent chapters the aspects of this transition, merely touched upon here, will be analyzed in full, and developmental variables accounting for them will be proposed. A description of the first phase of language in Chapter 3 will set the stage.

3

Entering Language: The First Phase

For most children beginning language production between the ages of 1 and 2 years, there is a significant period, usually several months in duration, when their language production is limited to single words. Why should this be the case? The nature and significance of the single words children express should provide clues both to the reason for the existence of a single-element phase and to understanding the subsequent period when they produce sentences. The single-word period begins for some but not all children with a few word-like vocalizations that occur only in relatively stereotyped situations (e.g., a word for "dog" only when such an animal is heard barking outside; a word accompanying pointing at an object of interest, e.g., *pretty*); a word consistently occurring only in a pretend event (e.g., *tea* in pretend drinking events). Such words, often termed context-limited (e.g., Barrett, 1995), probably emerge from exciting and repeated experiences with a parent, utilizing simple forms accessible from the babbling repertoire. They may drop out of use or change in meaning and application as the child's language develops (e.g., *rockie-rock*, Chapter 2). Such words are vocal aspects of a recurrent situation, participating in that situation rather than referring to it (Piaget, 1962).

Once single-word development is fully launched, two different types of word, both defined as referential, can be readily identified. Some words refer to entities in the environment distinguished by perceptual characteristics and adult class membership (e.g., *cup, cat*), while others, "dynamic event words," refer to the dynamic relational aspects of spatial and temporal events in which entities participate (e.g., *gone* to an empty cup; *up* as a cat leaps to a shelf). Words that occur as nouns in the adult language are prominent in the early vocabularies, but words occurring as verbs in the adult language are rare in English-learning children. Across six linguistic communities (Argentina, France, Belgium, Israel, the Republic of Korea, and the United States) Bornstein et al. (2004) found that nouns were the most prevalent adult category identified by mothers from a checklist as having been produced by their 20-month-olds, although proportions of nouns and verbs were close in some communities. Instead of developing a broad range of verbs in the single-word period, children express consistent dynamic aspects of events using a limited number of words that vary in form class across languages (McCune, 2006).

The division of early referential language into words that refer primarily to entities and those that refer primarily to dynamics provides a rationale for the single-word period. Each single word refers globally to the object and any dynamic, changing aspect evident at that time. Just as a single play act (e.g., putting a spoon to the lips) is the child's initial representation for the entire act of eating, the single word is the child's initial reference to a unified situation that will later be distinguished by a differentiated sequence of meanings and expressions. In order to produce longer utterances, the child must experience event meaning in a more differentiated way and learn to produce words referring to multiple aspects of the same event. (The initial holism of single words is addressed more fully later in this chapter.) In Chapter 5, we consider the cognitive basis of dynamic meaning and the reasons why dynamic-event words stand in for verbs, expressing the dynamics of the single-word period.

Bloom (1973) and Sinclair (1970) were the first to emphasize infants' single words referring not to objects themselves but across objects, as expressing consistent relational meaning regardless of the objects involved, although Werner and Kaplan (1963) had recognized the need for differentiation of meaning between entities and activities as a basis for combining words. These dynamic-event words—first termed "function words" (e.g., Bloom, 1973) and later "relational words" (e.g., Bloom & Lahey, 1978)—expressed meanings such as recurrence (e.g., *more*), disappearance (e.g., *gone*), or denial (e.g., *no*). Some years ago I analyzed the basis of these kinds of words in known aspects of sensorimotor cognition (causality, space, time, objects), recognizing their basis in potentially reversible aspects of motion in space and time (McCune-Nicolich, 1981). The lack of any linkage with later linguistic achievements originally limited recognition of the relevance of this analysis. Why should single words form two categories that would later be supplanted by mature linguistic word classes unrelated to this early distinction? Tomasello (1992, 2003) included dynamic-event words as "first verbs" and specified some early dynamic meanings that might provide building blocks for more general verb knowledge. My proposals are not in conflict with his but provide a more comprehensive analysis of initial dynamic-event meaning (see Chapters 4 and 5).

In recent work (Herr-Israel & McCune, 2006; McCune, 2006; McCune & Vihman, 1999), colleagues and I found a link between early use of these words and the transition to sentences by recognizing the relationship of both forms of language to children's expression of motion-event meaning (Talmy, 2000). Dynamic-event words have not been accorded status as a relevant *category* within the single-word period. The study of such words has been primarily limited to English, where they occur as particles and often are grouped by adult parts of speech (e.g., Smiley & Huttenlocher, 1995). In contrast, Werner and Kaplan (1963) considered these words as primitives for the dynamic aspect of language that would later be carried principally by verbs and hence worthy of consideration as a significant category of single words, distinct from those naming entities. Children's use of such dynamic-event words provides evidence of the child's verbal recognition of the significance of motion and change, the foundation for the verbs that will characterize their first sentences.

Gentner (1978) suggested that simple nouns (those referring to objects) and verbs differ in their relationship to the physical world. Noun meaning is "highly constrained by the physical world" (p. 990), as the items that infants encounter are perceptually bounded and concrete. Usually those called by the same name share perceptual and functional features. In contrast, verbs express relational meaning relatively unconstrained by the nature of objects participating in an event, and their meaning is extended in continuous time rather than embodied in a particular object. In learning verbs, children must intuit their more abstract meanings from highly varied perceptual situations. Gentner describes simple nouns as referring to entities, while verbs refer to relations among entities in events. In addition, verbs tend to include more than one semantic element in their meaning, with the conflated elements varying by language type. In English, for example, motion and manner of motion are often conflated: *The boy ran into the room.* The verb *ran* combines motion and the kind (manner) of motion, while direction (path) is conveyed by a separate particle, *into.* In contrast, Spanish often conflates motion and path: *El niño entro el cuarto corriendo.* The verb *entro* conveys path (English: *moved into*) as well as motion, while the manner of motion is conveyed by the gerund *corriendo* (English: *running*) functioning as an adverb. Because of this complexity, it may be more difficult for children beginning to learn language to interpret the meaning of verbs than of nouns in relation to the events they experience (Bowerman, 1989; Talmy, 1975).

Dynamic event word meanings are also constrained, albeit on a more abstract perceptual basis than early names and in a manner more directly akin to early cognition than the meanings of verbs. The words used may map directly to dynamic aspects of events accessible to children through image schemas (Johnson, 1987; Mandler, 2004). When verbs do occur early, as they do in Korean (Choi & Bowerman, 1991), the particular verbs learned in the early period tend to be those carrying the same kinds of meanings as the particles expressing dynamic events in English. Single dynamic-event words, regardless of adult form class, initially entail reversible spatial and temporal aspects of objects in motion or, if an object remains static, the potential for such reversal. Children first come to recognize these aspects of events before articulating the grammatically defined relational elements sufficiently to employ the verbs of their language.

Methods for Studying Children's Entry into Language

The study of children's spontaneous productions was the earliest approach to child language study. Parents, often researchers themselves, kept meticulous diaries of their children's language development (e.g., Leopold, 1939; Tomasello, 1992; Vihman, 1999). Beginning in the 1970s and 1980s, the first audio and then video recordings of children allowed detailed and careful analyses of the resultant language samples. Both diary studies and direct recording emphasize what can be learned from children's productivity; that is, from the freely given vocal productions of children as they make the transition into language. Diary studies can be comprehensive in noting all types of phenomena as they emerge. However, the actual productions themselves are not available for analysis, nor can the specific contexts of use be studied over and over again, as is the case for video samples. Unlike diary studies, recording approaches are limited in that they work with a sample of behavior. However, recording allows analysis of all vocalizations, including babbling, grunts, and words, along with other vocalizations such as sighs and cries. These may be accompanied by actions or gestures and occur against the background of the ongoing context, which can be captured on video. It thus becomes possible to interpret the children's meanings and communicative intentions more fully.

Two other approaches dominate early language studies at the beginning of the twenty-first century: (1) experimental approaches addressing focused questions such as identifying critical variables in children's word learning, often emphasizing learning names for objects, and (2) the collection of vocabulary data using the MacArthur-Bates Communicative Development Inventories (CDI) (Fenson et al., 1994).

Experimental Approaches

The experimental tradition provides information regarding what children know about language and how they learn words based on their reactions in experiments. Much of this research depends upon either the habituation paradigm and/or the use of looks and head turns as indicators of preference or expectation. This type of design is based on the well-established fact that infants engage visually with stimuli until they are successfully processed, at which point the infants look away (habituation). The infants' reaction to a subsequent "test stimulus" is used to judge their recognition of the distinction between the initial habituated stimulus and the test stimulus. If they show renewed signs of interest by attending to the new stimulus, experimenters judge that they have discriminated the tested from the habituated stimulus. Similarly, infants' preferential looking is taken as an indication of both their discrimination of and preference for the stimulus that elicits first and/or longer looks. Longer looking is also sometimes interpreted as "violation of expectation," or surprise (e.g., Baillargeon, 1993). Experiments are developed where stimuli and their presentation vary in ways defined by the experimenters as demonstrating a variable of interest.

In an ingenious use of such an experimental paradigm for studying word learning, Hollich, Hirsch-Pasek, and Golinkoff (2000) examined factors that promote word learning in young children between the ages of 12 and 24 months. In these studies, children were asked to show by their looking that they had learned a nonsense word associated with one of two novel objects. It is assumed that if they have learned the association, they will prefer to look at the associated object when the word is heard. The children had first explored the objects manually and visually for about half a minute, then witnessed the experimenter naming one of the objects, the target object. In the test phase, children who looked longer at the target object when the name was produced were interpreted as having learned the word associated with the object. This and other such experiments provide valuable information on the way language can be associated with objects and events, but it must be interpreted cautiously (Haith, 1998).

In these experiments, researchers assume that word learning occurs by simply associating a sound with an object or event, exemplifying "label theory" as distinct from a more constructive organismic approach (Werner & Kaplan, 1963). The research aims to determine what aspects of the ongoing situation are likely to promote or inhibit this association process. The assumption seems to be that the infant sees a familiar object or attends to a situation, hears a word, and learns that the word is a name or designator for the object or situation. Certainly learning of this sort occurs. Once children have recognized the possibility of designating meaning with a sound, perhaps by the processes described in the previous chapter, they readily learn new words, possibly by this association process, which is termed "fast mapping." As adults, we add to our vocabulary in exactly this fashion. However, adults know how language works and that new words are available. In the beginning infants do not know that they will learn language. An internal recognition of the possibility of linguistic reference is needed before young children can become word learners (Chapter 8).

Why do children begin to learn and produce words when they do? Answering this question is the goal of the present volume. Children's spontaneous behavior during the time when they make the transition to producing words and their first sentences holds many clues to the solution. As mentioned earlier, children we studied who were phonetically adept and whose parents involved them in plentiful language situations produced context-limited words between 9 and 12 months of age, but these early words seemed more a blind alley than a cornerstone of lexical development, and, in fact, not all children produce context-limited words in the months before referential word onset. Only subsequent to meeting criteria for referential word onset did we find stable vocabulary acquisition.

Parent Report Methods

Parent report approaches such as the checklists and elicitation questions on the MacArthur-Bates inventories provide normative data regarding parental experience of their children's language (Fenson et al., 1994). These data are particularly useful as a screening device because of the strong correlations achieved between such parental report data and children's recorded language (e.g., Feldman et al., 2005). However, this approach is of limited value in studying the details of individual children's initial entry into language or considering possible processes of acquisition, for two reasons.

First, the checklists do not recognize the critical significance of dynamic event words, placing these words in part-of-speech categories by language. This means that the extent of children's specific reference to the dynamics of situations cannot be captured until they begin using the verbs of their language.

Second, he identification of first words among children's vocal productions, a critical step in searching out the origins of language, is not easily addressed by this approach. The "moment" of transition into language is rather obscure Children's vocal attempts at language may or may not strongly resemble the adult form of the words they are trying to say because the phonetic structure of the production (its sound pattern) may vary considerably from the adult version, and/or the range of application for the "word" may differ greatly from that expected by adults, usually termed undergeneralization and overgeneralization (Gershkoff-Stowe, Connell, & Smith, 2006). To complicate the situation further, a child's productions of the "same" word probably do not all sound alike, and a word that is used for a few days may fade from use, leaving adults to wonder whether it counts as a word at all. A related difficulty is that adults, be they parents or linguists, do not necessarily agree on the criteria to be met by a putative word. These problems seem to be minimized in importance as researchers collect parental reports of words. Such studies are careful to define for parents the researchers' view of what should count as a word, but the potential for varied interpretation of child language by parents remains high.

Alternatively, the process used by the researchers themselves for identifying words is carefully delineated, so that the reader can know how decisions were made regarding "what counts" in identifying children's words; but researchers themselves differ in preferred definition (Vihman & McCune, 1994). These decisions inevitably affect the conclusions drawn by any study of entry into language, and they complicate the overall view of how children acquire language. It may be that the underlying reason for these difficulties is the seamless quality of children's development from a prelanguage phase to a phase clearly identifiable as linguistic.

Both experimental paradigms and parent-report data collection assume that researchers (and, in the latter case, parents) have a good sense of what it means for a child to comprehend or produce a word, but such understanding is often implicit. The experimental researcher establishes a context for testing the child's word knowledge or for training the child to establish new knowledge. The parent is asked to report in a checklist format based on informal observation. These strategies have proven useful in delineating children's performance in carefully controlled situations and in demonstrating the broad developmental sweep of children's language progress via large parent-report studies, despite the ambiguity inherent in assessing children's word knowledge. However, if the very nature of the earliest words differs from the words that adults speak in sentences, some important distinctions are lost in experimental and report paradigms of children's earliest word learning.

Technically, a *word* is defined as a linguistic constituent of a sentence (Ward, 2006; Werner & Kaplan, 1963/1987). Children's single-element productions are worthy of the term *word* by virtue of their relationship with the adult language, where similar elements do occur as constituents of sentences. Recognizing the unique linguistic role of early single words, Werner and Kaplan used the term *vocable* for early child utterances that "include a vocally articulated element" (p. 134). Vocables that are not incorporated into sentences—that is, those occurring only as single words—should not be confused with true words that are constituents of sentences. Without adopting this terminology, we can recognize the special status of single words. The omission of verbs from the early English-language lexicons, the length of the single-word period, and the existence of a notable period of two-word combinations all demonstrate that there is "something special" about single words. Words of the single-word period serve as a bridge to adult linguistic ability. Study of their special characteristics may clarify this bridging function.

When Is a Word a Word?

Vihman and I were faced with this question when we began our collaboration in 1985. Vihman, a linguist whose early focus had been on demonstrating continuity between babbling and early words (e.g., Vihman et al., 1985), was committed to determining the very beginnings of word use. I, a psychologist whose accomplishment was demonstrating relationships between steps in language and representational play (McCune-Nicolich, 1981; McCune, 1995), had little phonetic experience and favored the seemingly parsimonious view that a baby vocal form should not be credited as a word until it was easily recognized as highly similar to the adult word in form and use. The McCune and Vihman collaboration required careful delineation of criteria by both researchers and an eventual description of parameters that they and others could use to judge just how closely a given infant vocal form conformed to the notion of "word." This approach provides a useful yardstick in considering methods for describing children's beginning word use (Vihman & McCune, 1994) Findings from McCune and Vihman's collaborative studies of their two sets of participants, the Rutgers and Stanford samples, provide the basis for this chapter and Chapter 7.

In identifying potential child words, we proceeded as follows. Videotapes were first transcribed using the International Phonetic Alphabet (IPA). Where available, high-quality audio recordings were used to recheck the children's vocal forms. Next, each tape was screened for the purpose of nominating any possible words the child might have produced. A variety of criteria could lead to initial nomination. Nomination was assured for a vocalization exhibiting a plausible phonetic shape and occurring in a plausible context of use for the adult word in question. Nondictionary words such as onomatopoeic animal sounds (*meow, grr*) and those pretend sounds related to vehicles (*vroom*) or eating (*yum*) were included. Child productions that were apparently imitated from mothers' speech, or reformulated by the mother (Veneziano, 1981) also became word candidates.

Word candidates were then evaluated for word status using three types of criteria. First, we evaluated evidence based on context or contexts of use. If the vocalization occurred at least once in a context suggesting a given word and no other or the mother identified the word, this contextual evidence bolstered its candidacy. Multiple uses, even repetitions, also provided positive evidence. The strongest evidence would be use of the same vocal form in multiple episodes, where in each case a specific word and no other was suggested. However, given the variability in phonetic shapes produced by children and the often low frequency for given words, additional evidence proved important.

Vocalization shape provided the next source of evidence. Three types of evidence were considered. First, the child form was compared to the adult phonetic form to determine whether two or more segments matched the adult form, leading to what was termed a "complex match" (Vihman & McCune, 1994, p. 522). Table 3–1 demonstrates child variability in production of the same two words across participants and how match to the adult target was evaluated. Second, yielding to the needs of the untrained ear, we determined whether any production of the word was an exact and obvious match to the word in question. Third, we considered tuneful or prosodic match, or special vocal effects included across tokens (e.g., the rising/falling contour typical of *uh oh* or a whispered effect accompanying a word for sleep). Finally, we considered relationships across vocalizations. Imitation produced with understanding was positive evidence, although word types occurring only in imitation were not further analyzed. Both invariance of phonetic shape across candidate instances of a given word and all instances occurring in contexts plausibly suggesting the same word, with none in other contexts, provided further evidence in favor of word status. Finally, since our data were longitudinal, earlier sessions could be consulted to determine whether previous uses supported a word candidate.

Word status could not be determined by simply adding numbers of criteria identified for a given candidate. Rather, consideration of the criteria allows determination of the basis on which a given word is credited. We found ourselves well satisfied with this approach, although it tended to yield fewer words than Vihman's original criteria, and more than McCune's. (See the appendix for a list of all words accepted for each participant.) The truth is that children's vocalizations are "probabilistic words" for quite some time. That is, it is impossible in the early period to be sure that a child vocalization is "really" a word! The important methodological points are to be aware of the procedures for word identification in place in a given study and to recognize the consequences of criteria.

How do single words come to arise at all? It can be thought of as a case of apparently getting something from nothing! Werner and Kaplan provide a theoretical view of how the first word-like vocables arise—and how one might describe the development toward true words and sentences. Internal processes in linguistic and extralinguistic context operate on earlier constituents,

Table 3–1

Comparison of Child Word Forms to Typical Adult Forms

Example *a: baby*

Subjects	Adult Form:	'b	e	ɪ	b	i
	Child Forms					
Alice	[beibi]	+	+	+	+	+
Deborah	[p'e:bi]	+	+	(+)	+	+
Vido	[bobap]	+	[o]	+	[a]	[p]

Example *b: cock-a-doodle-doo*

Subjects	Adult Form:	k	a	k	e	d	u	d	ə	l	'd	u:
	Child Forms											
Aurie	[kakijali::]	+	+	+	[i]						[CV]	
Jonah	[əkakɛka] [ə]	+	+	+	[ɛ]						[CV]	
Sean	[dəlʊdəlʊ::]	[d]	+	[l]	+	+	+	+			[CV]	+

Source: From Vihman and McCune (1994, p. 527), with permission.

Matching segments indicated as +, feature-match (but not full segment) as (+). Mismatching segments set off by square brackets; matching syllable-count but mismatching segments indicated as [CV]. (All of these illustrative words were accepted and are included in the children's 16-month word lists given in the appendix #3A.)

providing a continuous flow from a period lacking words to a period where they become obvious. This explanation follows from that of the formation of vehicle-referent relationships discussed in the context of relationship in the last chapter.

Formation of Patterns that Represent Objects and Events

Werner and Kaplan proposed that in the first phases of language acquisition, children construct both representational meanings and vocal and/or gestural means of reference to such meanings as aspects of a single integrated schematizing process. These theorists emphasize bodily engagement in both meaning and form, such that meaningful gestures and vocalizations in the initial period of symbol formation begin in "coactive imitation"—bodily and/or vocal participation in the meaningful event. "That is, the infant does not [at first] represent an event, but responds to it by changes in bodily posture or limb movement" (p. 87). This is the first step in a developmental process leading to language. The dynamics of the world are, in a sense, gradually reflected in the dynamics of the infant's body. Language included in events by parents is only one part of this learning process. Recall the three-month-old infant learning to activate a mobile: this learning began with the spontaneous reaction of foot kicks in excitement and interest in the mobile. The kicks sets the mobile in motion, and a circular process involving infant and object then begins [exemplifying Piaget's (1954) definition of the "circular reaction"]. This natural link between bodily participation and objects forms the basis for meaningful expressions and eventually words. Piaget (1962) similarly proposed the gradual development of imitation and the eventual internalization of action as the means for developing initial mental representation.

Rather than merely learning which words apply in particular known situations, children, who have no capacity for symbolization at birth *develop a symbolic capacity* as both objects of reference (entities and events) and symbolic vehicles (words) emerge together in their understanding through the process of dynamic schematizing. This might, in contemporary terms, mean interaction among perceptual and action processing (such as coactive imitation), working memory, and associative memory, all supported by broadly interacting neurological activation and development (Edelman, 2000). Experimental work has demonstrated that object motion is essential to 14-month-olds succeeding in a task where they must associate a specific nonsense word, used in either a noun or a verb context, with an object or an action (Werker, Cohen, Lloyd, Casasola, & Stager, 1998) in the absence of social support. The object in question must be in motion whether the nonsense word is to be linked with the object itself (noun context) or with the motion demonstrated (verb context). This result highlights the fundamental importance of the dynamic and expressive qualities of objects that are conveyed by motion. These dynamic qualities may be essential to the child's development of initial word meanings. In their word-learning experiments, Hollich and coworkers (2000) allowed the children to manipulate the objects presented, creating motion in their manipulations.

Learning Words: An Example

In the classic *Child's Talk,* published in 1983, Bruner provides an extended example of a game that one mother and child frequently played. The mother structured the interaction in a way that offered opportunities for the child to observe, react, and participate. Over several months, the child developed understanding of the elements of the game and words that referred to those elements. The game involved mother hiding a toy clown and then having it pop into view, accompanied by lively vocalization from the mother: *"Boo!"* Bruner followed developmental changes in mother and child participation in this game over many months. The child, Richard, at first quietly observed his mother's preparation for the game as she held the clown and asked if he was "ready." He then watched the clown's disappearance and sudden reappearance, reacting with enthusiasm. He gradually became a participant in the three phases of the game (preparation, hiding, reappearance), such that, by 9 months of age, after 4 months of regular play, he contributed his own labial (produced with the lips) vocalization at the point where his mother had previously expressed an excited *"Boo!"* The type of movement and vocal participation, analyzed in detail by Bruner, constitute an outer form of dynamic schematizing activity structured by the mother. In Bruner's (1981) view, such routines are a prominent aspect of child language learning. This case example is particularly helpful as Bruner further documents the shift at 14 months to the addition of more conventionalized baby words, *allgone* at the hiding phase and *peek-a-boo* when the clown reappeared. At this same age, the child produced names for pictures encountered during book reading.

In Bruner's example, Richard first participated somewhat passively in a highly enjoyable social activity, showing his joy by laughter and excitement. His accompanying labial vocalization emerged in the game as a form of coactive imitation, where Richard used his dawning phonetic skill (labial production) as an aspect of his conscious participation, becoming, at this same time, a more active player, sometimes himself removing the cloth in a hiding sequence. Vocal imitation, primarily if not exclusively a human capacity, may rely on mirror neurons, thought to exist in Broca's area, that facilitate the production of actions matching environmental stimuli (Iacaboni et al., 1999). The simple labial production provides the initial phonetic material for Richard to eventually construct a fully articulated baby word, *boo.* At first this word might be limited to the particular game context, but should Richard begin to comment *"boo"* under other circumstances of disappearance/reappearance, it would seem that *boo* is becoming integrated with a more general meaning related to disappearance/reappearance and that "disappearance/reappearance" is being constellated as a known and articulated form of experience symbolized by the vocal form *"boo."*

A final step in establishing symbolic word/meaning relationships would be the beginning use of *gone,* a more conventional adult-like word to express the meaning "disappearance," a development Richard achieved by 14 months in the example. While *boo* might be elicited initially only in response to the specific game situation, later, in closely related circumstances, other similar but more distant experiences begin to elicit a related conscious state. During this same time period, the child is increasing his developmental capacity for mental representation. By the time the child is using the conventional baby word *gone,* experience with a variety of disappearance situations, occurring in the context of the word *gone* as spoken by adults, will contribute to an eventual integrated relationship between an internal meaning and this single word. The word can now function symbolically, as this meaning is instantiated under a range of varied experiences and related conscious states. As evidence for the continuity between such unconventional expressions as *boo* and the later conventional word, Werner and Kaplan cite instances from earlier diary studies where children used a combined word, partly a baby word and partly the conventional word (in this case it would be *"boo-gone"*), in a transitional phase. However, even conventional word use does not confirm a stable internal meaning delimited to the adult meaning "disappearance."

This example includes the three sorts of words or "vocables" typical of the entry into language. First, the nonstandard labial vocalization interjected where mother said "boo" would probably qualify as a context-limited word; that is, it occurs in a narrow context such as a particular game or routine. This labial vocalization is more a part of the activity of participating in the situation than of making reference to anything, and seems derived by imitation from the [b] sound of *boo.* Later the word *gone,* used in commenting on the changing dynamics or relational aspects of a situation, would qualify as a dynamic-event word. Words used to name or identify objects, such as pictures in a book, would exemplify entity words or nominals.

The Holistic Nature of Single-Word Utterances

One might wonder why Richard would not say "clown gone" if he had the vocabulary to do so. Werner and Kaplan proposed that the child's representational consciousness at the beginning of language is too holistic and not sufficiently differentiated to allow separate reference to interrelated objects and their dynamic movements. That is, since *gone* encompasses the entire situation (while emphasizing the dynamic aspect), as does *clown* (while emphasizing the object of focus), their overlap in meaning prevents combined but separate reference to the clown (entity) and its process of disappearance/reappearance (dynamic event). The interjection *boo* or the word *gone,* rather than being strictly delimited to the meaning "disappearance" or "reappearance," is embedded in, and in a sense refers to, the entire conscious experience, in this case including the disappearance and reappearance as focus, the identity of the disappearing clown, the cloth and the mother herself as periphery, the familiar game as background context, and joy and excitement as affective tone (Searle, 1992). The words of a sentence relate to one another not as elements in the physical world but in their linguistic context, as elements of a system. The linguistic system is related to the physical world only as a means of reference, predication, and communication. Because the early "word" is not really independent of its context, even when used referentially, the meaning is insufficiently abstract to enter into a linguistic system that is, by definition, separate from the pragmatic world of action and objects. In the earliest phase of two-word utterances, the meanings of each word become more delimited; but at first the words are related primarily by their occurrence in a unified contextual experience. Veneziano (1999) found that using two different single words (termed "expressive options") across similar situations is a precursor to combinations of two words.

Early words are phonetic expressions integrated with background consciousness of an ongoing active unified experience. Later, sentences will emerge based on the internal experience of more differentiated meaningful events. As the internal experience becomes more differentiated and complete, such that a sense of the meaning "disappearance" can be felt as a motion event that occurs or "happens to" various entities, the child will begin to mention both dynamic motion (e.g., for disappearance the expression *gone*) and the entity involved (e.g., *gone . . . clown*), perhaps initially with a pause between the elements (Veneziano, 1999; Herr-Israel, 2006). The initial limitation to single words supports the view that the child experiences the event holistically. The fact that these early words at first directly express either entity meaning or dynamic meaning and are later combined in utterances consisting in the two sorts of words supports the idea that earlier single-word occurrence encompassed both entity and dynamic meaning. While both kinds of words occur in the single-word period, their combination occurs only when the child can internally designate object and dynamic motion somewhat separately, representing each with a separate word.

Werner and Kaplan further distinguish the period of two-word utterances from that of true sentences. They define a single vocable stage including "monoremes" (single-unit expressions that are most word-like) along with other communicative vocables, and a subsequent period where "duoremes" (two-unit expressions) are produced along with continued use of the earlier forms. Again, without adopting this terminology, keeping these ideas in mind helps to emphasize that the period of single-word use is not homogeneous either within itself or with the subsequent period of early combinations. The single and early multiword expressions produced by children are not initially equivalent to adult words and sentences.

Context-Limited Words

The task of categorizing children's early words poses as complex a problem as identifying them. Consider context-limited expressions, for example. For adults, language is a medium of symbolic representation, but early lexical expressions (such as Richard's *boo*), although their phonetic form is derived from adult words, can be considered as *accompaniments to or integrated aspects* of relatively specific ongoing events, rather than symbolizing or referring to those events. Such words, limited in occurrence to specific contexts or objects, are considered nonreferential. Vihman and McCune (1994) identified several types of context-limited words (Table 3–2); the process of applying these categories is discussed later in this chapter. As Bates (1976, following Piaget, 1962) noted, "initially the child does not understand or objectify the vehicle-referent relationship . . . rather words are merely a subset of schemes for acting on objects" (p. 90).

Barrett (1995) reported controversy in the field as to whether such context-limited words occur earlier than referential words, with a number of authors arguing that children begin referential word use only after attaining "the insight that words can be used symbolically to represent referents" (p. 367; see also Bloom, 1993). By that time, they may or may not have already acquired a number of context-limited words. Criteria distinguishing context-limited from referential word use vary across studies, rendering comparison of results problematic. Bates (1976) distinguished a clear pattern of development from context-bound to referential word use in three children by examining the expanding range of uses for specific individual words in her diary study, as did Vihman (1976), Dore (1985), and Kamhi (1986) in case studies of individual children. Harris, Barrett, Jones, and Brooks (1988) found both kinds of words among the first 10 produced by the four children they studied but did not distinguish order of entry, so one cannot be sure whether context-limited words occurred first. Others—such as Goldfield and Reznick (1990), who used parental report of two occurrences each, not necessarily in differing contexts, to establish word use—do not distinguish context-limited and referential words.

In summary, context-limited words emerge in relation to highly specific objects/events and fail to generalize across a broader range of seemingly related situations. Referential words do generalize across situations where children encounter experiences that remind them of a given word meaning. A given referential word emphasizes one or another aspect of an event: dynamic-event words emphasize the aspect of observed or potential motion in space and time, while nominals stress the entity aspect. However, reference is still to the event as a whole, and during the single-word period, differentiation of word from event is considered to be slight. This early referential experience prefigures the more complex capacity for "event representations" of known experiences, such as "the birthday party event" or the "trip to the zoo event" which can then be narrated with language (Barrett, 1995; Nelson, 1973, 1985). The Werner and Kaplan position, and that espoused here, is that the child experiences an ongoing event consciously, in the moment, and references that

Table 3–2
Word Use Categories

Referential Words

Referential Nominals: Nominal forms used with reference to a range of entities, suggesting child awareness of type/token relationship.

Dynamic Event Words: Words referring to reversible temporal or spatial transformations in the environment, with use across contexts demonstrating type/token relationships. For example, *gone, back, more, up.*

Context-Limited Words

Limited Nominals: Nominal forms used in a limited way to refer to a single referent or part of a routinized context, such as labeling animals with their characteristic sounds while "reading" with mother.

Specific Nominals: Nominals used to refer to particular persons or entities. The category corresponds to the adult subclass of "proper nouns" but may refer to terms with broader adult use treated as proper nouns by the child (e.g., *mommy; num num* for a favorite blanket).

Social Expression: Words used to mark real or pretend social interactions (*please, hi, yay*).

Routine/Game: Words elicited as part of baby games or routines not supported by a larger situational context, including animal sounds in response to questioning out of context (*baa*) or games such as *peek-a-boo, how big is baby?* etc.

Pretend Event: Words or consistent sounds marking pretend events (feeding doll—*yum*; rolling vehicle—*vroom*; serving tea—*tea* to refer to a range of tea-related objects and actions but limited to the pretend situation.

Specific Event: Used in relation to nonpretend events that do not exhibit a reversible character. Includes verbs or action words (e.g., *jump* while jumping) as well as real-life events (hurt finger—*ow*; sliding—*whee*). Single-context uses of dynamic event words were interpreted as specific event words.

Attentional/Deictic: Words used to point out people, entities, or events of interest (*this, that*), or to mark interest in general (*aha, look, oh*).

Adapted from Vihman and McCune (1994, Table 4), with permission.

experience with a word. We do not assume internal "event representations" existing as stored content apart from the child's immediate experience. Later, children can reconstruct past experiences internally and use language as part of that representational experience. As Macnamara (1972) put it, "we regard an utterance as the embodiment of thought in language" (p. 3). These ideas will be elaborated as we proceed.

The Nature of Referential Words

Is the capacity for reference a human "given," available to infants when needed to allow language acquisition? Macnamara (1982) assumed that reference was innate because he could conceive of no way in which a prereferential organism could "learn" to refer. Hollich and associates (2000) similarly grant a "principle" of reference in their first tier of developmental lexical principles conceived as guiding the child's entry into language (see also Golinkoff, Mervis, and Hirsch-Pasek, 1994). In this volume, I propose a manner in which the capacity for reference develops on the basis of children's representational capacity and the experience of naturally occurring physiological sound/meaning correspondence (Chapter 8). Werner and Kaplan similarly included reliance on "natural symbols" in their view of the transition to referential language (p. 109).

Findings from Mills and colleagues (e.g., Mills, Coffey-Carina, & Neville, 1994) suggest that the shift to a referential vocabulary is characterized by differential neurological processing of language. They distinguished 13- to 17-month-olds who produced either no words or only context-limited words (range 0 to 9 words) from those who had made the referential transition (range 17 to 97 words, primarily names). The referential children showed more specialized differential event-related potential (ERP) activity to comprehended versus unknown words than those producing, at most, context-limited words.

Vihman, in a passage included in McCune and Vihman (1997), defined referential words as those that function to select an environmental or mental entity or event for joint attention and conversation (relying on earlier theorists such as Bruner, 1983; Macnamara, 1982; Moore and Dunham, 1995). Lyons (1968) defined reference broadly as "the relationship which holds between words and the things, events, actions and qualities they 'stand for'": p. 424). Macnamara offered a more restrictive definition: "Reference is the contact language makes with the environment; it is the device that enables us to talk about the things we see and touch" (Macnamara, 1982, p. viii). Although "referring expressions" in adult language are typically nominal, this appears to be a grammatical convention that extends nominal status to words that questionably represent entities. For example, "a whiff of perfume," "the collapse of the bridge," "the sound of chimes," or "the flush that spread over her cheeks" (to take as illustrative referents only perceptually accessible "events") are all equally awkward exemplars of "things we see and touch," demonstrating that vehicles of reference extend to dynamic intangibles.

In identifying referential word use in children, Vihman and McCune (1994) applied the following criteria: (1) conscious attention to some entity or event, (2) a voluntary intention to draw the attention of a listener to that entity or event, and (3) implicit recognition that a given vocalization (word) stands as symbol to symbolized in relation to one of a range of related entities or events while failing to apply to others—the principle of contrast (Bates, Benigni, Bretherton, Camaioni, & Volterra, 1979; Dore, Franklin, Miller, & Ramer, 1976; Golinkoff et al. 1994; Piaget, 1962). This definition includes both referential nominals and dynamic event words.

Do "names for things" dominate in the single-word period? Because many baby words take the form of object names from the adult language and because adults more or less expect children to be learning names for the important elements of their environment, object names—sometimes considered more generally as "nouns"—have until recently been the primary focus of research concerning children's single words. Nelson, Hampson, and Shaw (1993), in agreement with Werner and Kaplan, state that a word cannot be recognized as a noun outside of its role in a sentence. Nelson (1973) and others have used the term *nominal* to recognize the naming aspect of apparent nouns that occur only as single words, not yet as constituents of sentences.

Many researchers consider words apparently naming objects and referring to a basic-level category of entities—for example, *dog* as opposed to the superordinate *animal* (Rosch, 1978)—as dominant in children's early vocabularies. Golinkoff and colleagues (1994) proposed lexical principles specifying why a "noun bias" should be the case, spurring a flurry of confirming and dissenting studies. Nelson and coworkers (1993) reanalyzed a cross-linguistic evaluation of extent of nouns in early vocabulary (Gentner, 1982) and found that of the six languages studied, in only two—English and German—did the percentage of common nouns reach the 50% level. Nelson and associates' analysis of their own data, vocabulary use by 45 English-speaking 20-month-olds, revealed a mean of 38% common nouns, in contrast with 70% nouns reported by mothers for these same children on a checklist! Nelson and colleagues found that the checklist itself was biased in favor of common nouns—68% of items. However, this bias also reflects the general expectation among both parents and students of child language—an expectation that initially, the learning of language involves the task of learning names for things. Concerning names for basic-level categories, these comprised 52% of all nouns reported on the checklist in the study by Nelson and coworkers. Recent work on Korean suggests a bias toward verb use in Korean (Choi & Gopnik, 1995), in conflict with the analysis of Bornstein and colleagues. The dynamic-event meanings expressed in English with relational words are expressed in Korean with a set of verbs having similar meanings to relational words in English.

Bornstein and associates (2004) attempted to overcome the proportional predominance of nouns in checklists by omitting places and people from the operational definition of nouns (a conservative strategy) and including "actions, activities, games, and verbs" (p. 9), not just standard verbs, in their operational definition of verbs (a strategy that would presumably include many dynamic event words as defined here). They also credited children by percent of items available in each word class category rather than analyzing raw numbers using the Early Language Inventory (ELI), a precursor to the MacArthur-Bates CDI (Fenson et al., 1994). The procedure still finds a slight advantage for nouns across seven languages studied—including Korean, previously cited as an exception to the noun bias. The authors note methodological differences across studies and place the noun bias issue within the domain of universal versus language-specific effects.

Dynamic-event words are the child's earliest reference to movement and change, the dynamic aspects of events, with meanings that apply across a wide variety of objects. Parallel development of two classes of words, with different classes of words emphasizing entity and dynamic relational aspects of events that will later be referenced in sentences suggests that both aspects are salient to the child (Gentner, 1978; Lyons, 1968).

Recognition of the significance of dynamic event words might render the controversy concerning the part-of-speech categories "noun" and "verb" moot. The adult-form class of the words chosen may be of little relevance in interpreting children's single word speech if single words refer to entire events. The status of apparent naming words, or nominals, in early child language is only questionably related to the adult linguistic category *noun*. In discussing the problem of applying adult linguistic categories to child vocalizations, Maratsos (1998) suggested the terminology "prospective" category (e.g., "prospective noun" in this case). Children do attend to and manipulate objects, and it seems likely that the early nominal words mark the beginning of a trajectory toward reference to entities in the environment that will eventually be referenced by nouns in complete sentences.

Words are sometimes thought to reflect underlying categories, where instances of word use identify category members. This view, based on the cognitivist metaphor (mind as computer), assumes that categories are built up from experience and exist as mental contents. In contrast, I propose that words occur through a process of ongoing immediate experience, where a present situation reminds the child of past occurrences where he or others applied a given word. The difference between these views is that in the first the category is defined as existing brain/mind contents; in the second, there is no stored internal category. Rather, the child's word is based on immediate conscious reminding that instates some aspect of the conscious experiences when the word was previously heard and/or spoken. Werner and Kaplan discuss a shift from specific events eliciting words to elicitation by internal dynamic schematizing aroused across a widening variety of experiences. The more recently a word has been heard or said in circumstances similar to a given experience, the more likely the child is to produce that word (Gershkoff-Stowe et al., 2006).

An example demonstrates the underlying idiosyncratic basis for children's extension of some words. My granddaughter Brielle, at 18 months of age, was a highly successful word user who generalized her words in ways that are typical of young children but that can pose a challenge in relation to adult notions of categorization. The stars of the British-derived television show *Teletubbies* included four characters: Po, Lala, Dipsy, and Tinkie-Winky. These are bulbous figures, each a different color, varying in size and slightly in shape, all of whom have television screens in their tummies and antennas (shapes vary) coming from their heads. Brielle first developed the word *Po*, whispered perhaps because of the aspirated [p] sound appropriately applied to a large toy figure of Po among her toys. However, she rapidly extended this name to all four characters on the show. Some weeks later, presented with a Lala doll at 19 months, she learned the word *Lala*. Rather than dividing her characters into *Po* and *Lala* figures, she shifted and began labeling all of the figures, including both Teletubby toys and a request to view a favorite videotape, *Lala!* It seems that, at first, Teletubby experiences elicited the whispered sound *Po*. Later, similar events evoked *Lala*. It may be that *Po*, with its idiosyncratic pronunciation, was discarded in favor of a more fully formed adult-like expression.

Does this exemplify use of a basic category term? Perhaps, but it began with the name of an individual and then the whole basic-level group (if *Teletub-bies* can be so considered) was relabeled and her expression of desire to see them on video took the same vocal form! This and other examples (e.g., Bloom & Lahey, 1978; Bowerman, 1975) make it seem unlikely that theoretical distinctions between "basic"-level and other types of categories is pertinent to the single-word period. It is not clear that children's words are linked to "categories" in the same way that we often assume adults' words are. Gershkoff-Stowe, Thal, Smith, & Namy (1997), in studies discussed in Chapter 4, found no correlation between children's performance in categorization tasks and their lexical development.

For referential production, the child must experience a conscious state relevant in some way to a previous state when that word was comprehended or produced and must generate the word based partially on an internal sense of the external context. In situations of language comprehension where children hear a familiar word and react with understanding although they have never produced the word, a complementary situation ensues. Hearing the familiar word brings about a conscious state similar to that experienced in a previous encounter, perhaps calling the child's attention to a perceived element of the present context that reminds her, in some way, of the previous occasion on which she heard the word. In neither production nor comprehension cases is it necessary to assume that word and meaning, with their links, are stored. Rather, in comprehension, a familiar word serves as a reminder of previous meaningful situations. Occasions when a word not produced previously is imitated with comprehension may form a bridge for some word learning. In imitation, the child is using the adult form as a stimulus guiding his own production (McCune-Nicolich & Raph, 1978). Any of the previous production contexts can serve as the basis for extension of the word on future analogous occasions.

Rate of Lexical Development: The "Vocabulary Spurt"

Along with emphasis on experimental paradigms and the use of parent-report data, the possible universality and significance of a sharp spurt in rate of vocabulary learning during the single-word period has been a major preoccupation of language researchers, especially those studying English acquisition (see Barrett, 1995, for a review). Upon close examination of reports regarding this phenomenon, it turns out to be poorly defined and far from universal. Studies differ somewhat arbitrarily in their definitions as to what constitutes a "spurt." While some researchers base their findings on maternal reports only (e.g., Goldfield & Reznick, 1990), others use only words produced in the laboratory (e.g., Bloom, 1993). In either case, the goal is to identify new words (those that have not been reported or observed previously) in the child's production, with a sudden growth in the number of such words constituting the basis for identifying a spurt. The extent of new-word production required for a spurt also varies from study to study. Thus Bloom (1993) required observation of 12 new words in a monthly session, with a minimum base of 20 words previously observed. Ninio (1995) identified the spurt as the "observation in which the biggest vocabulary increase occurred relative to the previous observation" (p. 19) but presented no numerical data. Goldfield and Reznick (1990) considered any 2 1/2–week interval after which 10 new words were reported as a "spurt interval" (p. 175) and reported the timing and extent of spurting in individual children; Roberts (1998) required 12 new words in a 2-week interval by maternal report; and Mervis and Bertrand (1995) required 10 new words in a 2-week period by maternal report, 5 of which must be nouns. Given these varied criteria, it seems a stretch to consider the "vocabulary spurt" as a universal developmental phenomenon, although recent studies often define it as a turning point in development.

Variability in the timing of the identified spurt further suggests that the changes in rate of new word acquisition described by researchers may not entail a specific developmental effect. Bloom (1993), who followed 14 children (12 from 9 months of age and 2 more from 11 months) until they achieved a vocabulary spurt, reported that 5 children exhibited a spurt by 18 months of age and the others by 26 months. A spurt prior to using 50 different words was exhibited by 9 children and by 5 only after that milestone. Goldfield and Reznick (1990) reported that 13 of 18 children followed from 14 months on showed a vocabulary spurt, varying in age from 15 to 22 months, with the remainder showing sustained but slower growth. The base vocabulary in "spurters" ranged from 0 to 60 words at the outset of the spurt. Roberts (1998), who began observation at 15 to 16 months, identified spurts between 17 and 19 months. Mervis and Bertrand followed four "late spurters," who accelerated after 20 months, when their reported base vocabularies ranged from 89 to 112 words. Considering others' findings, 20 months is not particularly late for increased vocabulary growth. In summary, changes in rate of vocabulary acquisition over a child's course of development have been characterized in a variety of ways, all using the term *vocabulary spurt*.

Ganger and Brent (2004) addressed the methodological problems imbedded in searching for a vocabulary spurt directly. Following Bloom (2000), they state that a "spurt" requires a sustained change in rate rather than a single time span during which a larger number of words are learned than during a previous span. In order to confirm a spurt, longitudinal data from an individual child need to be tested to determine whether the resultant curve has an inflection point (i.e., a logistic curve rather than a quadratic curve), the statistical definition of a shift in rate of development. In a series of studies using the appropriate statistical analysis and involving 38 children, including both newly collected data and reanalysis of the Goldfield and Reznick (1990) data, they found only 5 children whose pattern of growth indicated a spurt.

An alternative and promising measure suggested by Pan, Rowe, Singer, and Snow (2005) is growth in diversity of vocabulary used in observation sessions. I will argue in what follows that more frequent word production, following the transition to referential word use, is the likely underlying change leading to the appearance of various spurt-like phenomena.

Words of the Single-Word Period: Analysis of Vihman and McCune Data

Vihman and I (Vihman & McCune, 1994) addressed a number of the questions raised in this chapter in a study of our pooled sample of 20 children studied from 9 to 16 months of age, summarized here. Data were collected in homes beginning before the occurrence of any single words, but collection methods differed somewhat based on the varying goals of the each investigator's research. Parents of children in Vihman's Stanford sample, studied at Stanford University, were informed that child language was of primary interest (Vihman, et al., 1985) and engaged in eliciting language in the observation sessions. This study focused on phonological precursors of early words. Parents of McCune's Rutgers sample, studied at Rutgers University, were told that the study emphasized children's spontaneous play but were asked not to influence their children's activities during the data collection sessions (McCune, 1995). Home visitors for the Rutgers sample were told to limit their interaction with participants during the taping and attempt to create a comfortable context for interaction primarily between parent and child. The Stanford children were visited weekly, continuing until 16 or 17 months; the Rutgers children, monthly until 24 months or beyond, depending on language progress. Rutgers children had been observed within a week of their birth date and then monthly. For purposes of the authors' joint research, Stanford samples were selected to be as close as possible to each child's month birth date.

Analyzing the Transcripts

Both referential and context-limited words were identified by the procedures described earlier and applied to the 20,711 vocalizations transcribed. Referential words were those that occurred across at least two different contexts and/or in relation to at least two different objects or events, where consistent properties could be identified that unified the observed uses. Words were considered context-limited unless they met these criteria. Words occurring only as imitations were not included in these categories or further categorized. In the rare cases where a word occurred both spontaneously and in imitation, occurrences were pooled and categorized according to the spontaneous occurrences. The referential transition was credited to the first session where the child produced two different referential words, with continued production of these or other referential words in subsequent sessions. These criteria were determined so that we would have confidence that a phase shift to referential language was occurring. Those wishing to distinguish the beginning of such a trend might employ less stringent criteria. For comparison, the context-limited transition was credited to the first session where two context-limited words were first produced, with continued production of any words in subsequent sessions.

Results: Referential Word Development Is Robust

We will first consider progress of the pooled sample of 20 children as they produced their first words and made the referential transition. Context-limited words were produced by all 20 children, while 13 children met criteria for the referential transition by 16 months of age (Table 3–3). Considering individual children who used both context-limited and referential words, mean age for onset of context-limited words was 11.15 months (±1.73), three months earlier than for referential words (14.50 mos., ±1.05; $t = -6.94$; $df = 12$; two tailed $P < 0.001$). The children not exhibiting referential words by 16 months all included one or more context-limited words in their repertoires, so they also exhibit a precedence of context-limited words. Earlier reports had suggested a gradual transition from context-limited to referential use of the same lexical items in the course of development (Bates et al., 1979). Our data failed to substantiate this suggestion. Numbers of context-limited word types used prior to referential word onset by the 13 children credited with the referential word transition ranged from 0 to 28. The number of these word types later produced in the sessions as referential words ranged from 0 to 6 per child, with 50% of the children who produced them failing to shift any words from context-limited to referential use. This suggests that for some children, context-limited words expand in meaning to become referential, but this may not be the typical pattern of early word learning. Careful diary study is more likely to identify such sequences than is periodic language sampling such as we used.

Large differences in numbers of words produced by the two samples were immediately evident. What could account for them? The Rutgers and Stanford samples differed in the frequency of observation, conduct of the sessions, and some goals of the studies. With the greater emphasis on language and more frequent home visits for the Stanford sample, we were not surprised that these children tended to be more voluble, producing many more utterances per session, on average, than the Rutgers sample. In fact, the mean number of utterances for the Stanford sample ranged from 107 to 298 across the 10 children, while the mean for the Rutgers sample ranged from 40 to 122! Similarly, at 16 months, their final observation, the Stanford children were credited with, on average, 16.8 different words, in contrast with 11.4 for the Rutgers children. It was natural for us to wonder what could account for this difference. We could be seeing a genuine intervention effect from the Stanford strategy. Alternatively, the McCune strategy may have suppressed children's language expression. Neither of these was exactly the case. Rather, our subsequent analysis demonstrated developmental importance of the distinction between context limited and referential words. To more fully understand the

Table 3–3
Age at Transitions in Single-Word Production and Number of Different Referential Words Observed across All Sessions

Name	Sample[a]	Age (Months) at Transitions to Kinds of Word		Number of Different Referential Words		
		Context-Limited	Referential	Dynamic Event	Nominals	Total
1. Alice	RU	10	14	4	28	32
2. Sean	SU	11	13	2	16	18
3. Molly	SU	10	14[b]	4	13	17
4. Deborah	SU	10	14	6	10	16
5. Timmy	SU	11	14	0	15	15
6. Emily	SU	13	14	2	10	12
7. Aurie	RU	14	14	7	5	12
8. Rala	RU	15	15[c]	1	9	10
9. Rick	RU	10	15	2	6	8
10. Jase	RU	14	15	2	4	6
11. Thomas	SU	12	16	2	2	4
12. Kari	RU	16	16	2	0	2
13. Ronny	RU	11	16	0	2	2
14. Andrew	SU	16	–	1	0	1
15. Camille	SU	15	–	1	0	1
16. Nenni	RU	11	–	0	0	1
17. Jonah	SU	14	–	1	0	1
18. Danny	RU	16	–	0	0	0
19. Susie	SU	13	–	0	0	0
20. Vido	RU	13	–	0	0	0

[a]"RU" designates children in the Rutgers Sample.
"SU" designates children in the Stanford Sample.
[b]No session was available for Molly that was within 1 week of her month birth date at 14 months. A session between 13 and 14 months (13 months, 2 weeks) detailed in Vihman and Velleman (1989) and Vihman (1996) demonstrated that she had made the referential transition by 14 months.
[c]No session was collected at 14 months for Rala.

production differences between the samples, we sorted each child's words, for each session, into one of three categories: referential words, context-limited words, and words used only in imitation and not further categorized. We then compared the total word types in each category produced by session across the months of data collection, pooling total number of types for each child within the Rutgers and the Stanford groups by month. Significantly, the trajectory for producing referential words was virtually identical for both samples, with none produced before 13 months. By 14 to 15 months, each group produced approximately 20 referential words, and by 16 months, approximately 60. In contrast, differences were apparent in the production of context-limited words and words occurring only in imitation, as can be clearly seen in Figure 3–1. Beginning at 13 months and continuing through 16 months, the Stanford sample steadily outpaced the Rutgers sample in numbers of context-limited words and those occurring only as imitations (Table 3–4 and Figure 3–1), while numbers of referential words were quite similar.

The similarity of growth in referential words across the two samples, in contrast with variation in context-limited and imitated words was striking as our published study indicated:

> It is likely that the different experiences the research afforded the parents at each site are relevant to the differences in numbers of early words produced. The Stanford mothers became close collaborators in monitoring their children's language acquisition. They focused on vocal production, encouraged by weekly inquiries from the observer. They also engaged in lively interchanges with the observer in the course of the session, resulting in a 'chatty' atmosphere which probably contributed to the children's higher vocal output. The Rutgers mothers were not encouraged to attend to any particular aspects of their child's development. The research team provided

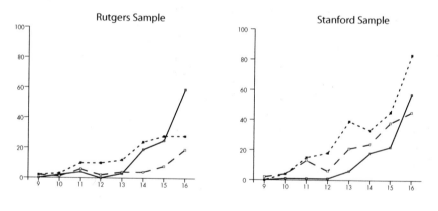

Figure 3–1. Numbers of word types summed across children by month for the Rutgers and Stanford samples. Although the Stanford sample produced many more words per session than the Rutgers sample beginning at 12 months, this difference resulted from higher numbers of context-limited and imitated words, while numbers of referential words remained similar for the two samples throughout the study. See the text for interpretation of this finding. [Adapted from Vihman and McCune (1994) p. 531, with permission.]

Table 3–4
Total Number of Words across Children in the Rutgers and Stanford Samples by Month

I. Rutgers	9	10	11	12	13	14	15	16
Referential	–	2	4	–	4	18	25	58
Limited	2	3	10	10	12	24	28	28
Imitations	3	1	6	2	5	5	9	19
Total	5	6	20	12	21	47	62	105
II. Stanford	9	10	11	12	13	14	15	16
Referential	–	1	1	1	7	16	23	55
Limited	–	5	14	17	39	33	46	84
Imitations	2	4	11	7	21	25	37	46
Total	2	10	26	25	67	74	106	185

general information about child development upon request, and did collect checklists of words used in the intervening month, but there was an explicit intention to minimize parental awareness of detailed research goals, lest these influence their interactions with the children. These mothers attended to their children's play and communication without attempting to elicit any specific behavior relevant to the research. They attempted to maintain children's interest in the toy set and rarely spoke to the observer. It is certainly plausible that weekly visits and emphasis on language contributed to a generally greater focus on language in the daily lives of the Stanford sample.

If, indeed the differences in the total number of words produced in the two samples reflects differences in parental experience, which thus had differential influence on the language environments of the homes, then the most notable finding here is the ABSENCE of a difference in flexible [here termed referential] word use in the two samples. This supports the possibility that the greater overall word production in the Stanford sample reflected an unintended "training effect" due to the focus on language, and at the same time suggests that such training is constrained by developmental limitations. Context-bound word use is susceptible to variation in parental efforts to encourage language, but adult-like referential usage will emerge in relation to developmental variables less susceptible to variation based on parental attention, participation in verbal games, book-reading and so on. (McCune & Vihman, 1994, pp. 530–31)

Reference, Frequency and the "Vocabulary Spurt"

As discussed, earlier studies often (but not always) report that children exhibit a sudden upswing in producing new lexical items, although criteria for and timing of the increase vary (Barrett, 1995) and individual children's data rarely fit the profile for a statistical rate increase (Ganger & Brent, 2004). Our group data show that a group shift in number of different (not necessarily new) word types produced in a given month was associated with the transition to reference. Rather than a shift in rate of development, this increase in production marked a qualitative shift in the language acquisition process. It may be that the various "vocabulary spurts" reported in the literature, most of which do not represent a true "rate shift," actually result from the shift to referential word production as defined here. In Chapter 7 we return to this possibility, considered from the perspective of enhanced lexical production facility.

Word Use Categories for the Single-Word Period

The categories we had identified were useful in capturing the variety of the children's early word use (see Table 3–2). The categories of context-limited words offer a window into the sorts of occasions children marked with their early words, and detailed study of these contextual uses over time might prove interesting. See Table 3–5 for numbers of children by month who produced words falling into each category and Appendix 3A for a list of their words. In the final session for the combined sample, at 16 months, 11 of the 13 children who were credited with the referential transition had used both referential nominals and dynamic event words. The data in Table 3–3 show that two children credited with the referential transition produced no dynamic event words in the course of the study, and one, Kari, was credited with no referential nominals. Inclusion of both types of words in the single-word lexicons is the norm, which was achieved by these children in subsequent months.

Bloom (1993), summarized evidence from previous studies, indicating that some children were described as beginning with more substantive (nominal) words and others with more relational (dynamic event) words, with often a later shift to balance, while still others showed no difference in distribution by these categories (1993, p. 197). Bloom also reported a number of words that did not conform to either category, some of which I would consider dynamic-event words and others that conform to one of the context-limited categories. Bloom's analysis confirmed the importance of two kinds of words, to an understanding of children's development of meaning in the single-word period: nominals and dynamic-event words. On the basis of her own longitudinal study of 14 children (Bloom, 1993) as well as an earlier case study (Bloom, 1973) and review of others' work, Bloom concluded that, with the exception of substantive (nominal) and relational (dynamic-event) words, additional categories applied to children's single-word speech are ill-defined. She concluded that "Relational concepts provide the underpinnings for much of the semantic structure of language" (Bloom, 1993, p. 229).

Conclusion

My central claim in this book is that by careful observation and analysis of children's behavioral development beginning prior to language. it should be

Table 3-5

Number of the Twenty Children Spontaneously Producing Words in Each Category by Month

Age in Months	Context-Limited Words						Atttention/ Deictic	Referential Words	
	Social Expression	Routine Game	Pretend Event	Specific Event	Specific Nominal	Nominal		Dynamic Event	Nominal
9	1		1	1					3
10	3	2	1		1	2			1
11	3	1	5	3	2	3		1	
12	2	1	4	3	3	5			
13	5	4	3	4	4	5	1	2	5
14	5	6	6	5	5	6	1	2	8
15	9	9	12	10	5	7	2	9	11
16	11	6	11	6	7	11	1	14	12

65

possible to predict when a given child will begin referential word use. Here I have established the critical distinction between clearly defined referential word use as distinct from possibly earlier context-limited word use, and the division of referential words into those that refer primarily to entities, often termed "nominals," and those that refer primarily to movement and change, here termed "dynamic event words." In the next chapter I will describe the cognitive trajectory that children experience during the time period of the transition to reference. This involves both the development of a capacity for conscious mental representation in contrast with a limitation to perception of the here and now and a related ability to predict and reflect upon moment-to moment events in space and time.

Appendix 3A

Word forms produced at the 16 Month session. Each child's word shapes are presented with frequency of occurrence and most common spontaneous phonetic variant. If the phonetic variants are equally distributed, the variant best matching the adult phonetic shape is presented. For Emily, Ronny, and Susie the 15 month session is used. One child, Nenni, who produced no words at 16 months, is omitted.

1. ALICE

Referential words
Nominals
apple (4) [ʔæ]
baby (7) [beibi]
belly (1) [vei]
blanket (1) [k'ɛt]
bottle (i4) [badi]
bunny (3) [bʌn̩n̩:i]
daddy (2) [da:di]
duck (1) [tæʔ]
egg (8) [ʔei]
eye (4) [ʔaɪ]
flower (3) [p'adi]
hat (2) [ʔa]
iron (2) [ʔāɪji]
key (1) [çi]
lady (4) [jɛ:ji]
man (1) [mæ̃:]
meat (1) [miʔ]
milk (1) [m̩mæ]
Oscar (= puppet) (6) [ʔaʔ]
plate (4) [p'ɛɪ]
shoe (1) [çi]
tea (1) [t̪i:]

Context-limited words
Limited nominals
bang (1) [pāi]
elephant (4) [ā:ɪjʌ]
nose (1) [n:æ]
Specific nominals
Grandpa (3) [p'a]
mommy (10) [ma:n̩i]
Social expression
bye (1) [baɪ]
Specific/Pretend event
clean (2) [ti:ni]
shiny (3) [ta:ji]
Imitation only
hello (1) [loʊ]

Dynamic event words
down (2) [dãʊ]
no (1) [næ]
up (2) [ʔʌ:p]

2. SEAN
Referential words
Nominals
bird (12) [bwɪ:ts]
block (16) [pak]
book (4) [bik]
bug (2) [m̩bʌkl̩]
butterfly (3) [pʌjʌ:]
cracker (2) [dʒak]
dog (3) [taǫ]
duck (4) [tʌk']
fish (4) [føtʃ]
horse (12) [ʔɪʃ]
moo sound (6) [ʔõ:ʰ]
mouse (9) [maʰ]
rabbit (3) [pʰæts]
Dynamic event words
more (29) [mɔ]

Context-limited words
Limited nominals
cock-a-doodle-doo sound (2)
[dəlʊdəlʊ::]
quack sound (5) [ʔaʔ]
vroom sound (3) [β::]
woof sound (2) [waʊ]
Specific nominals
mama (9) [ma:]
Routine/Game
baa sound (3) [baʰ]
blue (3) [bʊʰ]
Attentional/Deictic
look (4) [jɛkʰ]
oh (9) [ʔɔʰ]
this (6) [dɪs]
Imitation only
berries (3) [bɛbiʃ]
Ian (2) [niʰ]
stuck (1) [na:k']

3. MOLLY
Referential words
Nominals
baby (2) [pebi]
block (8) [pak]
book (13) [pʊk]
camera (4) [kamə]
ear (4) [he:]
glasses (29) [kaki]
meow sound (8) [miʌ]
nose (1) [no:]
Dynamic event words
stuck (1) [kak]

Context-limited words
Limited nominals
bead (8) [pi:]
piano (2) [paʊ]
picture (4) [pöpö]
Specific nominals
Brett (9) [pat]
Graham (9) [kɔn:i]
Grandma (1) [mɛʊwʌ]
Grandpa (1) [kæpɔ]
mama (7) [mama]
Nicky (2) [ɪn:i]
Nonny (10) [naṇni]
Ruth (6) [wʊt]
Social expression
hi (4) [ʔai:]
Routine/Game
baa sound (2) [pæ:]
cluck sound (11) [bʌʔbʌʔ]
neigh sound (8) [p'ʌ]
moo sound (13) [mʊ:]

3. MOLLY
Routine/Game (cont'd)

peek-a-boo (7) [pik]
snort sound (14) [ʔɛʔ]
three (2) [wi:]
two (2) [tʊ]
woof sound (17) [wʊ]
Specific/Pretend event
bang (4) [pan:ə]
choochoo sound (10) [tʊtʊ]
down (10) [taṇnə]
walk-walk (8) [wɔkæ]
vroom sound (12) [br̃ʌm]
Imitation only
click (11) [kik]
good girl (2) [gʊgə]
green (3) [kʏn:ɪ]
house (2) [haʊt]
in (1) [iḥni]
name (1) [nɛm:i]
oink sound (1) [ho:k]
open (1) [hɔpɔ]
pig (1) [pɪk]
red (2) [wat]
rug (3) [wa:k]
tail (26) [teʊ]
that (2) [tat]
work (6) [hʌk]

4. DEBORAH
Referential words
Nominals
baby (7) [p'e:bi]
ball (7) [bɔə]
bird (2) [bwa]
bottle (2) [ba:]
cheese (2) [ṣi:]
corn (5) [kʰɔ:]
duck (1) [tæ]
eye (6) [ʔaɪ]
kitty (4) [k'ekḷi]
Dynamic event words
down (4) [ta]
up (3) [ʔah]

Context-limited words
Limited nominals
moo sound (8) [bo::]
Specific nominals
monkey (1) [hṃmæ:]
Social expression
bye (1) [pa:ɪ]
hi (15) [haɪ]
Routine/Game
A (1) [ʔe:]
three (8) [ṣi::]
two (2) [tʰi]
Specific/Pretend event
water (5) [wawɔa]
hug sound (4) [ʔṃ :ṃ]
yum sound (12) [ʔṃ]
Imitation only
carrot (1) [kʰeɪwi]
cow (1) [kʰʔ:]
ear (1) [ʔi:ʔ]
crashing rock sound (2) [kx̣ ::]
hair (1) [ʔeəʔ]

5. TIMMY

Referential words
Nominals
baby (12) [pæpæ]
block (17) [gm̩bæ]
boat (2) [pæ]
bracelet (6) [pæpæ]
car (2) [kəɪ]
eye (5) [ʔæɪ]
fish (2) [s:æ]
light (15) [aija]
round & round (helicopter) (15) [ʌligʌligæ]

Context-limited words
Limited nominals
balloon (5) [bɛɪ]
toottoot sound (2) [dʌits:]
Specific nominals
daddy (2) [tadæ]
mama (2) [mʌmæ]
Nana (1) [ʔæ:nɛnæ]
Ruth (4) [hʌβæ]
Simon (6) [nʌmæ]
Social expression
hiya (3) [əɪjæ]
Routine/Game
D (1) [di::]
Imitation only
boy (1) [bʌɪ]
cookie (1) [kaki]
flower (1) [ʌøæ]
goodbye (2) [kæbæ]
please (3) [pai]

6. EMILY

Referential words
Nominals
beads (1) [pʰi:gɛ]
box (2) [pʰat:]
Dynamic event words
more (17) [mɔ:]

Context-limited words
Specific nominals
Marilyn (2) [mɛmɛ]
Routine/Game
tickle (5) [tʰitʰi]
Specific/Pretend event
yum sound (17) [ʔʌm]
daddy (7) [dædæ]
Attentional/Deictic
oh (2) [ʔou]
Imitation only
night-night (1) [na | næt]
open (5) [ʔap'pi]
patty-cake (3) [p'ak'æ]
up (2) [ʔʌp]

7. AURIE

Referential words
Nominals
apple (2) [ʔæbi]
book (1) [bʊk:ts]
dolly (2) [ʔadi]
shoe (2) [tsi]
Dynamic event words
bye (1) [bæbæi]
peek-a-boo (2) [p'iḥhu:]
up (5) [ʔap]

Context-limited words
Limited nominals
cock-a-doodle-doo
   sound (6) [kakijali::]
Social expression
hello (12) [hʌ:o]
hi (4) [hæi]
Routine/Game
open (2) [tʰʌ:ᵖpu]
tickle-tickle (1) [tɪkətɪk]

7. AURIE (cont'd)

Specific/Pretend event
ow (1) [ʔæʊ]
yum sound (2) [vʌm:i]
Imitation
orange (1) [ʔãwis]
stuck (1) [tæ]
out (1) [ʔaʊt]
uh-oh (1) [hʌʔʊ]
pretty (1) [pli]
whoop (1) [wʊ::]
yoohoo (5) [hʊhʊ]

8. RALA

Referential words
Nominals
baby (5) [p'epi]
ball (10) [bo]
beads (2) [ʔɛbi]
bottle (6) [hʌbaʊ]
car (7) [[hɛk'a]
comb (8) [hɛkɔm]
mouth (4) [mão]
shoes (2) [əʃə:ʃ]
spoon (5) [hɛbʊ:]
Dynamic event words
uh-oh (7) [ʔʌʔ]

Context-limited words
Specific/Pretend event
tea (11) [ti:]
do (6) [n̩htʊ]
go[es] (6) [Pɪk'oʊ]
Attentional/Deictic
see (20) [si:]
Imitation only
bye (3) [baɪ]
toe (2) [hɛthoʊ]

9. RICK

Referential words
Nominals
ball (3) [p'ʊ:]
doggie (2) [gʊ:dɪ]
eyes (3) [ʔaɪ]
spoon (1) [p'ʊ:p'i]
Dynamic event words
no (2) [noʊ]
open (17) [oʊp'i]

Context-limited words
Limited nominals
beads (1) [[pidʒi]
Specific nominals
daddy (2) [dægɪ]
mommy (6) [mam:]
Social expression
hi (6) [haɪ]
Specific/Pretend event
yum sound (1) [ʔʌm̩]

10. JASE

Referential words
Nominals
ball (1) [bɔ::ə]
dog (4) [dʊ:]
Grover (puppet) (3) [gɔ:]
juice (4) [dʒis]
Dynamic event words
more (5) [mɔ̃]

Context-limited words
Limited nominals
woof sound (5) [wʌp]
Specific nominals
mommy (7) [mam]
Social expression
no (2) [noʊ]

11. THOMAS
Referential words
Nominals
ball (23) [pakʰi]
glasses (6) [gæːti]
Dynamic event words
no (5) [nɔ]
up (2) [ʔap]

Context-limited words
Limited nominals
truck (4) [tʌkɪs]
woof sound (2) [ʔʌʔʌʔʌ]
Social expression
hi (4) [haɪ]
oh yeah (1) [hãːjaʰ]
Specific/Pretend event
down (1) [taː]
Imitation only
baby (2) [biː]
string (1) [tiʰ]
toe (1) [toʊ]
zoom (2) [zʊːːɫ]

12. KARI
Referential words
Dynamic event words
uh-oh (1) [ʔʌʔa]
up (1) [ʔap]

Context-limited words
Specific/Pretend event
car sound (5) [ʔm̩]
Imitation only
no (1) [nʌ]

13. RONNY
Referential words
Nominals
baby (7) [pˈebi]
woof sound (1) [waβa]

Context-limited words
Specific nominals
mama (1) [mama]
Social expression
hello (1) [[ʔalːo]
Routine/Game
sit (1) [sɪt]
Specific/Pretend event
vroom sound (1) [vř̩ːʊm]
Attentional/Deictic
this (1) [dɪ]
Imitation only
yellow (1) [ɪjæbɔ]

14. ANDREW
Referential words
Dynamic event words
up (3) [ʔæp]

Context-limited words
Limited nominals
spoon (2) [pˈʊ]
Social expression
no (1) [neːː]
Imitation only
bird (7) [be]
clock (3) [kæk]
mountain (2) [mʌ]
tail (4) [tˈe]

15. CAMILLE
Referential words
  Dynamic event words
  up (7) [ʔap]

Context-limited words
  Specific/Pretend event
  car sound (3) [ʤi::s]
  Attentional/Deictic
  (what's) this (7) [ʔəzis]
  Imitation only
  hello (5) [həhə]

17. JONAH

Context-limited words
  Routine/Game
  roar sound (9) [kɹ̆]
  Specific/Pretend event
  rock-rock (3) [wa:ʰwa]
  Imitation only
  cock-a-doodle-doo
    sound (2) [əkakɛk:a]
  cookie (2) [k'ak'a]
  no (2) [na::ʊ]

18. DANNY

Context-limited words
  Attentional/Deictic
  aha (8) [ʔæ̃hæ̃]
  that (6) [dæ:]

19. SUSIE

Context-limited words
  Specific/Pretend event
  kiss sound (7) [ʔm̩]
  Imitation only
  ice (cream) (1) [ʔaʔi]
  out there (2) [atats]

20. VIDO

Context-limited words
  Limited nominals
  baby (2) [bobap]
  Social expression
  thank you (8) [de:ɪde]
  unh-hunh (5) [[ʔə̃hə̃]
  Imitation only
  apple (2) [bapba]
  daddy (1) [daɦi]
  flower (3) [fa:βwa]
  good (1) [gʊ:ŋ]
  keys (2) [se:s]
  yellow (1) [dɛbloʊ]

4

Cognitive Bases of Language

As children make the transition to language, they are also making the transition from an obligatory perceptual mode of understanding the world to the capacity for mental representation, an essential development for reference. Change in one or only a few contributing variables, termed "control parameters," can lead to such systemwide reorganization (Thelen, 1989, pp. 79–80). The shift from primary reliance on perceptual processes to mental representation is gradual, and these modes of processing are not diametrically opposed to one another. Cognition is essentially embodied, and perceptual and motor processes are basic aspects of cognition. But as mental representation develops, broader possibilities for mental processing emerge. Piaget is sometimes cited as proposing abstract adult cognitive abilities as antithetical to earlier sensorimotor processes (e.g., Mandler, 2004). In truth, he was a great proponent of continuity, basing the emergence of logical thought on processes that originally serve to interpret real space, time, and motion. The ability to represent this early knowledge mentally, in the moment, serves, according to Piaget, as a bridge to analogous processes that, while more abstract, are continuous with earlier sensorimotor regulations (Piaget & Inhelder, 1969).

Studies of infant cognition in recent years have focused on the issue of "concepts"; that is, when they may be available to infants and what is their nature. Historically, concepts were seen as deeply related to language, but researchers currently investigate conceptual and category development in young infants who will not learn language for many months, infants presumed by many to rely on the perceptual and motor processes of the sensorimotor period. Typically, this research describes the infants' successful performance in familiarization/discrimination tasks as based on "representations" of categories and/or exemplars. This use of the term *representations* refers to information theoretically stored in the brain that forms the basis for internal computational mental processes, based on the "mind as a computer" metaphor. This definition is in stark contrast with my use of the term *mental representation*.

The Cognitivist Metaphor and Beyond

Mainstream cognitive science is grounded in the idea that the brain is a repository for discrete entities termed "representations." These are presumed to be formed by experiences in the world and are then subject to computational processes leading to behavioral as well as internal analytic outcomes. Freeman and Skarda (1990) describe this view as follows:

> [T]he human ability to understand the world is likened to the procedures for incorporating information on a tape into a machine by means of symbols. Cognitive operations are interpreted as manipulating these symbols according to certain semantic rules. At present we are all so accustomed to this metaphor that it seems self-evident. . . . Any other account appears to be "noncognitive" (Earle, 1987) and counterintuitive. In short, to question this commonsense notion seems quixotic, sophistic, and arbitrary. (p. 375)

Freeman and Skarda's tone, however, suggests that they do question this view. Their paper, entitled "Representations: Who Needs Them?" strongly opposes the metaphor of representations in the brain on two bases. "One is that no one understands how brains work," and the use of this metaphor "tends to obscure this fact," giving "us the illusion that we understand something that we do not" (p. 375). The other derives from their experience as neurophysiologists working initially within this representational framework.

In studying the olfactory system of the rabbit, Freeman and Skarda examined electroencephalograms (EEGs) of the olfactory bulb and cortex seeking regularities in spatial patterns that might correspond to specific sets of conditioned odorants. The representational approach led the researchers to "view neural activity as a function of the features and causal impact of stimuli on the organism and to look for a reflection of the environment within by correlating features of the stimuli with neural activity" (p. 376). That is, they expected a 1:1 correspondence between neural activity and the animal's experience of a given odor. Their results forced them to abandon this approach.

Rather than a given odor yielding a specific neural pattern, their findings were consistent with a dynamic systems view, as elements of behavior and context both clearly influenced the EEG responses. Rather than a given odorant leading to an identifiable EEG pattern in a given animal, stereotypical patterns of activity in response to a given odorant emerged only with training. Furthermore, the patterns were context-dependent, such that if the reinforcing stimulus or the required response pattern was changed, the patterned response to the odorant stimulus changed as well. When new odorants were introduced and trained, the patterned response to the original odorant was not maintained and a different pattern emerged (Freeman, 1991). No consistent pattern of brain activity could always be correlated with a given odorant, so one could not analyze an EEG pattern in relation to a presumed neurological "representation" of the odor in the animal's brain.

Recognition of these problems led the researchers to shift focus from "pattern invariance and storage capacity," based on the notion that brains contain representations, to asking "how these patterns could be generated in the first place from less ordered conditions" (Freeman & Skarda 1990, p. 377), questions more compatible with seeing the brain as a dynamic system in constant self-organizing interaction with the environment. These research findings do not necessarily invalidate the representational model, because there is no reason to suppose that EEG recordings would be the only or best way for determining the existence of discrete representations in the brain. The representational view of the brain, often termed "cognitivism," is still dominant in cognitive science. It is difficult to consider it as a hypothesis for brain function because research tends to assume and use this view rather than test its validity in relation to the enormous growth of knowledge regarding brain function since the 1950s, when computers were first invented to model the mind (Varela, Thompson, & Rosch, 1991).

Mental Representation as a State of Consciousness

The distinction between mental representation and perception is not concerned with stored contents of the brain (Piaget, 1962; Sartre, 1948). Instead, this distinction involves changes in children's capacity for ongoing experience of reality, as this capacity can be inferred from their spontaneous activities in real time. These different uses of the term representation can be a source of endless confusion (Haith, 1998). Some may question the distinction between perceptual experience and mental representation and the strong developmental transition between the two proposed by Piaget. However, no one would deny a distinction between the experience of looking at a white horse in a field and imagining that it is a unicorn. This is the distinction between perception and mental representation that I have in mind. In Chapter 6 developmental levels of mental representation are described in an analysis of symbolic play. In Piaget's view, learning and development, unfolding in a supportive social environment, contribute to the growth of the mental capacity for representational consciousness in contrast with perceptual consciousness, which is available from birth.

Children's Cognition at the Transition to Language

In my first analysis of dynamic event words (McCune-Nicolich, 1981), I recognized that children used these words in situations involving movement and change. I sought an interpretation of their semantics by analyzing them in relation to the real time transformations in space and time that, according to Piaget, children should comprehend at this period of development. My analysis confirmed Bloom's (1973) finding that these words made reference to presence, absence, location and negation. In addition I demonstrated interrelationships among the words' meanings based on their collective reference to reversible transformations in space and time. In this chapter I present a more complete perspective on the cognitive capacity evident in children's language and action at this point in development. In

Chapter 5 I demonstrate how this approach allows unified interpretation of the full range of dynamic event words observed thus far as single words across languages. This approach facilitates understanding the transition from single words to sentences.

Mental representation is derived from earlier purely perceptual and motor processes that will continue to affect cognition as later abilities develop. The proposed cognitive functioning guides children's movements, actions, and predictions about their world and serves as the source of dynamic image schema meanings (Johnson, 1987). This cognitive base is not a set of "representations" in the brain. Rather, this is implicit "possible knowledge" or "background," aspects of which spring to mind based on events, tasks, and experiences the child encounters. Similarly, Rosch (1999), despite wide citation of her early work on prototype-based concepts, more recently has suggested that "concepts" exist only at the moment when conscious human behavior engages them. The "background" for any given conscious meaning comprises assumed knowledge that is not consciously focused at a given moment, although its elements could, in principle, come to consciousness (Johnson, 1987 p. 189; Searle, 1992, p. 190). This background serves as the basis for specific conscious states such as those experienced when a child comprehends or produces a word. Critical features of this background are its basis in bodily experience and its function in unifying a number of what might otherwise be considered separate islands of infant knowledge. Piaget and Inhelder (1969) summarize the shift leading to this capacity as follows:

> In the course of the first eighteen months or so . . . there occurs a kind of Copernican revolution, or more simply a kind of general decentering process whereby the child comes to regard himself as an object among others in a universe that is made up of permanent objects (that is, structured in a spatio-temporal manner) and in which there is at work a causality that is both localized in space and objectified in things. (Piaget and Inhelder, 1969, p. 13).

This description contrasts with the initial attitude of infancy described in Chapter 2, where from the infant's perspective self, other, and object are not distinguished, "and the child's initial universe is entirely centered on his own body and action in an egocentrism as total as it is unconscious" (Piaget and Inhelder, 1969, p. 13). According to Piaget (1954) the source of the change is the infant's perceptual, motor, and social interaction which gradually allow the development of a sort of naïve physics . . . the child of 18 months to 2 years knows what to expect as he act on objects and observes the interactions of objects and others.

Figure 4–1 comprises two illustrations, the three circles in each representing self, other, and object. Figure 4–1A replicates Figure 2–1 in Chapter 2. Here, from the child's point of view, there is considerable overlap between the self and objects or other people as experienced in the environment. In 4–1B, showing later development, the separations between the circles symbolize the differentiation of self, other, and object developing over time. The curved double-pointed arrows connecting them

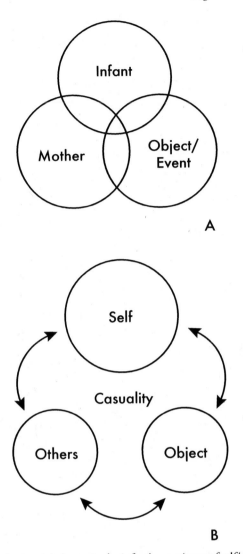

Figure 4–1. Developmental change in the infant's experience of self/other/object. A replicates Figure 2–1 showing the considerable overlap of constituents from the infant's perspective. B shows later development, the separations among the circles symbolizing the differentiation of Self, Other, and Object that develops over time. The curved double-pointed arrows connecting them show new cognitive and emotional understandings partly resulting from causal influences among them.

illustrate the continuing differentiation and integration of understanding in these relationships partly resulting from causal influences among them. Differentiation is a continuous process complemented by ongoing integration as more specific understandings of relationships among self, other, and the external world are forged.

During the second year of life the child becomes increasingly aware of forces and causal influences among these interlocking components. This awareness arises partly from the experience of force as the children themselves exert effort and as others affect the child and objects in the environment. Others can act causatively on the child, lifting him, for example, and thus providing experience of movement in a vertical plane. The child can act on objects by various manipulations and on others using language or gesture. The actions of all participants occur in ongoing, often repeated sequences that allow the child some prediction of next steps as well as recall of recent past elements of the sequence, leading to a sense of time.

Figure 4–2 shows the self/other/object matrix as imbedded in the larger world of spatial and temporal events. Analysis of children's dynamic event words (McCune, 2006; chap. 5) suggests that the child's spatial interest is centered on his own body, as he takes notice of objects' proximity to his own location (termed "deictic" in preparation for linguistic analyses in Chapter 5). Children's play activities and language also emphasize objects' position or motion on the vertical axis, possibly highlighted by the profound effects of gravity observed and experienced. Use of dynamic-event words highlights temporal and spatial changes affecting motion in relation to child location or access, and to motion and relationships in the vertical plane. Oakes and Madole (2003) have attributed even children's learning about the functional properties of objects to the emerging ability to integrate spatiotemporal information.

Double arrows in Figure 4–2 indicate the child's sense of potential reversibility in vertical and child-centered space and the child's dawning ability to experience past and future time as potential foci in contrast or comparison with the present. This sense of past/future is still dependent on close association with present reality. Emerging mental representation supports meanings useful to children in understanding and talking about their world. For example, a child who has drunk her juice must recognize the potential for future juice in order to make the request, "*more.*" Reversibility or the canceling out of one action by an opposite action (e.g., creep across a room; turn and creep back) characterizes the sensorimotor logic available when the child is making the transition to a representational mode of thought. Analogously, recall of the past and prediction of the future may involve an imaginal reversal of present reality (e.g., my cup is empty, but it might be full!). (This primitive sense of past and future is far from the explicit temporal comparison recognized in the tense expressions of a language.)

Piaget's (1954) observation of his daughter at 18 months of age illustrates functional application of knowledge based on the proposed background:

"Jaqueline loses a ball under a double bed. She bends down and sees that the ball is far under. Jacqueline gets up and goes around the bed and also around a bedside table [in order to retrieve the ball]" (p. 205).

Jacqueline demonstrates considerable world knowledge in solving this simple problem: (1) She understands motion in space, both hers and that of the ball, along varying directions of movement (paths) with equivalent

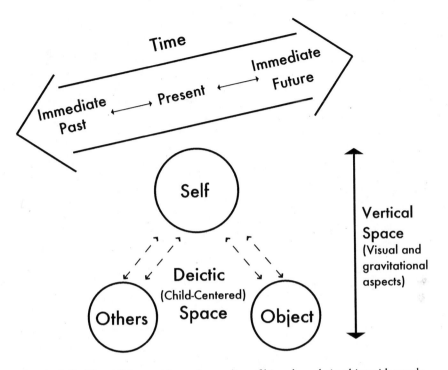

Figure 4–2. The child's cognitive understanding of his or her relationships with people and objects as these exist in space and time, illustrating the underlying knowledge that can be attributed to children at the culmination of sensorimotor development and the dawn of mental representation. Evidence for this knowledge is drawn from experimental findings and naturalistic events as described in this chapter. Double-pointed arrows within the self/others/object matrix indicate the child's sense of potential reversibility in child-centered (deictic) space. That is, objects and people can move in paths closer to or more distant from the child. (The curved linking arrows of Figure 4–1B are omitted for simplicity.) The vertical arrow to the right of the central matrix illustrates the child's sense of reversibility, in the vertical dimension encompassing potential trajectories or paths in the vertical plane. The broad double-pointed arrow above the central self/other/object matrix illustrates the child's beginning recognition of reversible mental focus (and sometimes action) across time. This figure illustrates the background underlying focused moments of conscious thought (Searle, 1992). Any given moment of consciousness encompasses several dimensions simultaneously, with specific content experienced against this background; for example, Jacqueline's search for her missing ball as described in the text.

end points. That is, the ball rolled under, but she walks around. (2) Mental representation is apparent in her seeking the "invisible" ball by bending and looking under the bed. She would be surprised at this age if, instead of the ball, she encountered a different toy when looking under the bed. (3) Variation in direction or path, in this case related to her own location (deictic path) is apparent in her recognizing the distance of the ball from herself and in overcoming that distance. (4) She also demonstrates knowledge of the object and of causality: the ball will not disappear or roll away on its own, yet she can retrieve it. Space is at her disposal for self-movement and manipulation of objects.

A child able to solve this problem, who has also attained the capacity for referential language (McCune & Vihman, 2001; Vihman & McCune, 1994), should be ready to incorporate understanding and expression of words such as *gone*, indicating the ball's temporary disappearance, or *there* as someone points out the location of the ball (designating the end point of a motion trajectory in relation to the child's own location). Words designating these meanings, along with naming words, such as *ball* are common in single-word speech.

The background exemplified in Figure 4–2 is meant to characterize the potential dimensions of consciousness for a child who has attained some capacity for mental representation. The figure emphasizes the dynamics of potential consciousness, while entities such as self, other people, and objects are merely designated without further internal analysis . Mental representation, of course, can include conscious attention to various levels of detail regarding objects and people. This vision of background knowledge is not suggested as literal mental contents but rather as descriptive of potential conscious states. As mental representation develops across the first year of life and beyond, the capacity for this level of mental representation of objects, space, and time gradually becomes available. The following sections will review research that supports this gradual development.

Experimental Findings on Space/Time Knowledge

Hakke and Somerville (1985) investigated children's ability to utilize a logical sequence of events in a problem-solving task that illustrates this background knowledge of space, time, and motion. The experimenter presented a sequential "invisible hiding task." Only by integrating sightings of the object with the movement of the hand during the hiding sequence could young children consistently find the object on the first trial. The procedure is as follows. With two screens on the table, the experimenter first enclosed an object in her hand as the child watched. Next the hand was passed under one screen, then emerged and was shown to the child (either empty or still holding the object); the hand then passed under the second screen and was again shown to the child (empty at this point, as the object had been left under one screen or the other) (Figure 4–3). In order to search logically and immediately find the object under the correct screen, a child must coordinate the last sighting of the object in hand, the screen next visited, and the first sighting of the empty hand, demonstrating space/time understanding. Infants 9 and 12 months old were capable of finding the object, but they did not lift the correct screen immediately at greater than chance levels, so they were not coordinating space and time in sequential logic. By 15 months, some children

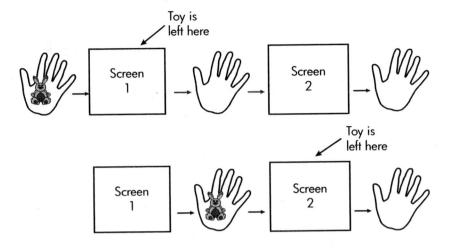

Figure 4–3. Search task demonstrating sequential understanding of hidden object trajectories. In the search task devised by Hakke and Somerville (1985), an object is hidden in the hand, then deposited under one of two screens as the hand is passed under the screens in sequence with the child watching. Between exit from screen 1 and entry under screen 2, the experimenter shows the child the open hand still holding (or no longer holding) the object; then shows the empty hand after screen 2. Immediate success in searching requires the child to integrate sequentially available information (object in hand or not and last screen visited when hand is first seen empty)—a characteristic attributed to late stage 6 of object permanence (Piaget, 1954).

were making appropriate inferences regarding the sequential trajectory of the "invisible" object; by 18 months, two-thirds of the children showed understanding of the object's trajectory in space and time by finding the object on the first trial. This success suggests that the children were able to remember and use a sequence of events that they had not directly witnessed—an aspect of dawning mental representation. The gradual nature of this development is shown by the changes with age. The 9- and 12-month-olds seemed able to infer that the object must still be in the environment, but they did not relate the trajectory of the hand and whether it still held the object to an immediate solution of the problem.

Experimental work in earlier infancy supports the gradual development of spatial understanding, which promotes logical inferences regarding space/time sequences. Studies have now demonstrated that infants effectively process spatial information as easily as they process perceptual aspects of objects. This ability is important to infants' development of the cognitive background sketched in Figure 4–2. Understanding relationships of objects to landmarks in vertical space has a known trajectory. Quinn (2003) found that by 3 to 4 months of age, infants reacted with a novelty preference to visual displays where an object was depicted as above versus below a horizontal line as long as object identity was constant across trials. By 7 months, infants were able to overcome this limitation, reliably distinguishing above versus below even when the object depicted varied (dot, dollar sign, plus sign, etc.). At this same age but not before, infants also distinguished the spatial relation "between," where an object was depicted between two horizontal bars, demonstrating a novelty preference to objects depicted as above or below the two horizontal bars. However, not until 9 to 10 months of age did infants show more general processing of "between" when object identity was varied. It is of interest that between 4 and 7 months, infants have gained experience handling and mouthing objects, providing opportunities for more complete experience of their spatial relationships than those available to 3-month-olds. By 9 to 10 months, in addition to greater experience in manipulation, most infants are mobile, leading to extensive experience of spatial relationships between themselves, landmarks, and various objects. Their generalization of spatial information across varied objects at 9 to 10 months indicates a beginning differentiation of spatial and object aspects of their world and the relationships between them. This spatial knowledge would contribute to the solution of the hiding task of Hakke and Somerville and Jacqueline's success in the example above. The analysis of dynamic event words in Chapter 5 draws on the background illustrated in Figure 4–2: evidence for children's knowledge of the space/time/motion dimensions of reality will be found in their use of these single words.

Knowledge, Concepts, and Language

Children's words express meanings based on their underlying knowledge and ongoing experience. What is the relationship between child words and child concepts? Context-limited words may be merely actions associated with a given situation (e.g., *byby* while waving a hand; *rm-rm* while rolling a toy truck; *Fido* while playing with the family dog). Referential words that occur with frequency over time in relation to varied objects and events must have a stronger cognitive basis. A child produces a single word when experiencing an internal meaning (a conscious state) and a desire to convey that experience to a listener. The word occurs because of the child's inherent interest in entertaining meanings and experiencing mutual understanding with the caregiver. Rather than being based on fixed concepts, these words follow from a reaction to current experience that calls to mind aspects of past experience with associated language. The child, from an adult point of view, may seem to extend a word meaning to exemplars of a category or concept, and differences between adult and child use are thought of as errors (overextensions where the child uses a word more broadly than adults; underextensions when child usage is narrower), but there is not independent evidence of the existence of such categories. Gershkoff-Stowe and colleagues (2006) propose that such "lexical errors" can be accounted for parsimoniously as "a product of similarity, previous activation [of a given word], and the strength of established links between object, concept and word" (p. 482). But how to define *concept!*

Controversy surrounds the nature of infants' concepts. Oakes and Rakison (2003) provide the following definitions of categories and concepts, based on the cognitivist metaphor:

> The mental representation that encapsulates the commonalities and structure that exist among items within categories is generally referred to as a *concept*. Thus in some sense categories are collections of things in the world and concepts are the internal mental depiction of those collections (Margolis, 1994; Smith, 1995). (p. 4)

An alternative perspective is offered by Rosch (1999):

> Concepts and categories do not represent the world in the mind; they are a *participating part* of the mind-world whole of which the sense of mind (of having a mind that is seeing and thinking) is one pole, and objects of the mind (such as visible objects, sounds, thoughts, emotions, and so on) are the other pole." (p.72; italics in the original)

Rather than existing as representations in the brain, Rosch sees concepts and categories as instantiated only in concrete contextualized situations. This view can encompass the rationale of Gershkoff-Stowe and coworkers (2006) for lexical errors and fits well with my thesis that language events occur because of the relationship between present context and thoughts evoked both by elements of context and by endogenous thought processes. When they are using referential words, children mentally represent word and meaning in the moment, experiencing the self and partner as participants in a world of which both are aware (i.e., the symbol situation described and illustrated in Chapter 2). This simultaneous awareness of word, meaning, and social context motivates language expression. We do not know the underlying neurological basis for such performances, although broad and deep brain involvement is implicated (e.g., Tucker, 2002). Another example from my granddaughter, Brielle, will anchor this discussion to real child language development.

Beginning around 16 months Brielle began producing a word for her shoes, roughly *kakun* ending with a nasal sound. This came from the Spanish language diminutive, typical of Costa Rican Spanish, [*zapotiko,* or "tiny shoe"]. This word was first applied to her own shoes and socks, in which she was so intensely interested for a while that she protested vigorously when they were removed at bedtime. Very quickly this form generalized to all sorts of feet as well as the lower segment of things, such as the bottom of a toy. Size variation did not present a problem: she pointed and used her word for the quarter-inch feet of a tiny toy animal. While we can follow her extension of this word, its use does not respect any typical adult categorization rules. In fact, the nominal aspect seems to be infected with a spatial interest in the lower portions of things. At 20 months, when she encountered her shoes when not on her feet, she would say *shoe*, but still responded to the question, "What's that?" with *kakun!* At 22 months, her family acquired a guinea pig. When pointing out its four tiny feet, each of which had four long pink toes, Brielle said, "*manos!*" ("hands!"), despite the fact that all four paws of her small fluffy dog (separate toes obscured by fur), continued to be termed *kakun!* Perhaps the last spontaneous extension of this term occurred at 27 months, when she was given footed winter pajamas. She collapsed in giggles, pointing at the pajama feet and saying, "*They have kakuns!*" Rather than thinking of children's words as a stored list or set of items, each applying to articulated categories or concepts, it is helpful to think of any given instance of a word as related to a conscious ongoing experience that probabilistically can bring one, another, or no word to mind.

Studies of Categorization

Findings regarding categorization and concepts in infancy tend to challenge the idea of a relationship between concepts as defined in infancy research and language. The same 4-month-old infant who may react categorically to cats as distinct from dogs in a novelty test will not be naming these animals for another 8 to 12 months. Even in the toddler years, relationships between categorization task performance and language are complex.

Infant Categorization: Familiarization/Novelty Testing

Infant behavior in experimental studies provides valuable information regarding development, whether one defines the infant's behavior as "categorical," "conceptual," or merely "discriminatory." Researchers studying infant concepts define infants' treating exemplars as somehow "the same" while treating nonexemplars differently as "categorical behavior." The approach is similar to that used in language acquisition studies described in Chapter 3, the familiarization/novelty-test procedure. To determine whether infants experience a group of exemplars as category members, they are first exposed to multiple trials looking at exemplar stimuli presumed to form a category, then, in the test, they are offered a novel item that is not an exemplar of the familiarized category in comparison to a novel item that does belong to the familiarized category. Longer looking at the nonexemplar of the original category is taken as indicating that the infant has formed a category based on the familiarized stimuli and hence shows renewed interest in an element of a "new" category. An alternative method applicable only after about 6 months of age, when children begin manipulating objects, is to present the child with sets of objects belonging to two different adult categories. Spatial grouping and/or sequential touching of like objects is interpreted as evidence of categorization.

Quinn (2005) identified a basic question regarding research using the familiarization/novelty preference procedure to describe infants' categories. Are infants utilizing category information available before the study (category possession), or are they forming categories "online" during the experiment (category formation)? Based on studies taking in the infants' home experience (e.g., for the cat/dog categorization: whether they have a pet at home), he concluded that the laboratory performances need not reflect preexisting knowledge. Rather, "the infants are demonstrating parsing skills in the laboratory that may be successfully deployed to form representations of real objects when these objects are encountered in the environment" (p. 111). Furthermore, boundaries being formed during familiarization can be manipulated depending on the information being presented during familiarization. In one study, Quinn found that cat-versus-dog categorization was asymmetrical, such that babies familiarized with color photographs of cats discriminated dogs in novelty testing, but those familiarized with color photographs of dogs did not discriminate cats. It turned out that dog exemplars tend to be more highly variable than cat exemplars; when variability within the dog category exemplars was reduced, infants successfully discriminated cats.

A link between infants' real-life experience and their performance in the laboratory was discovered when infants' capacity to discriminate human gender based on face stimuli was tested. An asymmetry in generalizing familiarization to male versus female faces raised the possibility that infants might prefer female faces, a possibility that was confirmed for the infants first tested, all of whom had female primary caregivers. When 8 infants were recruited who had male primary caregivers, 7 preferred the male faces. Quinn links the differences in children's responses to male and female faces to infants' early ability to discriminate their caregivers' faces (Bartrip, Morton, & de Schonen, 2001) and to cognitive and emotional processes related to attachment.

Quinn (2005) provides explanations for differences in findings regarding categorization of male versus female faces and human to other animals in terms of differences in the forms or types of "representations" guiding the infant. This way of thinking may be heuristic within the field of experimental work with infants, but there is no independent verification of such representations. In fact, the variation in categorical responding depending on stimuli presented argues against an interpretation based on stable represented information. If the "representations" are temporary, instantiated only as part of the experiment, perhaps *representation* is too strong a word for the phenomenon. Quinn and others in this tradition are generating valuable findings; however, their value does not depend upon the existence of "representations," and this type of interpretation may limit the search for links with later development. As Haith (1998) suggested, graded interpretations of infant knowledge are needed. When knowledge is demonstrated only by looking behavior, perceptual interpretations may be more parsimonious. Quinn's notion of "parsing skills" applicable in experiments and in real life is attractive.

Toddler Categorization: Touching, Grouping, and Imitating

Beginning at 9 months or so, it is possible to use children's manipulation of real (or toy replica) objects to study their categorization behavior. By this age, most children have been influenced by the ambient language, and this cannot be ruled out as a factor in their categorization behavior. Gershkoff-Stowe (2005) has shown that results from these tasks vary in their outcome. In the simpler task, the child is given a series of toy replicas of objects from one adult-based category, one at a time, and allowed to handle and explore them, then tested for novelty preference when given a member of a different category (e.g., contrasting "global" categories of "animals" and "vehicles") (Mandler & McDonough, 1993).

In the more complex task, children are given two sets of small replica objects (usually four each) varying on some adult-defined categorical dimension (e.g., Mandler & Bauer, 1988). Children's category knowledge is revealed when they sequentially touch objects from the same category or place matching objects in physical proximity in contrast with members of the alternative category. While Mandler and associates were able to show global category responses by 9 months in the simpler task, even at 12 months children failed to show this type of categorization in the more complex task. Oakes, Plumert, Lasink, and Merriman (1996) applied both procedures to a group of 10-, 13-, and 16-month-olds, confirming that the simpler task yielded "categorical" responding for all groups while the more complex task yielded categorical responding only for the older infants. This example is only part of an argument presented by Oakes (2005) for the strong effects of contextual aspects on results in these sorts of studies. This interpretation parallels that of Quinn for familiarization/novelty test procedures applied to younger infants. Children's apparently categorical performance is greatly influenced by context.

Children's knowledge of categories was considered as a possible basis for language long before the familiarization/novelty test began the attempt to identify infant concepts. Ricciutti (1965) found developmental trends between 12 and 24 months in children's tendency spontaneously to touch objects of the same kind one after the other and/or to place like objects in spatial groupings, and his procedures form the basis for the later studies. In contemporary studies, the emphasis has been on determining what sorts of categories infants either "possess" or can form. Therefore studies are designed, for example, to contrast perceptual with less obvious aspects of class membership (e.g., basic versus global categories). The assumption is made that a child touching two or more of one designated group in sequence or placing two or more together constitutes evidence of infant categorizing. This may be too strong an assumption.

Oakes and Madole (2003) have suggested that examination of the processes infants use in sequential touching and grouping may be more revealing than the content of categories demonstrated. Current research investigating kinds or contents of categories rarely examines infants' procedures in examining, touching, and grouping the objects, but such procedures provide evidence of internal processes that might be guiding the children's behavior. Changes in these procedures reveal developmental trends in strategy that are relevant to infants' categorizing ability.

Sugarman (1983) studied the nature of young children's classification activities between their first and third birthdays in considerable depth. Each child was given several sets of objects, one set at a time for 2½ minutes per set. Each set consisted of two groups: four each of two different kinds of objects. Unlike more recent studies, the emphasis was on children's strategies rather than on the nature of categories they discriminated, so each set consisted of identical items, although in some sets color variation was included. Sugarman first analyzed children's sequential contacts with the objects, whether or not these contacts resulted in a spatial arrangement, and then turned to analyzing the sorts of arrangements the children constructed with the objects.

One-year-olds tended to handle only one object at a time. Unlike the older children, they did not often use space as an organizing frame for grouping similar objects but more frequently expressed their knowledge of similarities and differences by spontaneously touching several objects of one kind with a hand or another object. But were these actions based on category knowledge, on pairwise similarity comparisons, or on preference for one type of object in the set over the other? The use of several sets of objects allowed Sugarman to determine that when 12- and 18- month-olds touched several of the same kind of object in sequence, the *children all tended to favor the same type of object:* for example, the dolls in the doll-and-ring task, the plates in the plates-and-block task. This type of selection suggests that, for both 12- and 18-month-olds, characteristics of a particular kind of object were more salient or appealing, biasing them to handle these objects to a greater extent than the others. Furthermore, *at 12 months, the same kinds of objects were contacted in sequence only when approximately three- quarters of the child's actions involved the single favored kind of object.* In other words, there was no evidence at 12 months that the children were comparing the items they touched or grouped with one another: rather, each item may have been selected independently due to preference rather than because of its similarity to the previous item touched. Sequential touching can be an artifact of touching only one favored kind of object most of the time.

Sugarman suggested that if the child systematically seeks out all or most of one kind of object, it seems more likely that similarity judgments are being made. If children simply prefer objects of one type, there would be no reason why they should contact all or even most items of a type. The shift toward such exhaustive selection occurred between 12 and 18 months, indicating significant growth in understanding of object similarities and differences in this developmental period. It is of interest that the very beginnings of referential language comprehension in carefully controlled studies are identified between 13 and 17 months (Oviatt, 1980; Thomas, Campos, Shucard, Ramsay, & Shucard, 1981). Children's recognition of categorical relationships should facilitate their learning of object names and, concomitantly, the availability of a word as an internal organizer should facilitate awareness of categorical similarities.

Sugarman (1983) found that some18-month-olds touched three or four of the less favored group of objects in some of their sequences, but this was not the case for 12-month-olds. For example, in playing with dolls and rings, in the course of a variety of moves, an 18-month-old would be more likely than a 12-month-old to enact a sequence of touching three or four rings in sequence, even though for both age groups their favored and more frequent manipulation in that task was with dolls. By 2 years of age, all of the children contacted three or four of one kind and then the other, demonstrating that their sequential selections were likely to be motivated by similarity judgments or even recognition of separate classes. These later strategies also suggest that in addition to the objects themselves, the logic of relationships among them is a particular focus of interest. Selecting all of one kind suggests an interest in the completeness of the activity as well as an interest in the objects as such.

Children's arrangements of classes of objects in space also revealed their ability to use knowledge of similarity and difference in making such constructions. From 12 months on, children tended to place two items of *one class* together, separate from items in the other class, a tendency that did not change with age, while forming *two groups* was infrequent until 18 months. When Sugarman examined each child's most complete sorting, few 12- or 18 month-olds produced any sorts involving three or four members of both sets, while most children 24 months of age and older did make at least one such arrangement.

When the children's construction procedures were examined, it was found that 12- and 18- month-olds produced most of their two class groupings by manipulating only objects from one class. Thus it appeared that, even in producing a two-class product, they may have considered only similarities shared by each pair of items contacted without considering membership in a class. In contrast, by 24 months, children produced most of their two-class groupings by manipulating objects from both classes, usually collecting one group and, then the other. This is consistent with the observation of Sinclair and colleagues of rapid exhaustive grouping of members of one of three classes at the same age (Sinclair, Stambak, Lezine, Rayna, & Verba, 1989). However, between 24 and 36 months of age, the tendency to create two-class groups by handling the objects in mixed order and placing each in its proper location based on kind as it was contacted became more frequent in the Sugarman study, which extended to this older age. In this last strategy, "kind" knowledge seems to direct the child's action.

Across all ages, children also made mixed constructions of objects from both sets that gave no evidence of grouping. It is of interest that the 12- to 18-month-olds tended to handle objects from both groups while making such mixed constructions, in contrast with their handling of only one kind of object at a time when grouping by kind was their apparent goal. This suggests that careful concentration on object-to-object similarity was an important grouping strategy for these younger children when they were sorting by kind. In contrast, beginning between 2 and 3 years of age, children were able to keep potential membership in either class in mind, evaluating objects from either class one at a time as they handled the objects. This suggests an internal cognitive focus on kinds and possibly a prior plan to create two groups. By 2 years of age, language comprehension is well advanced and the majority of children produce a substantial number of single words and some sentences. It is certainly possible that they may use words to mediate their grouping by this age. In fact, mutual facilitation of grouping by language understanding and language development by the experience of grouping is implicated.

These findings suggest the following sequence of developments of an understanding of kinds or categories. Perceptual testing of infants from 4 to 9 months demonstrates their ability to focus on object characteristics or spatial relationships in highly constrained displays and to discriminate objects according to many adult-defined categories in novelty preference tests. In this same time period they learn to discriminate vertical position of an object from landmarks, even if object identity varies across trials. In object manipulation tasks, by 1 year of age, children show their preferences for one kind of object over another by sequential touching or by placing two or more like objects of a favored type in proximity. It seems likely that this behavior serves to call the children's attention to the similarity across these favored items. This same attention to object-object comparative relationships could underlie findings from the object-examining tasks (Oakes et al., 1996). By 18 months of age, children are able to group all similar items together and seem to enjoy doing so. It then may be that the notions of similarity and comparison become particularly interesting to the children. However, even at this age, in order to achieve such arrangements, they seem limited to handling only one type of object in the course of the task, even if the eventual product involves two groups. Beginning at 24 months and continuing across the third year of life, children form two-category groups by selecting out all of one group, then the other. By 36 months, complete sorts could be made by picking up objects of either kind, one at a time, and placing them in a location the child has designated for that group. In this case they seem to be able to keep the notion of two kinds in mind while evaluating each item for membership in either. During this rather extended period, first in comprehension, then in production, children are developing and using words, suggesting mutual facilitation between language and the arrangement of objects by kind. The 36-month-olds may, as Rosch (1999) suggested, be guided by a concept, even if this is kept in mind only for the duration of the task.

Generalized imitation has also been recently used to test young children's category knowledge. This task exploits children's typical tendency to enact pretend actions with props. Mandler and McDonough (1996) pioneered this approach with an initial study of 14-month-olds. They showed that when an experimenter modeled an appropriate action with appropriate props (e.g., giving a drink to a dog), the infants showed recognition of what they term "global category" membership by offering a drink to a cat or a bunny (animals) but not to a vehicle when these were offered as props. The children's behavior is not surprising, given the sequence of developments in pretending (Chapter 6).

At 14 months, children spontaneously apply familiar actions to appropriate objects and resist application of inappropriate actions to objects. Whether recognition on a case-by-case basis that certain actions are appropriate with certain objects is indicative of category recognition is a matter of definition.

In summary, the earliest studies of children's categorical responses to objects show great sensitivity to the different groupings of stimuli offered by experimenters. Clearly infants find bases for becoming familiar with one set of visually presented stimuli and recovering response to "novel" presentations by 3 or 4 months of age. This "parsing ability" must form the basis for future consistent responding to members of the various "categories" of experience encountered in the real world. Similarly, children's manipulations show growing sensitivity to categorical similarities and differences across the second and even the third year of life. All of these responses are subject to experimental manipulation, varying with contextual variables including but not limited to particular objects, manner and sequence of presentation, and method of assessment.

Categorization and Language

Gershkoffe-Stowe and coworkers (1997) conducted three studies using variants of the Sugarman methodology to examine the relationship between children's category expression and language production. These investigators compared ages at achieving categorization milestones based on longitudinal versus cross-sectional methodology, age at beginning of longitudinal testing, and same versus different stimuli in the categorization task across sessions. This allowed assessment of the effects of these methodological manipulations. They found variation in performance attributable to all of these variables. Children who began longitudinal participation at an earlier age reached categorization milestones at an earlier age than either cross-sectional participants or longitudinal participants who began testing later. Repeated testing with the same category members also produced earlier achievement of milestones than testing with different objects at each assessment. In relating categorization to language, Gershkoffe-Stowe and colleagues found that "children's ability to classify objects in spatial or temporal order is independent of productive vocabulary growth" (p. 843) during the age range of 15 to 28 months. Rather than suggesting that children's growing category knowledge is truly unrelated to their development of vocabulary, they suggested that additional variables contribute to both sorts of performances and that a more detailed approach to past history and to contextual variables involved in testing would be helpful in elucidating the relationships.

Defining "Concepts"

Mandler (2004) considers the results of familiarization/novelty preference research as providing evidence for concepts based on representations. She defines concepts as "declarative knowledge about object kinds and events that is potentially accessible to conscious thought" (p. 1). This is described as "stored information" (p. 43) with long-term existence in the brain. Since she regards Piaget's ideas of sensorimotor development as implying only inaccessible procedural knowledge without conscious awareness on the part of the infant, Mandler proposed that "infants represent information from an early age at more than one level of description" (p. 91). The first type of representation results from "a perceptual system that parses and categorizes objects and object movements (events)" and is assumed similar to that found in many animal species (sensorimotor activity, in her view). A second system based on "perceptual meaning analysis" involves redescription of objects and events in ways that are "perception-like" but include only "redescribed fragments of the information originally processed." She continues, "These redescriptions are spatial and analog in form; we call them image-schemas" (p. 91). She considers image schemas existing in the brain, in support of the earliest concepts, to be available to infants' consciousness by 6 months of age.

But Piagetian sensorimotor intelligence does not exclude conscious awareness of ongoing activities. Rather, the infant's initial consciousness of the here and now allows for the gradual development of conscious mental representation, initially of the recent past and immediate future in contrast with the perceptual present. Over the course of the first 18 months of life, the potential for mental representation in contrast with perceptual consciousness emerges. Piaget considered the "image" as a state of mind distinct from perception rather than as a form of stored knowledge. Between 9 and 12 months, children show image schematic understanding of familiar objects by demonstrating their use out of context (e.g., cup to lips, comb to hair in play). Beginning at this age, the capacity for mental representation continues its own developmental trend in both object permanence and representational play tasks.

Piaget reserved the term *concept* for much more advanced cognition. According to Piaget (1962), "the concept implies a fixed definition, corresponding to a stable convention which gives the verbal sign its meaning.... The method by which one object is related to another is therefore different in the case of true concepts from that of the intermediary schema at this level" (that of single-word speech; p. 220). Piaget did not address the question of whether or how information is stored in the brain. Instead, he wished to show how children, by changing nonverbal and later also verbal behavior, advanced in cognitive performance. In Chapter 8 of *Play, Dreams and Imitation*, he goes on to say: "There still remains the problem of discovering in what ways language makes possible the construction of concepts, for the relationship is necessarily reciprocal and the capacity for constructing conceptual representations is one of the conditions necessary for the acquisition of language" (p. 221). (I interpret "conceptual representations" here to mean conscious states of mind reflecting upon concepts, compatible with Rosch, 1999.) In the following pages, Piaget provides examples of the changing use of language to refer to category members between about 18 months and 6 years of age, eventually showing that the idea of a conceptual category itself becomes accessible to consciousness and can be discussed with language. Piaget finds the source of this eventual level of conceptual development in the earliest schemas, first schemas of direct action on objects and later the image schemas of representational play.

This analysis is compatible with the current research on children's changing reactions to various tasks assessing category development. In his earliest studies of infancy, Piaget was interested in children's reactions when they encountered the same or different stimuli, although his work predates modern experimental methodology. It was not until children reached approximately age 3 that Piaget attributed to them the ability to keep class membership in mind as they sorted objects into two groups, as the oldest children in the Sugarman study did. However, he reserved credit for "true concepts" to the even later point in development where a child could complete classification of the same objects by differing criteria (e.g., sort geometric forms by shape and then by color) and recognize that one set could be nested in another (e.g., lilies within flowers). Like contemporary experimenters, he composed sets of objects that were amenable to these types of sorting judgments, not necessarily assuming that these kinds of categories were the only ones extant.

There are clearly developmental trends in children's responses to the various tasks arranged to examine the nature of their "concepts." The developmental trend may be of greater interest than the specific moment in developmental time when the term *concept* can best be employed. Mandler (2004, 2006) sees infant cognition as involving both sensorimotor procedures and a separate stored knowledge base organized into discrete concepts. Similarly, Piaget describes concepts as bounded and organized but attributes them to a much later period. While cognitive processes guide reactions to environmental stimuli in ways that become increasingly complex with development, available evidence does not seem to demand fixed categories of meaning at any level of development.

Malt, Sloman, and Gennari (2003) suggest that even adult conceptual knowledge is characterized by flexibility of boundaries: "At the conceptual level entities (objects, events, etc.) are represented as points in multi-dimensional feature-space (Rosch & Mervis, 1975). No fixed boundaries separate these clusters, and so conceptual categories are only implicitly defined...there is no fixed conceptual structure...[while]...linguistic categories are explicit, although their boundaries may be fuzzy" (Malt et al., p. 85).

Information from all methodologies examined demonstrates steady change in infant performance with development despite contextual variation in testing circumstances. This capacity for learning and change is no doubt the driving force that allows the eventual more broadly applicable cognition observed in the second and third years of life. According to Gershkoff-Stowe (2005), "Far from indexing the fixedness of children's categories, most studies reveal their extraordinary responsive to changing task demands (p.189)." In particular, the research reviewed by Quinn (2003, 2005) demonstrates the power of the infant mind to react consistently to stimulation and to vary that reaction based on both immediate and long-term context. Smith (2006) suggests that variability in findings can best be understood through the lens of dynamic systems, taking into account "nested time scales" to include development time (age), real-life experience prior to an experiment, and the experimental time scale itself as well as specific task demands.

Cognitive background common to all normally developing young children provides the basis for learning words of the ambient language. Research on category development testifies to the malleable use young children make of such underlying potential knowledge. Carving "fuzzy" semantic spaces for linguistic concepts begins at first by prelinguistic processes. As children begin to use words, the interaction of word and meaning becomes a powerful force in both cognition and language development. In the prelanguage and early language period, which is the focus of this book, there is extensive evidence of infants' ability to react with consistency to environmental stimuli in the laboratory and in the real world.

In the following section we consider hypotheses regarding the transition to mental representation as assessed in "object permanence" tasks and children's transition into language. Stage 6 of object permanence defines the earliest evidence of mental representation in contrast with perceptual responding. This means that a child is able to keep a specific object in mind when it is out of view and recognize it when it reappears. Xu (2005) defines "individuating" as "the process for establishing numerically distinct individuals that can be tracked through time and space" (p. 64). This capacity is implied in children's ability to mentally represent an object in its absence. Object permanence has become controversial owing to studies suggesting that very young infants demonstrate knowledge of object permanence by their looking behavior many months before manual testing demonstrates this knowledge (e.g., Baillargeon, Spelke, & Wasserman, 1985). However, findings of sequential changes in manual search behavior remain robust (S. Johnson, 2004), and visual preference tests have not addressed the stage 6 transition. Thelen and colleagues in a series of studies summarized by Thelen and Smith (2005, pp. 299–302) have demonstrated that 9- to 10-month-old children's performance on tests of object permanence are influenced by a number of task variables. Rather than simply demonstrating a change in beliefs regarding the permanent existence of objects, their ready ability to succeed at this task a couple of months later relies on several developments, including improved spatial memory due to locomotion, and to experiences perceiving and manipulating objects. This is compatible with a Piagetian perspective (e.g., Piaget & Inhelder, 1969).

Hypotheses Regarding Sensorimotor Development Milestones and Language Acquisition

When formal study of children's entry into language was seriously under way in the 1970s, Piaget's publications regarding sensorimotor development, in particular object permanence, were widely read in the United States, and there was great interest in the hypothesis that a child's level of object permanence might predict his or her level of language. This idea followed from the general view that learning language involved learning names for things. If objects could not be kept in mind when out of sight, how could children learn words signifying objects? Several authors organized Piaget's informal observations of his children into graduated sets of tasks (e.g., Uzgiris & Hunt, 1975), which were then used for a variety of purposes, including monitoring relationships between the development of cognition and language. The domains most fully investigated were "object permanence" and "means-ends" abilities (e.g., Bates et al., 1979). Researchers designed studies to determine whether either or both of these domains would be highly correlated with children's development of language. Although the sensorimotor period is often described as encompassing the first 2 years, stage 6 entry has been observed as early as 9 months of age in object permanence and a few months later in means/ends tasks.

A theoretical rationale for studies relating object permanence and language was that both performances depend on the child's developing capacity for mental representation (Bloom, 1973; Bowerman, 1978). Stage 6 of object permanence is defined by the onset of mental representation demonstrated in hiding tasks similar to but less complex than that of Hakke and Somerville (1985) described earlier. In a test of entry into stage 6, the object is first enclosed in the hand or a container, then deposited under one of two screens such the child does not witness the object's release. The child is credited with entry into stage 6 if he successfully finds the object over multiple trials and varied hiding location, even if he lifts the wrong screen first before successfully finding the object under the correct screen—a level of success achieved by 12-month-olds in Hakke and Somerville's studies.

Ramsay and Campos, in a 1978 study (replicating LeCompte & Gratch, 1972), demonstrated the validity of this task as a measure of mental representation. They presented a "surprise task" where children would see one toy hidden yet find a different toy when they searched. Ten-month-olds who had been pretested with the traditional stage 6 object permanence task to be at stage 6 but not those at stage 5 of object permanence showed surprise and persistent search when a given toy was hidden as they watched but their subsequent search yielded a different toy. By their surprise and continued search infants, showed the ability to keep in mind the perceptual characteristics of the object in its absence while they searched. The stage 6 infants recognized the discrepancy between the remembered and perceived objects when there was a toy switch. Converging evidence for a shift to mental representation of specific hidden objects is provided by Xu, Fei, and Carey (1996). They familiarized 10- and 12-month-olds with a scene where two different objects moved in and out from behind an occluder one at a time. When the occluder was removed to reveal either both objects or only one, the 12-month-olds but not the 10-month-olds looked longer at the single-object display. This suggests that the 12-month-olds (more of whom than 10-month-olds should have entered stage 6 of object permanence) expected to see both objects when the occluder was removed.

Representational development continues within stage 6, but Piagetian tasks devised to assess these later developments were unreliable, as a consistent methodology was not developed to measure later stage 6 (Corman & Escalona, 1969; Corrigan, 1979). The Hakke and Somerville (1985) task meets theoretical criteria for late stage 6 logical skill as described by Piaget (1952). From results of the Ramsy and Campos and Hakke and Somerville studies, it would seem that children may enter stage 6 as early as 9 to 12 months but do not begin to demonstrate the temporal and spatial memory for a sequential event with hidden components until several months later. In the Hakke and Somerville study of 12- to 18-month-olds, fewer than one-third of 15-month-olds, and two-thirds of 18-month-olds recalled the location of an object when locating the object required coordinating a sequence of sightings of the object versus an empty hand as the hand moved between two screens, leaving the object under one, suggesting that some children are still developing these skills between 18 and 24 months. Success in object search tasks is considered to be a sensorimotor skill because the child succeeds by a motor act. Although mental representation is necessary for success, no symbol/symbolized relationship is implied as there is no use of word or sign to refer to some entity or event.

Bates, Camaioni, and Volterra (1975) hypothesized that the development of means/ends skills (in contrast with object permanence) was the critical cognitive variable for language entry based on the importance of pragmatics, in particular the use of language as a means for obtaining desired ends. More recent analyses describe object permanence tasks as testing means/ends ability (e.g., Munakata, McClelland, Johnson, & Siegler, 1997). One might equally argue that means/ends skills such as "insightfully" using a stick to obtain an object out of reach (defined as a means/ends task), is achieved through mentally representing the solution. Piaget's work was observational as he used his own children's behavior to exemplify their cognitive development. He did not devise distinct testing situations for the different domains of sensorimotor function. These domains were seen as highly integrated, with separate descriptions used mainly to highlight different aspects of infants' knowledge.

Uzgiris and Hunt (1975), who developed the most widely used sensorimotor assessment instrument, considered both of these cognitive areas (object permanence and means/ends) to assess aspects of mental representation achieved at stage 6 of sensorimotor development. Both object permanence and means/ends achievements were described by Uzgiris and Hunt as part of an intercorrelated set of skills that "appears to be concerned with actions pertaining to objects taking place in surrounding space (p. 136)." They found that both object permanence and means/ends were correlated with gestural imitation, suggesting that "This constellation may be related to the development of representation for motoric acts (p. 136)." Uzgiris and Hunt did not include language in their analysis.

Corrigan (1979) examined theoretical and methodological issues in the large group of studies relating object permanence and language already available at that time, exposing a thicket of confusion. She found that studies differed in definitions of what constituted the relevant transitions in cognition and language and often failed to include sufficient scoring details for the results to be evaluated. She concluded, not surprisingly, that "different criteria yield different results" (Corrigan, 1979, p. 617).

Correlational Hypotheses

Bates and associates (1979) found that means/ends scores were correlated with language production at 13 months of age, while other sensorimotor scales, including object permanence, did not yield such correlations. The positive correlational findings regarding means/ends development and language in 13-month-olds, in contrast with object permanence, might as well be attributed to the generally later achievement of stage 6 items in means/ends and hence greater variability in means/ends at 13 months, when many more children might already demonstrate stage 6 entry in object permanence (Zachry, 1978). The difficulties identified by Corrigan (1979) were never solved, and owing to the null correlational findings, there was little research on the question beyond the 1970s.

Aside from the poor validity of tasks designed to assess later levels of stage 6 object permanence, there is little theoretical rationale for relating progress over time within stage 6 object permanence, the very earliest manifestation of mental representation, to advancing levels of language acquisition. Language is only beginning its extensive developmental trajectory at the point when stage 6 symbolic function is established. Language is influenced by a number of variables in addition to capacity for mental representation, as illustrated in this volume and elsewhere (e.g., McCune, 1992). Even if the onset of mental representation is required for language, later developments in language might rely on additional underlying skills other than those assessed by sensorimotor tasks.

Correspondence Hypotheses

Unlike a correlation hypothesis, which tests whether developmental progress in two domains occurs at similar rates within a sample group, a correspondence hypothesis seeks to evaluate the temporal correspondence in individual children of one or more transitions in each of two domains hypothesized to be related on theoretical grounds. Such correspondence may refer to limited steps and/or developmental points and is sometimes termed a local homology model (Bates et al., 1979). I proposed that the contribution of mental representation be evaluated by examining the timing of transitions between forms of language and nonlanguage behaviors considered to be equivalent in representational status (McCune, 1995; McCune-Nicolich, 1981b; Nicolich, 1975). Entry into stage 6 of object permanence implies that the child is able to keep the hidden toy in mind (using representational consciousness) and infer its location based on the trajectory of a container in which it is hidden. As in the Hakke and Somerville study, the hand passes under one or more screens, depositing the object under a screen in a manner hidden from the infant. Language defined as a representational process should require this capacity. I hypothesized that children should begin language production only following the entry into stage 6 of object permanence.

Evaluating hypotheses of correspondence, requires a case-by-case analysis of individual children aimed at determining whether children exhibiting a proposed cognitive skill are more likely than those lacking that skill to exhibit the hypothesized language behavior (cross-sectional method) or observing individual children over time and monitoring the emergence of the proposed abilities in cognition and language to determine whether they emerge "close in time" (longitudinal method).

The hypothesis of correspondence between entry into stage 6 of object permanence and language onset has received support (e.g., Corrigan, 1978). McCune-Nicolich (1981a) reported the development of a number of dynamic event words following stage 6 entry in five participants, and my unpublished data reveal that none of the five children studied longitudinally produced any words prior to entering stage 6 of object permanence. Bloom (1993), in a longitudinal study, reported that her 12 participants all began first words after entry into stage 6 object permanence. McCune (1992) reported stage 6 entry attained between 9 and 13 months of age, with lags of from 2 to 15 months between that attainment and development of a referential vocabulary in 10 participants studied longitudinally (Rutgers sample introduced in Chapter 3). The timing of the relationship between stage 6 entry and context-limited words was closer, with one child producing a few context-limited words in the month prior to meeting stage 6 criteria and the remainder with lags of from 1 to 3 months (7 children), and 5 to 7 months (2 children). Additional critical developments, such as phonetic skill and communicative competence (discussed in Chapters 7 and 8), may account for the delay between stage 6 entry and language onset. In summary, despite such delays, it is clear that children who have begun using words can be expected to show the level of mental representation indicated by entry into stage 6 of object permanence. Evidence for continued correspondence beyond stage 6 entry is lacking. It would be of interest to know whether children differing in logical search strategy in Hakke and Somerville's study would vary in any dimensions of language development.

Specificity Hypotheses

Gopnik and Meltzoff proposed more specific correspondences: (1) that the development of "disappearance words" such as *gone* is related to stage 6 of object permanence, and (2) that the development of "success/failure words" such as *there* upon completing a task and *uh oh* upon experiencing failure is related to the attainment of stage 6 of means/ends ability (Gopnik, 1984; Gopnik & Meltzoff, 1984, 1986; Gopnik & Choi, 1990). As object permanence and means/ends tasks are two approaches to assessing the same underlying skill, the specific correspondences proposed by Gopnik and Meltzoff would seem to be highly unlikely, although they report positive results from several studies. A larger data sample might have convincingly shown otherwise, but even in their most comprehensive study (Gopnik & Meltzoff, 1986), the sample included only a cross-sectional group of 30 children, all within 1 week of 18 months of age when tested, and a longitudinal sample of 19 children ranging in age from 13 to 19 months when the study began. Only16 of the 19 had complete data, and of those with complete data 5 also appear to have contributed data to earlier studies of the same relationships [Gopnik (1984) study 2 and Gopnik and Meltzoff (1984) Study 1].

Conclusion

Piaget's theory provides a comprehensive guide to children's cognitive development between about 6 months and 2 years of age, the time of transition into language. Results from experimental approaches provide support for gradual cognitive developments during the same time period. Findings from a Piagetian approach integrate well with the notions of embodied cognition and a dynamic systems view of development. Two related sorts of cognitive ability emerging during this time are essential for beginning referential language: (1) the capacity to process an ongoing event as it occurs in real time and space and (2) the capacity for mental representation of meaning. Children's behavior in naturalistic situations, (as when Jaqueline searched for the ball that rolled under the bed) and their solution of logical tasks, such as that presented by Hakke and Somerville (1985), demonstrate use of mental event sequencing. Dynamic-event words display this sequential ability along with expression of meaning. Language develops in the context of more general development of mental representation, of which stage 6 object permanence is the earliest easily tested evidence. However, the natural and universal unfolding of representational play provides the most comprehensive index of children's gradual development of the capacity for mental representation of meaning. In Chapter 5 we consider the expression of meaning with dynamic-event words; we turn to representational play development in Chapter 6.

Acknowledgments

Material quoted on pp. 93–94 appears with permission of Oxford University Press, The citation is as follows: Freeman, W. J., & Skarda, C. A. (1990). Representations: Who needs them? In J. L. McGaugh, N. M. Weinberger, & G. Lynch (Eds.), *Brain organization and memory: Cells, systems, and circuits.* New York: Oxford University Press, p. 375.

5

Motion Events, Dynamic-Event Words, and the Transition to Verbs

Two goals are addressed in this chapter. First, I wish to establish the inter-relationships among single dynamic event words and their relationship to the cognitive background established in the last chapter. Second, I propose that the semantic analysis offered by Talmy (e.g, 1975, 2000) is so compatible with my cognitive interpretation of dynamic event words, as to provide a bridging function between single words and early sentences.

Assuming that all children rely on similar underlying cognitive bases for their early expression of dynamic-event meaning, how can we account for variation across languages in the way children talk about the dynamics of their experience? As early as 1989, Bowerman questioned the reliance of initial language on ready-made categories. Languages do not encode critical meanings in areas such as spatial knowledge in exactly the same ways, so reliance on universal prelinguistic meanings seemed unlikely. While recognizing that a nonlinguistic understanding of, for example, space, was an important prerequisite for spatial language, she wrote, "It is not clear exactly what this nonlinguistic understanding consists of" (Bowerman, 1989, p. 142). Mandler refers to "developmental primitives" in place from birth or learned early enough to serve as prelinguistic concepts (2004, p. 256). Paradoxically Piaget (1962) considered the development of prelinguistic sensorimotor knowledge of object, space, causality, and time to be nonconceptual and yet to form the basis for language. A unifying possibility is that initial cognitive organization relying on sensorimotor schemes, the bodily understanding described by Piaget, provides a foundation for broader image schematic understandings, like those initially described by Johnson (1987) and elaborated for the infancy period by Mandler (1988, 1992, 2004). This underlying background forms the basis for more delimited meanings expressed in each language.

The underlying background of child knowledge presented in Chapter 4 (Figure 4–2) provides a framework that can unify dynamic-event words as a linguistic category characterizing single-word speech across the world's languages. Many of these words in English (e.g., *out, down, there*) include a spatial meaning. Talmy (1983) termed the abstractions underlying "individual spatial expressions such as English prepositions . . . schemas" (p.258), which, along with schemas underlying other sentence constituents, could be analyzed in terms of properties and relationships to elucidate the bases of sentence meaning. Analysis of children's use of single dynamic-event words in relation to ongoing events suggests that they give early linguistic expression to the motion-event dynamics described by Talmy (1975, 1985, 2000), providing a foundation upon which first verbs can grow. The motion-event view is, in turn, compatible with both Piagetian cognitive processes and image-schematic descriptions of underlying meanings (Johnson, 1987; Mandler, 2004; Piaget, 1954, 1962).

Body and Mind in the Experience and Expression of Meaning

Sensorimotor stage 6, in addition to its role as the culminating level of the sensorimotor period, also defines the child's initial transition into mental representation, such that, for example, the child can keep in mind the physical properties of a toy that was hidden; the child will therefore continue to search in a toy-switch task when a different toy from that which was hidden is found (Ramsay & Campos, 1978). This ability to mentally compare a present object with one that was recently in view and is now absent is followed shortly by the ability to make inferences regarding the hidden trajectory of an object as it is moved (Hakke & Somerville, 1985). These skills of imagining both absent objects and absent motion demonstrate the ability to "imagine" elements of the dynamic sensorimotor knowledge illustrated in Figure 4–2. In Piaget's view, sensorimotor knowledge becomes internalized as "the image," where by *image* he implicates not merely a visual-mental picture but rather all of the senses, including vestibular, hearing, vision, audition, and so on, allowing projection of meaning beyond the here and now. Piaget's major interest in this new capacity was as an internal mental sense of reality that would allow the formation of mental operations. Piaget's analysis reflects Kant's view that "imagination *always* involves a temporal ordering of representations" (Johnson, 1987, p. 153). It is this temporal ordering that allows children to recognize potential reversibility in space and time, eventually developing the concrete and later the formal operations of thought. The first manifestations of this process of imagination are in representational play and in single-word language.

Both Werner and Kaplan (1963) and Piaget (1962) relate the development of language to the nonlinguistic construing of objects and events as meaningful. The child's handling of objects in representational play and in sorting tasks during the course of the emergence of language demonstrates a developing understanding of object appearance, function, and meaning that guides the development of object names gleaned from the ambient language. Similarly, organizational arrangements of objects and attempts to relate them as, for example, container and contained, demonstrate the child's sensitivity to causality, space, and time.

Johnson (1987) proposed that "the *human body,* and especially those structures of imagination and understanding that emerge from our bodily experience," ignored in previous accounts of "meaning and rationality" (p. xiv), provide the key to understanding the development of knowledge.

Meaning, according to Johnson, arises when image schemas focus attention on some aspect of bodily experience. "An image-schema is a recurring dynamic pattern of our perceptual and motor programs that gives coherence and structure to our experience" (p. xiv). He gives the example of the *verticality* image schema that emerges from experience of an up–down orientation and our tendency to pick out meaningful aspects of our experience in relation to this orientation. Considering the background knowledge portrayed in Figure 4–2, the verticality image schema would be engaged in conditions where the child's focus is on actual or potential vertical movement. He may see an object above him and comment, "*up.*" He may desire to be lifted in his mother's arms. The verticality image schema would form the basis for the use of a word such as *up* in these circumstances. A sense of time would also be involved in the image schema underlying *up* in the latter case, because the child would be comparing present circumstances (being on the floor) with a potential future situation (being held in mother's arms). Most 12-month-olds are able to pull to stand and many are walking; therefore they have experienced changes in bodily orientation, which would contribute strongly to the development of a verticality image schema. Quinn's (2003) results regarding children's developing discrimination of the spatial relationships "above," "below," and "between" in the period of 4–9 months suggests that spatial understanding emerges gradually in infancy.

I propose that the nonconceptual knowledge underlying children's early words is carved from the underlying background of potential meaning shown in Figure 4–2. Image schemas such as verticality do not necessarily rely on stored "underlying knowledge representations" as proposed by Mandler (2007). Rather, they can be considered *potential processes* of instantiating meaningful conscious states. *Because the body and its orientation provide continuing awareness of the background knowledge that forms the basis of such image schemas, these processes may be evoked by interaction between self and environment without the image schemas necessarily having a stable existence when not activated.* That is, there are always mind-in-world cues available to support these processes. These potential processes are available to be engaged when the child's focus is on matters that draw out a particular image-schematic meaning.

In English-learning children, the particle *up* is broadly generalized to a range of situations involving verticality (as is *down* for opposite situations), although few children in the early period use both words. A verticality image schema is likely to arise for these children across these multiple occasions. In contrast, Korean does not have such a general word usable for the many occasions where verticality may be salient for a child. Yet Korean-learning children tend to talk about the same sorts of events and desires as English-learning children. In Korean, more specific verbs—different verbs for spontaneous and caused motion—convey these several meanings. Because an image schema includes a bodily sense of meaning as well as the internal mental focus, children learning either language should experience variation in the instantiations of the verticality image schema, even though the English language learners use the same word across situations that are differentiated in the Korean language. Werner and Kaplan discuss variation in underlying schematization across homonyms in early child speech. Johnson writes: "Unlike templates, schemata are flexible in that they can take on any number of specific instantiations in various contexts" (p. 10).

Barsalou (1999, 2005) makes the case, from a theory of embodied cognition, that "simulations" (partial and potentially combinatorial neural reenactments of past experiences) can form the basis for complex mentation. His discussion of entity, property, and relationship simulations is compatible with Johnson's 1987 views regarding image schemas as organizers of meaning. Barsalou further suggests a neurological basis for integrating information from such image-schematic simulations, citing Damasio's (1989) and others' views that perceptual and motor properties, both experienced and remembered, involve the activation of brain regions involved in modality-specific experiences, with integration dependent on a neurological "convergence zone."

Johnson's approach goes beyond image-schemas of direct bodily experience by recognizing the "metaphoric" extension of meaning beyond literal sensory aspects. He defines metaphor as "a pervasive mode of understanding by which we project patterns from one domain of experience in order to structure another domain of a different kind" (pp.xiv–xv). (This useful technical definition must be distinguished from the more complex linguistic metaphors of mature speakers and writers.) The metaphors of embodied cognition rely upon the structured nature of our physical experiences, and the fields of metaphoric projection are not arbitrary. The verticality scheme provides an example in which many abstract quantifications invoke a metaphor of verticality (e.g., "*Prices keep going up . . . Turn down the heat.*") Johnson relates this metaphor of quantity projected on verticality to physical experiences: adding blocks to a pile makes the pile higher; as you drink from a glass the amount of liquid goes down. "MORE and UP are therefore correlated in our experience in a way that provides a *physical basis* for our *abstract* understanding of quantity" (p. xv; emphasis in the original). Notice that reversibility characterizes both of these phenomena, and young children often include both of these words among their dynamic event words.

Mental representation is available to children by the time they begin to use single referential words. In their representational play, they show the capacity to extend meaning from one simple experience to another—for example, illustrating the act of real drinking from a cup by simulating this activity with various concave objects in the absence of a real beverage. This extension exemplifies an embodied cognition "metaphor" (considered by Johnson, 1987, as an essential aspect of thought). As in play, image-schematic meanings that are correlated with words in one set of circumstances will arise in analogous circumstances even where different objects and events are involved. Dynamic-event words such as *up* and *more* must rely upon this imaginal "metaphoric" process, as there may be no exact similarities across the instances of their use except the analogical relational aspect. Naming words benefit from these processes as well. In order to extend a word to new and varied situations, a child does not need either a stored "concept" to unify perceptual experiences or a stored set of images (e.g., of all dogs previously encountered) in order to extend the word *dog* to new instances. Dynamic image-schematic processes, in addition to automatic "natural" metaphoric extension, allow online activation of meaningful consciousness and potentially appropriate words in newly encountered situations.

The sensorimotor control of time, causality, space, and objects achieved as the child first gains representational ability is a global cognitive ability that allows inference of one part of a temporal sequence of movements from an immediately prior or subsequent event. Children's single-word speech encodes meanings well described by Talmy's (1975, 2000) motion-event analyses of linguistic expression. Entity words typically encode the figure— that is, the entity in motion—while dynamic-event words encode an aspect of dynamic movement. Children at this period recognize that movements in space can be cancelled out by reverse movements. One can also imagine that something that has disappeared (such as the clown in the Bruner's hiding game, described in Chapter 3) can reappear. These are the kinds of situations that children remark with dynamic-event words. In every use, these words imply real, potential, or imaginal reversibility of movement or dynamic state. Such recognition of reversibility implies the capacity to mentally represent a situation different from the perceived present. Sinclair (1970) proposed that dynamic-event words reflect the child's operative knowledge, the stable patterns of cognition that organize reality for the 1- to 2-year-old (Piaget, 1954; Piaget & Inhelder, 1969). This is illustrated in Figure 4–2. Image-schematic meanings derived from this background form the basis for words that encode the entity and dynamic aspects of motion events.

Motion Events According to Talmy

Talmy (1975, 1985, 2000) presents the "motion event" as a fundamental basis for structuring language expression by adults. A motion event is an aspect of ongoing overt experience that can be delineated from that stream of experience and referenced with language. That is, the event as experienced or witnessed can be carved from the ongoing stream of experience and coded with linguistic elements standing in for the major elements of the "real" experience. A motion-event approach to the construction of sentences allows a direct analogy with the real-world events that young children enact in their own movements and observe in the movement of people and objects around them.

The following components are core:

- Motion—"refers to the presence per se in the event of motion or location (only these motion states are distinguished by language)."

- Figure—"a moving, or conceptually move*able* object whose site, path, or orientation" is the focus.
- Ground—"a reference object (itself having a stationary setting within a reference frame) to which the figure's site, path, or orientation receives characterization."
- Path—"the course followed or site occupied by the Figure object with respect to the Ground object."(Talmy, 1985, p. 61)

According to Talmy the basic motion situation can be symbolized as follows:

Motion situation: figure + motion + path + ground

Talmy's conception of the motion event as a primary organizer for the meanings expressed in a language provides a vehicle for describing the relational language typical of children at the one-word stage. While these elements are lexicalized differently by different languages (Bowerman, 1994; Bowerman & Choi, 2000), words articulating meanings that serve to structure this domain are, along with words naming people and objects, prominent in children's single-word speech in all languages studied thus far.

Additional situational aspects affecting a motion event and relevant to this discussion are:

- Deixis—the direction in relation to nearness or distance from the speaker (Talmy, 1985, p. 61).
- Manner—for example, walked versus skipped.
- Force—Talmy (1988) recognized force dynamics as (at that time) a neglected semantic category that is central to the "traditional notion of causative." His analysis begins with the basis of opposing forces in the physical world and shows the extension of force concepts to the expression of internal psychological conflict and social pressure (Talmy, 1988, p. 53). Culicover and Jackendoff (2005) describe the range of predicates characterized by force dynamics as those in which "one character, the agonist or agent, is involved in influencing the execution by another character, the antagonist" (p. 447). Talmy (1988) gives the "tendency toward rest" (p. 54) a potential role as antagonist in force dynamic interaction. This is relevant to children's word use as they comment when objects resist their actions.

From a developmental perspective, recognition of one's own and others' role as potential forces in the physical and psychological world may be a necessary prerequisite to the experience and expression of agency. Lack of this understanding might limit children's ability to express agency with verbs. Johnson (1987) recognized that all of our causal interactions with the environment require "the exertion of force. Either as we act upon others or are acted upon by them" (p. 42). He specified critical defining aspects of force. Force is experienced through interaction with others or the physical environment (e.g., gravity). It has a vector quality that influences path of motion and degrees of power or intensity. It is characterized by sources or origins and can be directed to targets by agents.

A critical developmental question concerns the consistency across children and languages of the motion-event elements initially encoded. Should it be the case that children's single dynamic-event words express common motion-event meanings across languages despite variation in language typology, strong developmental continuity would be implied. McCune 2006; presented evidence of such cross-linguistic commonality. Vihman (1999) identified these same dynamic-event meanings in Estonian. Initial analyses of early word combinations with verbs in English and Hebrew reveal the same categories of motion-event meaning as earlier single dynamic-event words, adding recognition of self as agent or experiencer (Smiley & Huttenlocher, 1995; Herr-Israel & McCune, 2006; Ninio, 1999a,b). This cross-linguistic semantic correspondence spanning developmental accomplishments suggests that earlier single dynamic-event expressions provide partial knowledge contributing to initial combinations with verbs.

Cross-linguistic studies (e.g., Bowerman, 1994; Bowerman & Choi 2000; Choi and Bowerman, 1991) have demonstrated that dynamic-event words, while arguably based on common universal understandings, respect children's ambient language, carving up the world with dynamic-event words somewhat differently across languages. However, the aspects of events and situations that children choose to talk about with dynamic-event words are common across languages. The characterization of these words as reflecting reversible sensorimotor knowledge (raised to the level of mental representation) indicates the basis of such words in child cognition. However, such an analysis does not suggest the manner in which these words might direct the child toward complete linguistic expression in sentences.

Talmy's (1975) formulation of motion-event expression as a fundamental semantic model for linguistic analysis offers the potential for linking dynamic-event words as a transitional behavior to later complete sentential expression. The use of these words demonstrates the child's primitive understanding of motion events and a dawning ability to refer to salient relational aspects of those events. At the same time, some dynamic-event words will be found to refer to relationships between basic elements expressed in the Talmy formula or to specify their cognitively interpretable meaning within a more generally conceived motion-event construct. By following Talmy's interpretation of motion events as semantically and syntactically organized, we may be able to analyze the sequential steps from singleword expression to initial syntactic development. *From this new perspective, the defining feature of dynamicevent words, complementary to their cognitive basis, is that each refers to some aspect of one or more reversible motion events extended in time and involving spatial relationship(s) between entities.* In this way the single words that refer to the dynamic aspects of experience serve both to anchor word meaning in infant cognition and point the way to more complete linguistic expression.

Image Schemas with and without Language

Image schemas, internal processes potentiating conscious mental representation of meaning, arise spontaneously, bringing about various internal states for children who have attained this representational capacity. As children attain the capacity for mental representation, they begin to use their broad foundation of nonspecific sensorimotor understanding to develop linguistic meanings. Aspects of experience are shaped and emphasized as words begin to function as symbolic vehicles capable of expressing these newly shaped and mentally represented meanings. As children interact with objects and people in the environment, their image schemas support the internal mental representation of particular experiences. The experiences based on image schemas encompass the broad areas recognized as interesting by a particular child, with some commonality across children ensured by underlying cognitive commonalities as well as the biological and social similarities characterizing all human infants.

Adult reactions add emphasis and strength to a subset of these internal mental representational states: those that adults mark with language in a given culture. Often adults, attuning to the child's focus, might produce words expressing the meaning they intuit in the child. For example, a child who finishes eating a cookie might, due to image-schematic processes, consciously experience (imagine) the possibility of another cookie. An adult, intuiting the child's goal, might say *more* or *cookie* as the child is experiencing this internal state, emphasizing an aspect of the child's internal meaning. Because of the flexible and analogical aspect of image-schematic processing, the adult word might become part of the "possible future cookie experience" when this internal experience occurs on another occasion. Taking the word *more* as an example, the child might also have experiences where an adult, having paused in tickling him, then asks "*More?*" and proceeds to tickle him again, perhaps leading to an image-schematic experience of the word *more* accompanying a different experience of iteration.

The range of image schemas arising for a child, apart from any adult linguistic accompaniment, would reflect a given child's personal and highly varied individual nonlinguistic experiences. At various times, these image schema–based experiences would be likely to include most of the wide variation of situations encoded by dynamic-event words across the world's languages. The situations emphasized by accompanying parental words in a given setting would prompt the child to build understandings of the meanings distinguished in the ambient language.

A critical feature of the image schema is its imaginal and analogical quality. Once a child has experienced an adult word in the context of a given image schema, that image schema is transformed to include the word in its schematizing properties. Additional experiences recognized as "similar" by the child (not necessarily by adults) will now also call to mind the word as part of the image schematic process. Children's creative use of language (sometimes termed "overextension") is a result of this process. Korean provides some interesting examples.

The Korean language does not encode containment with highly general seemingly simple particles like *in* and *out* as does English. Rather, as exemplified in Table 5–1, in Korean, tight versus loose fit is a critical distinction

Table 5–1
Categories of Early Dynamic Event Verbs in Korean

Spontaneous Motion	Caused Motion
1a. Vertical Path	
Ancta [sit down]	*Ollita* [cause to go up]
Ilineta [get up]	*Naylita* [cause to go down]
Nwupta [lie down]	*Anta* [carry in arms]
Ileseta [stand up]	*Epta* [carry on back]
Ola kata/ota [go/come up][a]	
Nayle kata/ota [go/come down][a]	
Ttelecita [fall]	
1b. Deictic Path	
Kata [go]	*Nohta* [put on surface]
Ota [come]	
2. Figure/Ground	
Attachment and Containment	
Na kata/ota [go/come out][b]	*Kkita* [fit] (tightly)
Tule kata/ota [go/come in]	*Ppayta* [unfit] (tightly)
	Yelta [open]
	Tatta [close]
	Pwuthita [juxtapose two surfaces]
	Kka(k)ta [peel off]
	Nehta [put in] (loosely)
	Kkenayta [take out] (loosely)
	Pesta [take off] (clothing)
	Kkocta [put elongated object to base]
	Ipta [on trunk] (clothing)
	Sinta [on feet] (clothing)
	Ssuta [on head] (clothing)

[a] Numbers refer to the named categories more fully described in a following section.
[b] These expressions are identified as two words in Choi (1997).

that crosses the notions of containment versus support as coded in English. Korean-learning children have been shown to respect these distinctions using a variety of specific containment/attachment verbs to express what would be *in* and *on* relationships in English (Choi & Bowerman, 1991). They do generalize the earliest learned transitive verbs beyond adult uses, but in directions that make metaphorical sense within the Korean linguistic structure. For example, *ppayta* 'removal from tight fit' was used by several children in the following situations where other more specific verbs were required: to request the removal of clothing (*pesta*), trying to take a toy from another child (*cwuta*), and asking someone to peel a banana (*kkata*). The verb *kkita*, meaning "to cause to fit tightly," was used concerning sticking a fork into an apple (*kkocta*), being held tightly by an adult (*anta*), and attaching magnetic fish to the magnetic mouth of a duck (*ppwuthita*). Bowerman (1989) reported extension of Korean *kkita* and *ppayta,* appropriate for containment and its opposite in situations of tight fit, to putting magnets on surfaces and peeling stickers off surfaces where *puwthita* and *tteyta,* joining/separating flat surfaces, would be appropriate. All of these are examples of "tight-in" situations; it is of interest that *kkita* and *ppayta* do not tend to be overextended to "loose-in" situations, such as an apple in a bowl. The construct of an abstract image-schematic base for word meanings accommodates these appropriate metaphorical extensions despite their "overextended" status.

Image schemas as defined here (and by Johnson, 1987) are abstract processes providing an underlying capacity for a momentary conscious mental experience. The utility of any given image schema for engendering a given conscious mental state might be fleeting. The number and kinds of coherent mental states that might be engendered by a child in this way would be limitless, being constrained only by their basis in an underlying cognitive background , such as that illustrated in Figure 4–2. The ambient language would work its distinctive developmental magic by emphasizing, by more frequent accompaniment, those image schema—based mental states reflecting important distinctions within that language. In other words, fleeting and uncategorized mental states experienced by the prelinguistic infant provide a basis for shaping linguistic and conceptual development. Differential accompaniment of such states by parental language shapes the child's range of expression to the ambient language. Within a language, the child would build internal meanings and internal word forms that encompass the appropriate distinctions of the ambient language while failing to build such differential meanings expressed in other languages. (e.g., McDonough, Choi, & Mandler, 2003). Mandler (2004, 2007) finds evidence for many of the image-schematic meanings, described below for single dynamic-event words, in younger infants' responses to experimental situations. On this basis she attributes greater stability and more discrete meaning to infants' cognition during the first year of life than I do. Alternatively, discriminatory abilities displayed in earlier infancy provide a foundation for continued development, including expressing a variety of dynamic meanings with words. Talmy identified a linguistic "microcosm" dealing with the categories of "space, time (and hence also...location, and motion)," among others, where a limited number of expressions, the closed-class forms express "the structure of those domains." And "Thus the closed-class forms of a language taken together represent a skeletal conceptual microcosm. Moreover this microcosm may have the fundamental role of acting as an organizing structure for further [linguistic] conceptual material" (Talmy, 1983, p. 228). (I interpret "structure" here as "linguistic structure" not necessitating stable physiological brain structures) Talmy's "linguistic core" is compatible with a foundation in early cognition (Piaget, 1954). Development of a set of dynamic event words for initial reference to aspects of the microcosm of meaning portrayed in Figure 4–2 may prompt the child's additional acquisition of more complete linguistic constructions.

Children's referential words as defined in Chapter 3 are of two kinds: names for things, or entity words, and dynamic-event words. Children's dynamic-event words express the logical and reversible nonconceptual understanding established through their observations of and participation in events in the real world. This understanding includes understanding of vertical space or the ability to predict gravitational effects (e.g., what happens when objects are dropped or placed in a location) as well as possible relationships of closeness or distance between objects and self, and topological notions, such as containment and attachment, as well as the location of the child's body in space. The dawning of mental representation allows the child to understand brief time sequences of past, present, and future and to incorporate such meanings into relational language regarding ongoing events.

When a child uses a single word in a given situation, that word makes reference to the child's entire conscious experience of the ongoing situation; therefore use of a given dynamic event word includes a sense of the entity involved. Similarly, use of an entity word implies ongoing awareness of any movement or dynamic aspect involved (Werner & Kaplan, 1963). Recall that, in experimental situations, young children succeed in learning nonsense words for objects or actions only if the salient object is moving or being manipulated—that is, if the object is participating in some sort of motion event (Hollich et al., 2000; Werker et al., 1998). A child can often use either an entity or dynamic-event word for the same communicative goal. A child who has eaten a cookie might comment on the situation at time 2 below, saying *gone*. If she wants another, she can say either *cookie* or *more*. Use of the word *cookie* at time 2 to request another cookie conveys the child's desire and implies recognition that the cookie eaten can be replaced by a similar cookie (categorical recognition of entities). *More* conveys additional meaning. In using *more,* the child shows awareness of three time points in the event of interest, exhibiting the cognitive background that I proposed in Chapter 4:

Time 1. cookie present₁

Time 2. cookie absent

Time 3. cookie present₂

    Use of the word *more* specifies the child's implicit sense of the prior situation (cookie present), the current situation (cookie absent), and the potential future situation, having another cookie. Use of the single-entity word *cookie* specifies the desire for a cookie while failing to linguistically reference the underlying motion/time event sequence and so provides less evidence regarding the cognitive basis of the request. By using a dynamic-event word interpretable as such by adults, the child specifies a complex meaning more fully. The overlap in implied understanding for *more* and *gone* is of interest, as both reflect the child's comparison of at least two time points. The type of sequential-event knowledge that should underlie such word develops between 12 and 18 months of age, the time when most children begin to use referential words (Haake and Somerville, 1985).

Categories of Dynamic Event Meaning

In integrating Talmy's linguistic categories with child knowledge available at the beginning of language learning, we identified the following superordinate categories of dynamic words (Herr-Israel & McCune, 2006; McCune & Vihman, 1999; Vihman, 1999). These categories were formed by parsing the children's word uses into groupings that link well with Talmy's analysis and/or form a coherent group of meanings in relation to children's underlying knowledge of object, space, causality, and time. Divisions across the categories are somewhat arbitrary: see *allgone* below. The utility of this particular organization will be determined only by future study relating children's dynamic-event words to probable cognitive bases and later more complete linguistic expressions. My initial analysis of early verbs supports this organization (McCune, 2006). In the following sections I describe the motion-event meanings underlying common dynamic-event words in English and include examples from additional languages based on Talmy's semantic analysis. Recall that motion, figure, ground, and path are primary in the Talmy system and that deixis and force are also important. Children's single dynamic-event words can be interpreted based on the contexts where they are used either through the cognitive background described in Figure 4–2 or in relation to motion-event semantics. I have chosen an analysis in relation to motion-event semantics (although the cognitive underpinnings are often transparent) in order to emphasize the relationship between the use of single dynamic-event words and the earliest verbs. This relationship is described at the end of the chapter. The categories of dynamic-event words are not mutually exclusive, as often a given word refers to more than one aspect of a motion-event situation and reflects more than one feature of the cognitive background. Some expressions require consideration of a motion event prior to and/or predicted by their expression, thus encompassing two or more related motion events. These single word expressions in the particular contexts provide opportunities for children to recognize situations that will later be more fully expressed with sentences. Three super-ordinate categories are described: (1) Path, (2) Figure/Ground, and (3) Motion-Event Sequence. A following section provides examples for these categories. Table 5 summarizes the categories and documents the generality of their use across children learning several languages.

1. Path: Spatial direction or path in the vertical plane (e.g., *up, down*) or the "deictic plane," involving movement toward or away from the child's body (*here* used in exchange; *there* accompanying placing actions). The words *up, down,* and *here* in these cases seem to refer to the path of a figure in a single reversible motion event, without direct reference to ground. When *there* accompanies placing actions, some sense of the ground, as end point of the path, is implied. Such placing actions, accompanied by the word *there,* are often iterated sequentially with multiple objects, bringing multiple motion events into play.

2. Figure/Ground: Spatial relations between entities in relation to child action or access, including reversible aspects of containment (*open, closed, in, out*), and attachment (*stuck, off*). Use of these words implies a single motion event where the topological relationship of figure and ground is the primary focus. In situations of occlusion, relationships between figure and ground are also implied. But *allgone,* the most common English baby word in occlusion situations, is also used in cases of absence to request a recurrence (similar to *more*). For convenience, therefore, it is included in the following category.

3. Motion-Event Sequence: Event sequences, where the dynamic-event word indicates a mental comparison of the ongoing state of affairs to a prior, expected, or desired reverse alternative, again in relation to child action or access: iteration or conjunction (*allgone, more, again*) and potential reversibility or negation (*no, uh oh, back*). These situations seem simultaneously to reference two or more distinct but related motion events involving the same ground and the same or an equivalent figure where at least one event is either remembered or anticipated. Table 5–2 summarizes the number of these meanings expressed by each of 10 children learning English, 3 of whom were developing bilingually, learning Estonian or German in addition to English.

Children's direct experience of their own movement—either in the vertical plane, when being lifted and lowered, or horizontally through locomotion or the approach or retreat of people and objects from the child's location—promotes knowledge of path. Figure/ground relationships are accompanied by words coding specific relationships in space, either static or the subject of ongoing motion on the part of the figure. These words specify the relationship

Table 5–2

Dynamic-Event Words Used by 10 Children: 7 Learning English and 3 Bilingual Learning English (E) and Estonian (S) or German (G)

Motion Categories	Participants												
	1	2	3	4	5	6	7	8E	8S	9E	9S	10E	10G
1. Path													
a *Vertical Path*													
down	X	X			X	X	X	X	X			X	X
up		X	X	X	X	X	X	X	X	X	X	X	
b *Deictic Path*													
here/thanks	X	X	X	X	X		X		X		X	X	X
mine						X	X						
there	X	X	X	X	X		X	X		X	X		
2. Figure/Ground													
a *Containment*													
open	X	X	X		X	X	X	X	X			X	X
closed									X			X	X
out				X		X	X	X	X			X	X
in								X	X			X	X
b *Attachment*													
stuck/fitted	X		X			X	X	X	X		X		
unstuck (invented)								X	X			X	X
3. Motion Event Sequence													
a *Occlusion*													
allgone		X	X	X	X	X	X	X	X			X	X
'bye	X	X		X		X	X	X					
peekaboo							X						
b *Iteration/Conjuction*													
more	X	X	X	X	X	X	X	X	X		X	X	
again								X	X				
c *Negation (Reversal)*													
no	X	X	X	X	X	X	X	X			X	X	
uhoh	X		X	X	X	X	X	X					
back	X					X					X		

between figure and ground without indicating additional details of the motion event, such as action by an agent, although the child may herself be acting on the objects at the time. Words spoken in relation to motion event sequences indicate the child's cognitive awareness of the reversible character of such events as they unfold in space and time and the linguistic ability to mark with a word the central element of the event for the child at that time. All of these expressions tend to focus on situations where the child is physically involved. The development of dynamic-event words is the child's first step to specifying these relationships cognitively and expressing them linguistically. Most examples in English are taken from McCune (1981), a study that comprised all dynamic-event words of five children throughout the single-word period. Examples from other languages are cited in the text.

1a. Vertical Path: Reversible Spatial Direction in Relation to Gravity

Linguistic reference to events involving spatial reversibility is apparent in uses of *up* and *down*. In English-learning children, *up* is the most common and early dynamic-event word expressed.

Examples: *up*

Mira—Lifting workbench and bouncing her body, pointing up

Trying to sit up with book

Trying to lift cover and open book

Meri—Climbing on a chair

Sitting up higher to look in toy bucket

Tracy—When front of truck is up in the air

In all of these examples there is a sense of motion and of the dynamic possibility of vertical movement in opposing directions against gravity. The image of Mira, simultaneously lifting, bouncing up and down, and pointing, strongly demonstrates this contrast.

Note: Each of the children studied included one or more words from each dynamic event category in their repertoire of single words, although nuances of meaning varied across languages. Children's words in each category are marked with X in the row for each meaning they exhibited.

Sources: Data sources are as follows: 1 (Shanti), 2 (Mira), 3 (Meri), 4 (Janis), and (5) Tracy are drawn from McCune-Nicolich (1981) who provide many of the examples of dynamic event word use in the text; 6 (T) from Tomasello, 1992; 7 (Aurie), from McCune (1995), 8 (Virve) and 9 (Raivo) from Vihman (1976, 1985, 1999); 10 (Hildegard) is from Leopold (1939).

Examples: *down*

Shanti—As she sits down

Throwing cheese on the floor

Bringing hand downward

Mira—Patting floor prior to mother putting jack-in-the-box down

Patting high chair tray as mother holds out cookies

Uses of *down* include the sense of vertical motion from a higher to a lower location, as shown by Shanti lowering her hand and Mira patting a surface indicating the terminus of vertical movement anticipated, a sense more often verbally encoded with *there*.

In Estonian, various words are used in vertical-path circumstances: for example, *sülle*, "up (into arms), into lap"; *alla*, "to down" (from highchair); *all*, "at down"; *maha*, "to down, to the ground" (throwing things); and *maas*, "at down" (Vihman, 1999). In French, *tombe*, "fall," first in experiences of falling and later generalized, and *en haut*, "up," were used by one French child studied (McCune, Veneziano, & Herr-Israel, 2004). Korean presents a seemingly more complicated situation (see Table 5–1). Motion in the vertical direction is expressed by a variety of different words influenced both by whether the motion is spontaneous or caused and by different characteristics of the objects involved. Different verbs are always used in Korean for spontaneous and caused motion, and children have been found to respect this, not generalizing meaning across this transitivity boundary. Choi and Bowerman (1991) found that the Korean-learning children they studied were later than the English-learning children to refer to vertical motion in general. While many English learners say *up* or *down* by 16 months of age, the general transitive verb *ollita* ("cause to go up") was used by few Korean learners even at 24 months of age. They used instead a variety of more specific transitive and intransitive verbs to express more specific notions of vertical motion. These include intransitive posture verbs such as *ancta*, "sit down," and *ilenata*, "get up," as well as transitive verbs such as *anta*, "carry in arms," and *opta*, "carry on back."

Early use of *ollita*, "cause to go up," was observed in only one child, from 18 to 19 months. He incorrectly used this verb in situations where objects were replaced in their former location or placed in a customary location regardless of any notion of verticality. This is a meaning common to English-learning children in their use of the word *back*, as in "put it back." The authors traced this error to his mother using *ollita* as she placed an object in its customary place in a high cabinet. This example is of interest for two reasons. First, it demonstrates the notion of reversibility underlying dynamic-event words: this overlap in meaning motivates the child's error. Second, as Choi and Bowerman report, he was learning a number of transitive verbs that included "ground" in their meaning, so he may have generalized this notion, assuming that "customary location" was an aspect of the meaning of *ollita*. This "misuse" supports the claim made here that dynamic-event words share a deep connection to cognition: in this case the reversibility of vertical motion is confused with the reversibility of placement at (or not at) a typical location. It is of interest that children learning different languages pick up words that, while differing cross-linguistically for adults, are used for some of the same dimensions of meaning by the children. The connection to the situation (and aspects of the situation attended by the child) is critical.

1b. Deictic Path: Reversible Spatial Direction in Relation to Self

Closeness and distance of objects and people with respect to the self is of critical interest to babies. They extend objects to their mothers, using the word *here,* in English, and attempt to keep or gain control of objects, saying *mine. Mine* has sometimes been considered an expression of possession, but its spatial basis should be clear (Mandler, 1992; Smiley & Huttenlocher, 1995). In the single-word period. *mine* frequently occurs as a child seizes an object and attempts to bring it into proximity with himself. Both *here* and *mine* are sometimes used as a generalized exchange word when passing objects back and forth, again emphasizing the notion of reversibility.

Examples of *here* in situations of object exchange:

Shanti—Throwing elf toy to her mother

Janis—Putting bottle to doll's mouth

Mira—Giving purse to mother

Tracy—Putting cow puzzle piece in mother's lap

The child's implicit understanding of the empirical reversibility of situations coded with *here* is apparent because the child must learn the word under circumstances that are the exact inverse of conditions under which he or she produces it. When transfer to the child is anticipated, a parent is likely to say *here* while holding an object extended toward the child. The child is expected to use the word while holding the object toward the mother, anticipating potential transfer to her. Children using *here* seem to do so while they are in control of the object. In French, *tien* (used similarly to English "here it is." reduced to *ta* in child speech) serves this same purpose (Veneziano, personal communication).

Estonian-learning children code similar meanings with various words: *kätte,* "into hand"; *aitäh,* "thanks" (used in exchange); *siin,* "at here"; *siia,* "to here"; *kaasa,* "take along with self"; *ees,* "at ahead." The meaning "take along with self" does not seem to be expressed by English-learning children, but the dynamics of an object sharing the child's trajectory seems compatible with deictic path, demonstrating that an accessible word for a meaning can prompt early learning.

For Korean-learning children, *kata,* "come." and *ota,* "go" are their earliest intransitive motion verbs, referencing movement of themselves toward or away from others and movement of others toward or away from themselves

(Choi & Bowerman, 1991). The transitive verb *cwuta,* "give," is also a common early verb in Korean, probably with a similar exchange function to *here* in English (Gopnik & Choi, 1995).

Path–End Point

Related to both vertical spatial direction and/or spatial relation to the child's body is the use of words as the child places an object on a surface near herself, necessarily involving a downward vertical movement, and seeming to have a particular location in mind (marking "end of path"), or a sense of completed action (see Gopnik & Meltzoff, 1986, for a similar interpretation emphasizing successful completion of an action).

Examples of *there* (placement/end point/completion):

Shanti—Lifting and lowering doll blanket

After nesting the last cup

After opening a small box

Meri—Holding jack-in-the-box: her mother has closed it

Janis—Straightening (lifting and lowering) cloth she has put over book prior to ironing it

The contexts of occurrence for *there* could in some cases have called for *up* or *down* (lifting and lowering a cloth). Rather than the vertical movement in relation to gravity, the children seem to emphasize the completion of their own actions and possibly the successful reaching of a desired end point for an object (nesting a cup, opening a box, orienting one object to another—cloth and book). In similar placement and completion contexts, some children use the word *okay,* possibly following a parent's model.

In placing a sequence of objects, the child may accompany each placement with the word *there,* or, in some cases, a consistent nonword vocalization. Occurring where like objects are selected, moved, and placed, the actions may suggest preference for a type of object, similarity of a class of objects, or the beginning of class knowledge, as suggested in Chapter 4. However the use of *there* or some other vocalization accompanying sequential placement suggests that the iterative sequential aspect of the situation, a repeated motion event, is the child's focus. Placement and/or location is also expressed by the words *there* and *here,* although the contrastive use typical of English-speaking adults is not characteristic of this early period.

Examples of *here* (placement/location):

Shanti—Bringing pants to doll's leg

Janis—Setting toy dog on ledge

Meri—Pulling purse out of bucket

Mira—Laying doll on piano bench

Tracy—Pointing to iron in response to mother's question: "Where is it?"

Examples of *there* (placement/location):

Meri—Touching doll's mouth

Taking out and holding up plate

Tracy—Answer to the question, "Where's the baby?"

In French, *là bas,* "there," was used, and in Estonian, *siin,* "at here," or *siia,* "to here." It is not clear from available literature whether or how this meaning is coded in early Korean, but *nohta,* "place object loosely on a surface," is a possible candidate (Choi & Bowerman, 1991).

2. Figure/Ground: Reversible Figure/Ground Relations: Containment, Attachment, and Occlusion

A group of dynamic-event words in English specify types of relationship between figure and ground that can be altered in reversible motion events. Children's manipulation of objects includes great interest in placing objects one inside the other (Sinclair et al., 1989). The object in hand that is moved is considered the "figure," while the primarily stationary object serving as container or surface where the object is placed is considered the "ground."

The relationship of containment includes the notion of an accessible receptacle. Accessibility versus its opposite is noticed by babies with the words *open* and *close(ed).* In the single-word period, *open* is common in English-learning children, while *close* is rare. The examples below seem to emphasize a desire on the part of the children for access to occluded objects and/or the desire to create an opening, potential detachment, or to reveal a concave space.

Examples of *open:*

Shanti—Gesturing at toy milk bottle she wants mother to open

Prior to opening the jack-in-the-box

Taking bottle after mother opens it

Janis—Pushing on cover of workbench, trying to open it

Trying to open book

Mira—Trying to get object out of bottle that is already opened

The words *in* and *out* express the containment relationship between figure and ground directly in English, accompanying placement in and removal of objects from containers. *On* and *off* in English are more likely to refer to donning and removal of clothing rather than placement and removal of an object (figure) from a surface (ground) in the single-word period.

Figure/ground relationship can also involve a close fit or apparent attachment between the two objects. English does not offer an obvious and common word for the act of joining or putting together. Raivo, developing bilingually, used Estonian *kokku,* "put together," for this purpose (Vihman, 1999). In Korean, the English-language categories of "containment" and "support" are divided differently in ways that often conflate the English senses of support versus containment. Individual verbs also may incorporate aspects of figure and/or ground, expressing more specific relationships covered globally by *in* or *on* in English. Consequently, in Korean, a long list of spatial verbs is needed to cover the territory of *in* and *on* in English. Nonetheless, Korean-learning children make reference to the same types of situations as English-learning children do with their short list of relational words (see Table 5–1). In Korean, the earliest learned motion verbs are *kkita,* "cause to fit tightly," and *ppayta,* "take apart tightly fitted objects."

English-learning children say *stuck* in situations where it is difficult to remove objects from tight fit, but they may use *out* or *open,* generalized from situations of containment, lifting lids, and so on as a request to take apart tightly attached objects. The word *stuck* is of particular interest because it is an early acknowledgement of force, as objects resist children's application of effort.

Examples of *stuck* (Herr-Israel & McCune, 2006):

Aurie—Pulling on lid which has fallen into pot

Trying to push piece into puzzle

Pushing small man into truck

Struggling to get small man out of truck

After trying to take nesting cups apart before giving them to mother

One French-learning child used *difficile* (where English-learners would say *stuck*) at 17 to 19 months, and at 20 to 22 months, *c'est dur* or simply *dur.* Estonian-learning children say *kinni,* "closed"; *sees,* "at inside"; *sisse,* "to inside"; and *välja,* "to outside" in situations of opening, closing, and placing and removing from containment. English-learning children say *off* for the removal of clothing. Both Korean-learning and Estonian-learning children include the body part concerned (i.e., the ground) in words for donning clothing (Korean: *ipta,* "on trunk"; *sinta,* "on feet"; *ssuta,* "on head. Estonian: *jalga,* "onto foot"; *pähe,* "onto head." Removal of clothing in Korean uses a single verb, *pesta*).

Considering available data on Korean, eight different transitive verbs were used by the majority of children in one or more studies to refer to situations that, in English, are covered by three or four spatial particles. Similarly, Estonian seems to employ a broader range of lexical items than English, although the extent of their generality has not been studied. Nonetheless, the commonality of the spatial movements and relationships that the children choose to encode are highly similar across languages, testifying to a common underlying preverbal cognitive understanding of space, time and motion.

3. Motion-Event Sequence Including Previous and/or Anticipated Motion Event:

While all dynamic event words imply potential reversibility, the words discussed in this section (e.g., *allgone, bye-bye, more*) compare two or more reversible motion events. In the examples below where the children said *allgone*, showing their mothers empty cups and implying a request for more juice, they seem to point both backward in time to the emptying of the cup (one event), show awareness of the present state of affairs (a second event), and point forward in time to its potential filling (a third event). Two of these events are aspects of representational rather than perceptual experience, anchored by the perceptual presence of the empty cup. In the first two examples below, *more* used in similarly sequential circumstances points to the past event, where the figure popped out of the jack-in-the-box, and a potential future motion event where something previously present and currently absent will be restored as the figure pops out again.

In the remaining examples. *more* expresses iteration of a sequence of actions with objects: multiple motion events in relation to one another.

3a. Occlusion/Absence

Allgone is expressed by children when some entity is expected to be present but is indeed absent as well as on occasions when something is occluded or hidden from view. In both cases the notion of reversibility from absence to perceptual presence is implied. It is interesting to note that as commonly used by parents, this expression is more likely to denote true occlusion or absence; children seem to extend this by analogy to "absence from an expected or alternative location." Absence in a location—for example, when all objects have been removed from a container but are perfectly visible on the floor—can be an occasion for *allgone*. The word *bye-bye*, no doubt generalized from situations of departure, is used in this context by some children. Note below that Meri says *allgone* while looking in the empty bottle, having removed the small objects to the floor around her, and Shanti says *allgone* while looking around the floor when she has put all of the objects in the bottle!

Examples of *allgone and bye-bye* in conditions of absence, absence in a location, and occlusion:

allgone

Tracy—Taking lid off and looking in empty pot

Closing a box over a book

Janis—Showing mother an empty juice cup

Looking in empty bucket when toys have been removed

Setting a book down when finished with it

Meri—Looking in empty bottle after removing objects

Holding up blanket; answering mother's question, "What happened to the baby?"

Mira—Looking in empty cup;her juice gone.

Shanti—Waving her empty juice glass in the air

After dumping an object from the large bottle

Searching for a doll

Looking for more objects to put in the bottle after the appropriate ones have been put in

bye-bye

Janis—Dropping lid in pot

Before and while closing the lid on the jack-in-the-box

Putting objects in the bottle

Covering mother's face with her hair

Typically, English-learning children use *allgone* in situations of absence or disappearance, although they sometimes say *bye-bye.* In Korean, *epista*, "not exist," is used for disappearance situations, although no detail is available on the use of this word (Choi & Gopnik, 1995). In Estonian, *kadunud*, "to be lost, gone" and *otsas*, "at an end." have been observed in typical *allgone* situations (Vihman, 1999).

3b. Iteration/conjunction

Examples of *more:*

Tracy—Pushing button before jack-in-the-box pops up again

Shanti—Requesting another portion of juice

Reaching for and picking up a second toy fish

Janis—Giving two doll bottles to her mother

Meri—Trying to take the last piece from a puzzle

Finding a second small bottle and putting it next to the first

Mira—After finding one puppet, searching for another

English-learners use *more, again,* and *another* in these situations; recall the example regarding request for another cookie. Estonian-learners use the terms *veel*, "more," "again"; *teine,* "other" (breast, for nursing; hand, for washing); and *jälle,* "again" (Vihman, 1999); French-learners say *encore,* meaning "again" or "more." Sometimes *there* is used with repeated placement of objects, marking deictic path repeatedly.

3c. Representation of Reversible Sequence/Negation

Reversible and repeated actions form a common core of children's play with objects during the second year of life. They fill a container and dump it; they stack blocks and knock them over; they complete a simple puzzle, disassemble it, and complete it again. Uses of the words *no, uh-oh,* and *back* confirm children's ability to compare present with past or potential future circumstances, implying simultaneous consideration of a state of affairs and its inverse.

Examples of *no:*

Mira—Trying to put lid on pot and failing

Throwing book down

Shanti—Protesting as her mother tries to take cookie box

Shaking her head and looking at her mother after failing to gain the observer's attention

When her mother tries to put the shoe on the wrong doll

Janis—When one cup will not fit in another

Looking at a puzzle piece she has put over the wrong hole

Tracy—Protesting because her mother is trying to interest her in a puzzle

In contrast with *no, uh-oh* is often used when failing to achieve a goal, implying the alternative possibility of success (Gopnik & Meltzoff, 1986). *Uh-oh* is also used to predict disaster, as when an item is about to fall. Such prediction implies comparison of a present to a potential subsequent state.

Examples of *uh oh:*

Shanti—Trying to touch a bug on the floor and missing

Janis—After falling on the floor

Looking at cover and box that are apart

Meri—When the lid comes off the pot

Comment on empty purse

Tracy—Letting her mother know her shoe is coming off

Uses of *back* sometimes imply return to a habitual location, as in "Put your toys back," but may also accompany playful reversal of actions such as opening and closing a toy car, as in the example below.

Examples of *back:*

Meri—Picking up hammer before putting it away in the toolbox

Searching for elephant's hat, which she has broken off and is trying to replace

Shanti—Before putting objects back in the bottle

After closing the toolbox, wanting mother to open it

Trying successively to open, close, open, etc., the door of a small car

In English, *no, back,* and *uh oh* were used in circumstances where conditions in the environment conflicted with the child's expectation, desire, or effort. These words imply simultaneous consideration of a state of affairs and its inverse. If the child says *no* when a lid will not fit on a pot, awareness of the alternative possibility that it would fit is implied. In Estonian *ei,* "no," and *tagasi,* "back," seem most common, with *valest,* "wrong," also occurring. In French, *non,* "no," is used. These words imply the child's sense of cognitive disequilibrium.

Dynamic-Event Words and Cognition

Children's dynamic-event words express the logical and reversible understanding established through their observations of and participation in events in the real world as shaped by the organization of meaning in the ambient language. This understanding includes the ability to predict gravitational effects, such as what happens when objects are dropped (vertical path) or placed in a location, as well as possible relationships of closeness or distance between objects and self (deictic path). Topological notions relating figure and ground—such as containment and attachment as well as the location of the child's body in space—are also demonstrated. Mental representation allows the child to understand brief time sequences of past, present, and future and to incorporate such meanings into dynamic language regarding ongoing events. It seems likely that dynamic-event words are selected from the ambient language because each expresses a simple dynamic meaning relevant to the cognitive background derived from earlier sensorimotor experience. As aptly demonstrated by Bowerman and Choi (2001; Choi & Bowerman, 1991), the meanings will emerge in accord with those of the adult language.

In research with convergent findings, Smiley and Huttenlocher (1995) studied the contexts of use for "event" words (those termed "dynamic-event words" here) by 10 children recorded monthly for 5 hours each across the single-word period (median age range 13 to 19.5 months). They identified 14 event words used by four or more children, 10 of which overlap with the words and meanings analyzed here (*down, up, off, out, open, more, mine, there, allgone, uh oh*). They examined (1) child range of use and (2) potential sources in the input, including parental frequency and range of use. Parents made frequent use of the words identified, but more broadly than in the uses adopted by children, suggesting developmental influences on semantic expression. Smiley and Huttenlocher's analysis of the meanings intended is compatible with that presented here. For example, "directed vertical motion was most common for *down*. Occasionally, movements in the opposite direction occurred (e.g., . . . going up for *down*)" (p. 31). (This finding supports the notion of reversibility that I have identified as a common element across all dynamic event words.) For words not directly related to paths of movement (*open, allgone, uh oh,* and *more*), they note the perceptual salience of the outcome. For *more,* "children may group instances on the basis of replication (perhaps a non-appearance-based category) of interesting effects, regardless of the entities involved" (Smiley & Huttelocher, 1995, p. 29). The cross-linguistic findings reviewed here replicate the meanings reported by Smiley and Huttenlocher. But the analysis goes further, demonstrating (1) that the sets of dynamic-event words that children use can be seen as semantically interrelated based on infant cognition and (2) the meanings can be interpreted through motion-event semantics potentially linking these single words with later verbs in sentences.

The generality of meaning across children and languages attests to the basis of early language in underlying cognition. At the same time, the variation across children and languages in the qualities and range of situations likely to be referenced by a given dynamic-event word attests to the fluidity of language relationships with cognition at this period of development and the effects of the ambient language. The common element underlying all of these words is their application in conditions of spatial and/or temporal reversibility. It may be that in differentiating entities from their dynamic aspects, reversible states are both highly salient and very common. The child's beginning development of mental representation allows both recall of very recent situations and prediction of simple highly likely events. Therefore children are attracted to adult words that accompany these most easily recalled and predicted transformations. At the same time, as they learn these dynamic-event words, they are learning about the salience for language of paths objects take, figure/ground relationships, and so on. The use of single dynamic-event words points the child in directions useful for future linguistic development, a fact that becomes obvious when language is considered from a motion-event perspective. Herr-Israel and McCune (2006) found that children's first sentences with verbs replicated the meanings previously expressed with dynamic-event words.

Dynamic-Event Words and Early Verbs

Dynamic event words are single-word predicates codifying reversible events in the environment. The entities involved are linguistically unspecified at the single word period (Bloom, 1973; Werner & Kaplan, 1963). Although Tomasello (1992) included dynamic event words as "first verbs," they do not conform to the category of true verbs even when they exploit verb forms of the ambient language, as in Korean (Choi & Bowerman, 1991). These single word utterances demonstrate the linguistic capacity to refer to dynamic aspects of the ongoing event, but not the ability to sort out either the linguistic or non-linguistic relationships among the constituents of the event and/or the potential sentence. Linguistic specification of this core dynamic information across a range of diverse motion events may provide learning experiences promoting linguistic expression of these more complex relationships in sentences (Vihman, 1999).

Smiley and Huttenlocher compared children's use of single dynamic event words with their subsequent use of verbs. Single dynamic event words accompanied rather than preceded events of interest and occurred in the context of both own and others' activities. This finding suggested to the authors that the movement or change itself was the focus of these expressions, rather than the child's intention to act. When verbs began to appear children spoke almost exclusively about their own actions, and often before the event occurred. This finding suggested to the authors that the children were beginning to experience themselves as potential agents or experiencers. They further found that "self words (i.e., the child's name, first person pronouns, self-action meanings of change verbs) were acquired simultaneously in the early multiword period, regardless of differences in salience in parent utterances or in linguistic complexity. Verbs were extended to include others' actions after several months without a change in distribution of parental uses (Smiley & Huttenlocher, 1995, p. 53)." So true verbs were, at first, limited to expression of the child's own action, and usually said before such action occurred.

The sense of oneself as a causal agent may be derived from earlier image schematic experiences of one's own force across a variety of action situations. Thelen and Smith (1994), following Johnson (1987) provide a model for the child's development of an embodied sense of force (Figure 5–1; from Thelen & Smith, Figure 11.4, p. 326). They describe the child's experience of reaching, kicking, crawling, and walking as four clouds of physical, mental, and neurological experience. With time and the experience of many such events, the sense of force that is part of all of these activities (and others) would come to have a more abstract and general aspect, yet still be connected to the bodily sense of action. A sense of self as a source of force might emerge earlier than knowledge of others as sources of force. Dynamic event words express movement and change over time, but they do not linguistically encode action or force. Smiley and Huttenlocher's finding that the earliest verbs are limited to self action supports the view that a bodily sense of "self as force" may underlay the first expression of agent's action. Considering the kinds of verbs children first use further supports this notion.

In studying Hebrew-learning children's first-acquired transitive verbs, Ninio (1999a) found that these comprised three general categories: "obtaining" verbs (*want, get, give, take, bring, find*); "creating" verbs (*do, make, prepare, build, draw*); and "consumption/perception" verbs (*eat, drink, see, hear*), all

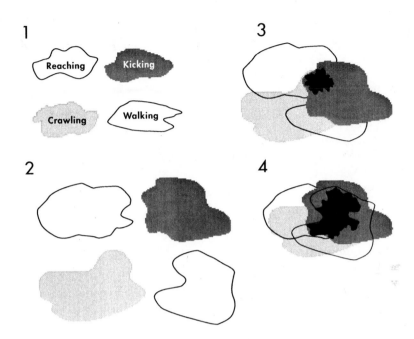

Figure 5–1. Model for the embodiment of the concept of force. Thelen and Smith model the embodiment of force as initially involving separate "clouds" of experience. As children experience and gain control of force in varied circumstances, solutions to the problem of experiencing and managing forces of and on the body come to overlap, so that a sense of force develops its own central focus. This sense may be a prerequisite for true verb use, which is at first limited to actions related to self. [Adapted from Thelen and Smith (1994), Figure 11.4, p. 326, with permission.]

involving relationships of objects to the child's body. According to our analysis (Herr-Israel & McCune, 2006), these verb meanings replicate, either directly or by analogy, motion-event categories already described here as characterizing single dynamic-event words. For example, *want, get, give, take, bring,* and *find* all literally involve deictic path (spatial location or movement of an object in relation to child location), with *find* additionally implicating figure/ground relationships. The creating verbs involve a metaphorical deictic path *from* the self, while the consumption/perception verbs involve a metaphorical deictic path *to* or *into* the self. In Ninio's study there was substantial overlap in first verb use across children. In verb/object combinations only 11 verb types were observed among the first two produced by 16 children and in subject/verb/object combinations, 13 verb types.

In complementary work on intransitive verbs, Ninio (1999b) examined the frequency of 48 mothers' use of intransitive verbs with their young children in relation to the verbs first used by 20 (independently studied) children. Intransitive verbs used first by 17 of the children are equivalent in meaning to dynamic-event words commonly used prior to verbs: *come* (expressing deictic path toward the self), 13 children; *fall* (expressing vertical path), 2 children; *go* (expressing deictic path from the self), 2 children. These same three verbs (*come, fall, go*) accounted for 35 of the 60 first three verbs used by the 20 children, with the remainder spread across 13 other verbs. They were also the intransitive verbs used most frequently by the mothers studied. Huttenlocher, Smiley, and Charney (1983) found that translation equivalents of the first verbs identified by Ninio (e.g., *find, want, go, get, put, come, open, give*) comprised the majority of the first verbs their children used.

Why do these particular verbs (transitive and intransitive) tend to be learned first? It may be because they draw on the same underlying motion-event meanings as the single dynamic-event words just described. Aspects of the meanings identified by Ninio may have existed in the children's repertoires earlier, encoded by dynamic-event words. The developing sense of "self as force" may further contribute to the initial use of verbs in relation to self action.

Herr-Israel and McCune (2006) studied both dynamic-event words and all verbs produced by three children from 16 to 24 months of age to establish the relationship between dynamic-event meaning expressed in the single-word period and verb use in the period of early combinations. We first identified all combinations including a verb, a previously identified dynamic-event word, or both. We then classified those verbs with meaning substantially overlapping previously identified dynamic-event words as "primal verbs" based on both their developmental primacy and the foundational nature of their meanings. The verbs identified are listed in Table 5–3. It can be seen that these verbs overlap substantially with first verbs identified by

Table 5–3
Dynamic-Event Categories of Primal Verb Meanings

Category of Meaning	Verbs
deictic path	*Come,*ˈ *Drink, Eat,*ˈ Feed, Feel, *Give,* Gave, *Get*ˈ
	*Go,*ˈ Have,ˈ Help,ˈ *Hold,*ˈ Like,ˈ *Look,*ˈ Leave, Need
	Put,ˈ See,ˈ *Take,*ˈ Took, *Want*ˈ
figure/ground	*Close,*ˈ *Find,* Found, Hideˈ
Agency in motion	Can, Do, *Make,*ˈ Playˈ

Note: The verbs with an asterisk are those that were used by all three children. Those in italics were also identified by Ninio (1999a, b) in Hebrew translation equivalents.

Ninio and verbs reported frequently as "first" in previous literature (e.g., Bowerman, 1978; Clark, 1978; Huttenlocher, Smiley, & Charney, 1983). We then calculated the frequency of each child's combinations that included a previously identified dynamic event word, a primal verb, or both. For each of the three children studied, the total proportion of combinations including a dynamic-event word, a primal verb, or both was 83%, 84%, and 88% respectively. The motion-event meanings expressed by dynamic-event words in the single-word period continued to be the primary meanings expressed in combinations. The earliest verbs, overlapping in meaning with earlier dynamic-event expressions, additionally encode self as agent or experiencer. See Table 5–4 for examples of early single-word expressions and later comparable combinations.

These first verbs rely on context and/or on an accompanying dynamic-event word for their communicative effect. Many of them are considered to be "general-purpose verbs," highly frequent in the input, and some are potentially effective in linking semantics with syntactic roles in sentences (Goldberg, 2004). The interpretation offered here links these same verbs to early cognition. In comparison with dynamic-event words, the added element in using these verbs is the notion of self-intention, action, experience, or desire.

Table 5–4
Examples of Transition from Single Dynamic-Event Words to Primal Verb-Word Combinations

Child Language	Context
1a. Path: Vertical	
Alice	
16 months: *down*	(drops Ping-Pong ball)
20 months: *go down*	(closes elephant J-box)
21 months: *put down for baby*	(puts bottle on table)
22 months: *get down play*	(asks researcher to join her in play)
2b. Figure/Ground	
Aurie	
17 months: *off*	(wants doll's diaper off)
21 months: *off, off*	(takes doll's shoes off)
22 months: *off diaper . . . off clothes*	(wants mom to take them off)
24 months: *take diaper off . . . I want to take it off*	(Aurie is the agent)

Source: Examples are taken from Herr-Israel and McCune (2006).

Conclusion

Central problems in the study of early child language include connections between (1) children's underlying knowledge and the language they are learning at any point in development and (2) the relationship between their single-word expressions and adult sentential expressions. I have described the cognitive status of children at the transition to language in a manner that exposes relationships with the semantic elements included in a motion-event analysis of adult language (e.g., Talmy, 1975, 2000). Empirical investigation of the kinds of dynamic-event words children use during the single-word period supports both their basis in early cognition and the suitability of their meanings for motion-event interpretation. At the same time, the cross-linguistic variability in early dynamic-event meaning as well as children's "errors" in using these words demonstrates the interaction between cognition and ambient language that is essential to acquisition. In a simple way, one can consider the young child's life as an ongoing set of motion events, experienced or witnessed. The use of verbs may await the child's embodied understanding of "self as force." It should not be surprising that a system of linguistic analysis organized in this way should facilitate interpretation of children's meanings. It may be that this approach to linguistic analysis achievese a certain verisimilitude with real-world experience. In such a case early understanding of concrete motion-event expression could form the basis, by analogy or metaphor, for more abstract linguistic meaning (Lakoff, 1987; Talmy, 1996). This approach to analysis enriches the investigation of the transition to sentences.

6

Representational Play and Language

If representational play and language both reflect advances in the young child's emerging ability to represent reality mentally, play and language skills would be expected to develop in parallel, with corresponding transitions to more advanced levels occurring close in time. I have identified such correspondences on theoretical grounds and proposed the achievement of certain levels of mental representation—as observed in spontaneous symbolic play—as control parameters for analogous achievements in language, based on common levels of mental representation across domains (McCune, 1992).

Werner and Kaplan introduced the idea that meanings and the symbolic vehicles (more simply "symbols") that refer to them are barely separate in the beginning, with distancing between them developing over time until the relationship between symbol and meaning can seem quite arbitrary. This process is further elaborated by considering both representational play and language as symbolic modes affected by differentiation (distancing) and increasingly abstract modes of integration between symbols and the meanings they represent. Differentiation of meanings from sensorimotor actions involves gradual transformation and eventual elimination of the child's own bodily participation as representations of meaning become abstract. For example, in pretending at one's own everyday activities, bodily action is nearly identical in the real and pretend situations. Integration is achieved by unity or high similarity between meaning and representation of meaning. In play, a child might mentally recreate eating by merely putting spoon to lips and making "eating sounds." The entire experience of eating is bound up in this simple gesture and its vocal accompaniment.

As the child's understanding of eating as an event to be symbolized becomes more complex and differentiated, this meaning may be expressed more fully by a variety of bodily gestures rather than encompassed only in a given motion and sound. In pretending, for example, that a doll eats, the child uses very different bodily action to convey eating than that characteristic of real self-feeding, stretching the spoon toward the doll rather than turning it toward himself. The single act of pretending to feed mother or doll is the first indication of this greater differentiation. Later, stirring in a pot, spooning imaginary food into a dish, and then raising spoon to lips with sound effects provides a more elaborate expression for a more abstract and complete sense of the meaning of eating. More varied play acts involving eating can express additional meanings involving other potential actors and longer sequences, with more varied actions and types of food verbally specified. In these more elaborate cases, integration is achieved by the child's ongoing internal sense of the pretended eating experience.

Similarly, in language, context-limited words may occur early as part of real-world events. As differentiation between word and meaningful aspects of events proceeds, the child may refer to multiple aspects of an event, using different words in a given situation on different occasions, and eventually put the different words together in sequence. So, when the child wants another cookie, instead of being confined to the single word *more* or the single word *cookie*, the child might now express *more cookie*. The two aspects of the situation are differentiated by the distinct meanings of the words. The meaning of the entire message is integrated by use of a single intonation pattern. However, this two-word utterance conveys the same message as either single word in context. A more complete differentiation between events as experienced and ways of talking about events with language will eventually be achieved. In complete sentences, meaning is expressed through the systematic properties of language rather than the kinship between a one- or two-word expression and an event. The sequence of words within a sentence does not conform to the sequence of an event in real time; rather, integration of the elements of a message is achieved by the grammatical patterns varying by language. Transitions in representational play exemplify distancing, or the gradual liberation of children's mental representation from close linkage with perceptual reality—a liberation that is essential to systematic expression of meanings through language.

Piaget used the development of play as a model for describing the sequential development of more highly differentiated and integrated qualities of mental representation, while Werner and Kaplan describe the effects of these processes on language. Piaget drew his examples from observations of his own children during the second year of life. Werner and Kaplan (1963) mined the rich trove of diary studies of child language available at the time of their writing. These theorists stressed that both systems, language and play, develop in relation to general progress in the semiotic function, the cognitive capacity that accounts for mental representation across such modalities as play, language, drawing, and mental imagery.

The Development of Representational Play

The most appropriate indicator of the capacity for mental representation in the second year of life, apart from language itself, is the development of representational play. Object permanence is useful as an indicator of readiness for language onset but reaches a ceiling at the point when language begins; it is therefore less valuable as a predictor of developmental milestones. Careful study of the child's changing relations with objects and social partners in representational play demonstrates developmental steps that follow from

Werner and Kaplan's theoretical framework regarding the development of symbolization. In their view, the internal process of symbol making, termed "dynamic schematization," involves a close external and internal working through of meaning relationships, including the intention that some externally apparent behavior (vocalization or action) stands as symbol to symbolized in reference to some meaningful content. This meaningful content is an internal mental condition and, in adults, may or may not involve some specific external focus of joint contemplation. Language is characterized as the "medium of reference par excellence" (Werner & Kaplan, p. 15) because the systematic principles of syntax and semantics inherent in its structure allow revelation of the complex connotations and interrelationships among the meaningful elements referenced. Parallel developments between representational play and language can be expected only in the initial phases of symbolic development, before the child enters into the deep systematic meanings expressed in fully formed adult sentences.

Piaget (1962) did not propose detailed correspondences between the domains of play and language. Since my dissertation (Nicolich, 1975) proposed specific relationships based on the structure of underlying symbolic ability expressed in language and play productions, research has offered significant supportive evidence, including my own (McCune, 1995), confirming longitudinal and cross-sectional study. In this chapter I first propose a common underlying structural organization for the domains of language and play, presenting evidence for cross-domain correspondences at certain critical phases. I then address the child-mother-object relationship, Werner and Kaplan's primordial sharing situation, as both reflecting and facilitating these developments. In the course of their pretend play with mother, children demonstrate increasing recognition of intersubjectivity in their actions and words (Schactel, 1954; Werner & Kaplan, 1963).

The gradual articulation of meanings through real and simulated actions with objects is displayed in sequential levels of play first recognized by Piaget (1962). He identified the "symbolic scheme" in play acts having an element of mental representation (p. 98). My organization of five levels that exhibit increasing distance between the play act and the underlying meaning conveyed (McCune, 1995; McCune-Nicolich, 1981; Nicolich, 1977) was adapted from Piaget's original analysis (Table 6–1). At each level the child uses both object and action to depict meaning. The action and object are inseparable in the earliest symbolizing situations. Eventually characteristic action alone will serve to express meaning. For example, a child might first pretend at tooth brushing with a toy in the shape of a brush; later the gesture of tooth-brushing with an empty hand can convey this same sort of pretend meaning in action. Similarly, in language, both object and activity are at first expressed with a single word, often the object name used in an appropriate context. The actions depicted in representational play are quite specific: a tooth-brushing gesture will not be mistaken for another meaning in a tooth-brushing society. Words for such specific actions are rare in the single-word period. In contrast, a wide variety of

Table 6–1
Levels of Representational Play

Piaget (1962)	McCune (1995) Nicolich (1977) Levels and Criteria	Examples
Sensorimotor period	Level 1: Presymbolic schemes: The child shows understanding of object use or meaning by brief recognitory gestures. No pretending. Properties of the present object are the stimulus for action. Child appears serious rather than playful.	The child picks up a comb, touches it to his hair, drops it. The child picks up toy telephone receiver, puts it to his ear, sets it aside. The child gives the toy mop a swish on the floor.
Prior to stage 6		
Stage 6	Level 2: Self-pretend—(autosymbolic schemes): Child pretends at self-related activities while showing by elaborations such as sound effects, affect, and gesture—an awareness of the pretend aspects of the behavior.	The child simulates drinking from an empty toy baby bottle. The child eats from and empty spoon. The child closes her eyes, pretending to sleep.
Symbolic stage I	Level 3: Single representational play schemes	Child feeds mother or doll (A). Child grooms mother or doll (A). Child pretends to mop floor (B). Child pretends to read book (B). Child moves toy car with appropriate sounds of a vehicle (B).
Type IA (assimilative)	A. Including other actors or receivers of action, such as doll or mother.	
Type IB (accommodative; imitative)	B. Pretending at activities of other people and objects such as dogs, trucks, trains, etc.	
Piaget does not distinguish single acts from simple multiple-act combinations.	Level 4: Combinatorial pretend 4.1 Single-scheme combinations 4.2 Multischeme combinations	Child combs own, then mother's hair (single scheme). Child stirs in pot, feeds doll, pours food into dish (multischeme).

Type IIA

Type IIB

Piaget distinguishes the assimilative case, where the child identifies one object with another, (A) from the accommodative or imitative case, where the child identifies his or her own body with some other object or person (B).

Type IIIA

Level 5.1: Hierarchical pretend

An internal plan or designation is the basis for the pretend act. The child exhibits double knowledge: real and pretend. Evidence is of three types: (1) the child engages in verbalization, search, or other preparation; (2) one object is substituted for another with evidence that the child is aware of the multiple meanings expressed; (3) a doll is equated with a living being and treated as if it could act independently.

Level 5.2: Hierarchical combinations

Any combinations including an element qualifying as level 5 are included here.

Child picks up a toy screwdriver, says "tooth-brush," and makes motions of toothbrushing.

Child picks up comb and doll, sets comb aside, removes doll's hat (preparation), then combs doll's hair.

Child places spoon by doll's hand.

Child picks up the doll, says "baby," then feeds the doll and covers it with a cloth. Child puts play foods in a pot and stirs them. She dips the spoon in the pot, says "hot," blows on spoon, then offers it to mother. She waits, says "more," and offers it again.

socially defined actions occur in play, perhaps assisting the child in mastering these more specific meanings through appropriate action.

Play is a natural but special aspect of child behavior. One cannot direct a child to play but must arrange circumstances to allow the child's natural inclination to play to come forward. Consequently children's level of representational play development must be assessed with care. Presenting children with toys and suggesting activities may or may not elicit play. A better and frequently used approach is to structure a situation conducive to children's natural tendency to play. Because children's representational development is bound up with relationships and interactions with the mother (or primary caregiver), the most valid form of play assessment is in the presence of mother where she can provide support, even act as a prop, but is not an immediate source of the play meanings upon which the child's play assessment is based. Play evolves from a situation of comfort and interest. A seminaturalistic approach to assessment is best, combining some standardization with some organized structure. In the research summarized here, I videotaped children at play in their homes with a standard set of toys (see Table 6–2). Mothers sat on the floor near their children. When presented with a bucket of toys, a young child first explores, removing the toys from the bucket. After this familiarization period, he or she then engages with particular objects, often inviting mother to join. This situation proved ideal for eliciting a broad range and high frequency of play actions in the course of 30 minutes. We instructed mothers to "play as you normally would, but let the child take the lead," knowing this might be a paradoxical instruction. Ideally, for assessment, mothers should be available yet nonintrusive. We found mothers' levels of activity quite variable, but in every case there were a sufficient number of child actions to be coded where mother was not the instigator of the action.

I hypothesized correspondences in representational development in the domains of play and language based on apparent similarities in structure across the sequential developments in these domains. Following a period of presymbolic expression in both domains, single representational expressions (words or play acts) are observed. Subsequently both language and play involve sequences of elements, and finally, each exhibits a hierarchical aspect. These aspects of play and the extent of correspondence in development with language milestones are described in the following section, where my (McCune, 1995) findings are summarized and additional supportive evidence is reported. I observed 102 children once (6 at each month of age from 8 to 24 months), and followed 10 longitudinally through the same age span (the Rutgers sample described in Chapter 3). The sequential development of the six levels was confirmed in the longitudinal and cross-sectional samples. Scale analysis showed that 85 of the cross-sectional sample fit the predicted ordinal pattern (coefficients of reproducibility = 0.93 and scalability = 0.75. The levels of play observed were as follows.

Table 6–2
Toys Used in Play Assessment

Doll baby wrapped in blanket	Jeep—toy
Doll blanket	Mail truck—Fisher-Price
Blocks	Man—2-inch Fisher-Price
Book—*Baby's Thing*	Mirror—small
Book—*Pat the Bunny*	Mop—toy
Scrub brush	Matchbox—sliding
Brush—small	Monkey—7-inch stuffed
Comb—large	Napkin
Comb—small	Bottle cover
Cup—toy	Necklace—white plastic
Saucer—toy	Nesting cups
Teapot—toy	Ping-Pong ball
Teapot cover—toy	Sponge
Teaspoon	Purse—toy
Doll baby's clothes:	Popbeads—snapped in necklace
diaper, jacket, and bonnet	Sunglasses—Child's—lenses removed
	Puzzle with five pieces: chicken, pig, donkey, cow, duck
Doll—Ginny doll	Slippers—pair of women's size 6
Ginny doll's clothes:	Telephone—toy
blue pants, red jacket	Toolbox—toy
with hood, red shoes.	Tools—toy hammer, screwdriver, wrench, saw, pliers
Doll bottle with soft nipple	Dump truck—12 inches
Stuffed dog—brown, 9 inches	Finger puppet (Grover)
Drum with bell inside	Finger puppet (Oscar)
Dumbo jack-in-the-box	Iron—toy
Dumping bottle—clear plastic bottle	
Dumping bottle pieces:	
apple, grapes, banana, lemon,	
doll bottle, two fish, butter,	
milk, orange juice, red bottle,	
corn	

Source: Toy list from McCune (1995), with permission.

Presymbolic Play (Level 1): Typically Attained at 8 to 11 Months of Age

The earliest level of representational play depends upon the child's internal understanding of some real-world experience that is recalled to consciousness upon encountering a familiar object. Figure 6–1 illustrates the gradual changes in differentiation and integration characterizing the sequential levels of play and the language hypothesized at each level. Where there is an internal component, a mental experience somewhat separate from the act itself, this is designated by a broken-line circle inside the circle depicting a play act at a particular level.

Play at level 1 merely imitates the expressive acts characteristic of use of particular objects but does so out of context. These are brief, isolated actions without evidence that the child is aware of the relationship between the played acts and the routines of life they mimic (sometimes termed *enactive naming*; e.g., Bates, Camaioni, & Volterra, 1975). Rather, play seems differentiated from real actions merely by displacement in time and omission of the realistic goal ordinarily entailed. Examples of these recognitory gestures include:

The child picks up a cup, touches it to her lips, and sets it aside.

The child picks up a comb, touches it to his hair, and drops it.

The child picks up the toy telephone receiver, puts it in ritual conversation position, and sets it aside.

The child gives the toy mop a swish on the floor.

The child hammers with a toy hammer.

The child rolls a small truck on the floor.

These actions depend on present objects and their manipulation for conveying understanding of a common daily activity. The entire action represents the corresponding "real" activity, involving a subset of the constituent movements of that activity, so there is substantial overlap between the expressive action and the meaning it represents, as illustrated by shading in Figure 6–1.

At level 1, the presymbolic play act is shown as a solid line circle within the outer circle standing for the real act of, for example, drinking from a cup. The representational act (inner circle) is an abbreviated form of the real act (outer circle). The action of this presymbolic behavior completely overlaps in execution with the real behavior, which is differentiated from it only by omission of swallowing and other consummatory behaviors integrated with the real act by their overlapping content. For both real and presymbolic acts, the internal component is consciousness of the act itself. Only actions the child has performed occur and only realistic objects can elicit the behavior.

Level 1 acts are considered presymbolic and sensorimotor in nature. The child's expression is serious rather than playful, and he seems more

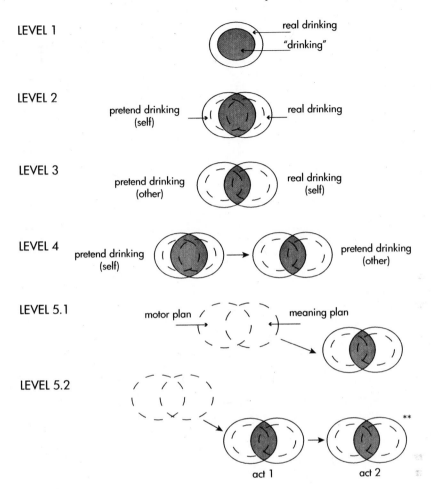

LEVEL 1

real drinking
"drinking"

LEVEL 2

pretend drinking
(self) — real drinking

LEVEL 3

pretend drinking
(other) — real drinking
(self)

LEVEL 4

pretend drinking
(self) — pretend drinking
(other)

LEVEL 5.1

motor plan — meaning plan

LEVEL 5.2

act 1   act 2 **

**Not every act on a level 5 sequence must be planned.

Figure 6–1. Gradual changes in differentiation and integration characterizing successive levels of representational development. The concentric circles illustrating level 1 show that the representational play act (inner circle: "drinking") is an abbreviated form of the real act (outer circle: real drinking). At level 1 there is no evidence of an internal mental component differentiating the representational act from the real act. The representational play act at level 2 is differentiated from the real act, as indicated, for example, by simulated "eating sounds." This suggests a mental awareness of the distinction, shown by broken lines inside the overlapping circles (as in Figure 2.2), illustrating the representational play act in relation to the real act. Broken lines indicate the internal component at all of the following levels. At level 3, where others' acts are pretended and dolls can be incorporated as recipients of play action, there is further differentiation between real and pretend acts, shown by the diminished overlap between the concentric circles illustrating the real and pretend acts. At level 4, two or more related representational play acts occur in sequence. At level 5.1, the internal component is evident prior to the representational play act and continues during enactment. At level 5.2, one or more representational play acts follow from the initial planned act.

concentrated on understanding the action than on conveying a meaning to someone else. To the extent that a child's underlying capacity for representation influences play and language performance, language is not expected at this level. However, the distinction between the presymbolic play of level 1 and the next level, self-pretend (level 2), rests on inclusion of subtle clues indicating that the child is aware that "this is pretend" as opposed to realistic activity (differentiating symbol or signifier from symbolized or signified). It is merely lack of such evidence that distinguishes the less advanced level 1 from the more advanced level 2, rendering the distinction between the two problematic. Symbolic referential language is not predicted when play is limited to presymbolic level 1.

During the period when their play remained at level 1, only 3 of the 10 Rutgers sample used any words at all, totals for those children ranging from 1 to 5 words, and in all cases these words were either imitated or context-limited in use.

Self-Pretend (Autosymbolic Play, Level 2): Typically Attained at 11 to 13 Months of Age

Pretend is distinguished from presymbolic play by evidence that the child recognizes the distinction between the real and representational acts. The child essentially imitates her own behavior out of context, using realistic objects, while indicating by facial expression (e.g., pretend smile), sound effects, or other elaborations an awareness of the distinction between the literal (signified) and the played (signifier) actions. For example,

The child simulates drinking from a toy baby bottle.

The child eats from an empty spoon.

The child, with closed eyes, pretends to sleep.

Sound effects and exaggerated gestures (such as throwing the head back to drink deeply, making slurping sounds) that accompany these actions supply, in a pretend manner, some of the missing aspects from the literal behavior. This suggests a mental comparison between the play action and the conscious experience of the remembered real behavior and an effort to represent the literal behavior more faithfully. The symbolic vehicle is the child's total action: rather than a particular object (e.g., toy cup) symbolizing a real cup, the child's action symbolizes the total real activity: ("what drinking is like" or "what lying down to sleep is like"). The played action is still in part a nearly exact replication of the literal action (e.g., the child refers to a generalized notion of real drinking by lifting a cup to the lips), but this is distinguished from the real act not only by the omitted consummatory behaviors but also by the addition of a creative element, the simulated sound effects. This addition of sound effects corresponds to Werner and Kaplan's notion of a deliberate act of denotation as the child chooses to express the meaning of drinking in this way. In Figure 6–1, level 2 pretend action is differentiated from real action by, for example, the addition of sound effects of drinking or eating, yet there is still a large overlap between the child's real act of eating or drinking and pretending at the same act. There is a somewhat separate inner mental experience accompanying the pretend act, which is designated by the broken-lined inner circle.

Pretend sounds are often shaped to become some of the first context-limited words. For example, the vocalization *num num* or some similar sound may evolve from the sounds the child experiences during actual eating to have a function in pretend and/or to signal an interest in real food. It may even be shaped by adults. Thus a sound derived and only slightly differentiated from real eating sounds may be included in conversations with baby: "*Are you ready for your num-nums?*" These language and play acts both show beginning differentiation of representational acts from what they represent or signify. The integration between signifier and signified is still achieved by great overlap between the two. Both representational play acts and initial words at this level are specifically dependent on elements of the child's own bodily action and represent activities also reflective of sensorimotor stage 6.

"Other" Pretend (Decentered Symbolic Play Level 3): Typically Attained at 12 to 13 Months of Age

When the child pretends at activities—typical of adults—that he has only observed rather than performed himself or when he applies his own ordinary acts (drinking, grooming) to others, it is clear that the internal meaning of these acts is now differentiated from the specific motor acts of the real behavior. For example:

Child feeds mother or doll.

Child grooms mother or doll.

Child pretends to read a book, turning a page and babbling.

Child pretends to clean the floor with a sponge or mop.

Child moves toy car along with appropriate sound of real vehicle.

A critical fact is that real drinking involves holding a cup to one's own lips, while pretending that a doll or the child's mother drinks requires different motoric activation—that is, holding the cup away from the self toward the mouth of the other. So the action comprising the symbolic vehicle is distinct from the action of the child in the real activity. This is a significant element of differentiation. Play at "cleaning with a sponge" or "reading" a book involves meaningful actions that never have practical significance for babies and have not previously been performed for realistic purposes. Therefore this play gives evidence of the child's internal process of articulating and representing a meaning separate from his own typical action. In a sense, the behavior indicates that a certain type of generalized action can stand in for a variety of analogous meaningful actions of this type. The additional differentiation is illustrated graphically by less overlap between the conjoined circles in Figure 6–1.

This form of play still exhibits a global representation of an entire meaningful situation by a single action performed by a single actor. This same level of representational ability was hypothesized to characterize referential words used symbolically: for example, generalizing a pet name to a variety of animals or using *more* to request another cookie. The nominal or dynamic event word at this level stands as symbol to symbolized for a total meaningful situation. Thus even children using both *more* and *cookie* as single words would be unlikely to combine these words in a request at this level of symbolic ability because each word is closely tied to the total situation, including both entity and the dynamic relational aspects in its meaning.

Bloom and Tinker (2001) reported that children showed an advance in language subsequent to exhibiting play behavior similar to that described by level 3, as my hypotheses would predict. She reported frequent expressions of positive emotion following these acts, relating this to the smile of recognition or achievement (similar to what I term the "pretend smile." Level 3 acts of pretend involving others were more frequent in my (1995) data, and often occurred earlier than self-pretend acts with sufficient confirming evidence to be considered level 2. Recall that self-directed representational play acts are considered presymbolic (level 1) unless there is specific evidence of pretend awareness such as sound effects, other elaborations, or a "showing-off smile" to mother. At level 3, where actions are either derived from or applied to others, the evidence of the symbolic aspect of the performance is apparent from that role differentiation rather than requiring additional behavior by the child. It may be that some acts identified as level 1 support a greater extent of internal symbolic differentiation from the real activity than the child's external behavior indicates. That is, some of these acts may be "false negatives," where evidence falls short of that needed to allow coding at level 2. It may also be the case that the particular play assessment situation, with mother available, tended to make other-pretend more likely than self-pretend, level 3 acts more likely than level 2. In analyzing relationships between play level and language level, I found it useful to consider single pretend acts (levels 2 and 3) together, because self-pretend was scored much less frequently than other-pretend. Often levels 2 and 3 would be first observed in the same session.

The 10 longitudinal participants in McCune's (1995) study showed pretending at level 2 and/or level 3 before the referential language transition. Of the cross-sectional participants, 27 failed to show pretending (level 2 and/or level 3; 8 to 14 months of age). None of these children used words referentially. Three additional studies contribute evidence supporting the proposed relationship between onset of pretending (level 2 or 3) and the onset of referential language. Kelly and Dale (1989), who studied 12 children in the age range of 12 to 24 months, reported that the 5 children not yet using words (all 12 months old) also failed to show symbolic play, while the other 5 single-word speakers all produced self-pretend or other-directed pretend play. Folven and Bonvillian (1991) observed 1 child who was deaf and 8 hearing children learning sign as their first language and reported that 6 of 7 children for whom data were available showed their first referential sign after self-pretend had been observed. Ogura (1990), in a longitudinal study of 4 children learning Japanese, reported use of "first names" at level 2, when the children were 12 1/2 to 13 1/2 months old, but they did not reach a milestone of 10 words (perhaps more diagnostic of the referential transition) until they were between 13 and 16 months of age, when they were between levels 4 and 5 play.

Although play acts can be coded at a given level, development of mental representation must be thought of as gradual and continuous. Children tend to exhibit a variety of levels in a play session, not all at their highest level. Many children by 24 months will continue a play theme for many acts, taking up the majority of a 30-minute session with a single sequence. Although my hypothesis that single pretend acts would precede referential words in development was confirmed, in practice, for some children, a number of months intervened between these milestones. In fact, children tended to make the referential transition closer in time to their first play combination than to onset of pretending (Table 6.4 in McCune, 1995). The significance of this finding is discussed in Chapter 9, where we consider interrelationships of dynamic system of variables contributing to the referential transition.

Combinatorial Pretend (Level 4): Typically Attained at 13 to 18 Months of Age

Eventually the child begins to combine play schemes into sequences, indicating an internal shift in representational ability. A combinatorial symbolic ability supports portrayal of a variety of signifier–signified relationships one after the other. The simplest form of combination is the repetition of the same act with varying participants (level 4.1 . Each single act would be scored as level 2 or 3 if it occurred in isolation. Only one action scheme is played, but it is repeated with variations. Two or more different level 2 or level 3 acts may also be combined in sequence (level 4.2). For example:

Child combs own, then mother's hair. (4.1)

Child drinks from bottle, feeds doll from bottle. (4.1)

Child kisses doll, puts spoon to its mouth. (4.2)

Child stirs in pot, feeds doll. (4.2)

Child puts necklace on, grooms hair. (4.2)

In combining pretend acts, the child shows recognition of differentiated components of an event that can be referenced separately by, for example, pretending to drink from a cup, then pouring "liquid" into the cup or offering a drink to mother or doll. The elements of play at this level are linked by a more complex and flexible internal sense of meaning. The first act of a play combination represents pairing of a given action and a specific actor. To yield a combination action and actor must be differentiated so that a subsequent act can pair a new actor with the old action (e.g., self drink + mother drink) or extend the meaning with another action (e.g., kiss doll + put bottle to its mouth). Figure 6–1 illustrates this differentiation and reintegration process by the combination of two sets of partially overlapping circles, each set with its internal aspect (broken lines) representing one act of the play combination.

It is not unusual for a child to apply a pretend scheme to all available appropriate participants in a long sequence—for example, doll, mother, and experimenter are all given a drink, exhibiting something like a categorization of animates [Mandler (2004) proposed "animate" as an early image schema–based meaning]. Similarly the child may comb two dolls' hair or comb using two combs. These aspects of sequencing are reminiscent of Mandler and McDonough's (1996) studies of functional class membership.

Earliest word combinations also recognize differentiated components of events. For example, a typical early combination, *allgone cookie* refers to an entity (a cookie) and its state (current absence, previous presence) at the time of the utterance. Such combinations are linear in the sense that the elements are joined only by virtue of reference to aspects of a common event (as play elements are) rather than by internally specified rules. Linear word combinations are likely to develop at the same time as or later than when play combinations are observed. Only children in the McCune (1995) study who exhibitedtwo or more representational combinations in their play produced any word combinations, supporting the notion that when children begin to combine words they are also capable of nonverbal representational combinations. Additional studies provide evidence for sign or word combinations that lack a syntactic basis occurring contemporaneously with level 4 play combinations (Folven & Bonvillian, 1990; Kelly & Dale, 1989; McCune-Nicolich & Bruskin, 1981; Ogura, 1990). Further analysis of the McCune findings regarding play and language combinations follows discussion of Level 5 representational play.

Hierarchical Pretend (Level 5): Typically Attained at 18 to 24 Months of Age

Play is considered hierarchical when the external action follows from internal mental processes rather than being dominated by perceptual aspects of real objects in the environment. Werner and Kaplan (1963) describe the distinction between a symbolic mode of designation and earlier processes:

> In our attempt to determine the nature of symbolization we concluded that the central distinguishing feature of a symbolic vehicle as opposed to a sign [presymbolic designator closely linked with what it represents] lies in its representational function: the vehicle is exploited by the organism to represent

or depict a referent. Such representation, we concluded further, comes about through schematizing activity of the organism; it rests on the establishment of an inner-dynamic, rather than external, similarity between the total articulatory processes entering into the formation of cognized objects, on the one side, and symbolic vehicles on the other. (p. 25)

The earlier activities of play culminate in the ability to first designate a meaning internally and then devise the appropriate means for its expression. The hierarchical structure is derived from the relationship between the internal designation or "plan" that is held in mind and the external acts that follow from it. In the early forms of representational play discussed thus far, children's pretend actions and internal representational intention are assumed to arise simultaneously, often in response to some object that reminds them of a given meaning. The concave property of a cup may suggest drinking, so the child picks up the cup and pretends to drink. At the combinatorial level, perhaps self-drinking in mother's presence gives rise to the notion that mother also is a potential "drinker," so an additional act ensues, leading to an apparent combination. The acts of level 4 combinations may be linked to one another by the child's growing ability to shift attention across varied elements of meaning, but there is no sense of a prior internal mental state guiding the initiation and continuance of the activity. Rather, there is close integration between perceptual and motor activity and the ongoing representational consciousness supporting pretend play. Eventually a child's representational intention can arise without external perceptual support, with internal plans (dynamic schematizing) guiding external action. As in adults, mental life flows between perceptual and representational interests, often in directions quite divergent from present external reality.

The structure of representational behavior is considered hierarchical when external acts are based on a separate and prior internal intention. That is, some internal designation is the source and organizational framework for the external behavior. Object substitution (using an inappropriate rather than appropriate object) for a given action is the obvious and most commonly discussed form of hierarchical pretend. This behavior is deemed hierarchical because a prior mental act determining, for example, "this block is a cup," is the ongoing guide to pretend activities in which the block is treated as a cup. Implied in this analysis is that the child continues awareness that "this block is a block," so hierarchical pretend is assuming ongoing double knowledge, an intentional ongoing representational state equating what is known materially to be different from a cup with "a cup." This behavior corresponds to the criterion Werner and Kaplan established for symbolic acts: awareness that the symbol (block) is separate from what is symbolized (cup) and the ongoing intention to represent one by the other, a phenomenon termed "decoupling" by Leslie (1987). In Figure 6–1 the overlapping broken-line circles illustrate the internal component that precedes and continues to guide the level 5 pretend act. This internal act defines the hierarchical quality of this level. A planned level 5 act may be followed by a second act (not necessarily separately planned), yielding a level 5.2 sequence. Referring back to Chapter 2, Figure 2–2 illustrates a rather mature state where addressor, addressee, object, and symbol have achieved maximum differentiation and remain integrated through the activity of a given communicative event. Level 5, where the internal aspect of symbolization attains some independence from the literal, designates the child's initial capacity to interact in such decontextualized situations.

Experimental studies have been undertaken in which experimenters model play acts using a variety of objects as substitutes to determine the extent to which real object properties influence children's tendency to choose or accept a given object as a substitute for another more typical object in producing a pretend play act. It turns out that children's willingness to treat one object as a pretend substitute for another object (once they have achieved the developmental capacity to substitute at all) is highly correlated with adult judgments of similarity between the two objects in question (Jackowitz & Watson, 1980). Furthermore, children in these experiments first show the ability to substitute neutral objects, such as blocks, in pretend actions; they will then, somewhat later, mimic pretend actions without an object (e.g., brush teeth with a finger) prior to pretending with a counterfactual object that has a function of its own (e.g., pretending to comb hair with a toy car).

These experimental results follow from the developmental principle of "distancing." Initially symbol and symbolized are nearly identical, "toy cup = real cup." With development, increasing divergence from similarity is possible. In the case of counterfactual objects, the representational intention is in direct conflict with the perceptual understanding of a given object, so effort is required to maintain the representational designation. Mandler and McDonough (1996) used children's willingness to generalize imitation of pretend acts across objects as evidence of their category knowledge. Level of symbolic development should influence this task, with children who have achieved level 5 showing greater willingness to generalize outside the expected category than younger children.

I have defined hierarchical play by evidence that the child has *planned the play act prior to execution*. In addition to cases of intentional object substitution, the child's prior representational intention or planning can be identified by verbal announcement or inferred from search or from intervening preparatory behavior, including speeded movement toward an object at a distance that is then used in representational play. When a doll is treated as a center of its own action (e.g., placing the cup in the doll's hand rather than to her mouth), the implicit internal designation of "doll = animate agent" provides the hierarchical structure for ensuing activities. Planned representational play may occur as a single act (5.1) or be incorporated into a sequence (5.2). Examples labeled 5.1 below would be considered level 2 or 3 without the hierarchical aspect, while those labeled 5.2 would be 4.1 or 4.2.

Some examples of hierarchical pretend observed at the transition to this level are as follows:

Child picks up the bottle, says "*baby*" then feeds the doll and covers it with a cloth. (5.2)

Child finds the iron, sets it down, searches for the cloth, tossing several objects aside, finds it and irons it. (5.1)

Child picks up comb and doll, then removes hat before combing doll's hair. (5.1)

Child puts play foods in a pot, stirs them. Then says "*soup*" or "*mommy*" before feeding the mother; waits, and says "*more*" offering the spoon to the mother. (5.2)

Child picks up play screwdriver, says "toothbrush," and makes the motions of tooth brushing. (5.1)

Child puts scrub brush to ear, saying "*hi.*" (5.1)

This level of play demonstrates the capacity to entertain symbolic material that is distinct from external action. The internal plan itself, for example, designating "block = cup" as an internal meaningful relationship, demonstrates the child's capacity for distancing symbols from material content. In Werner and Kaplan's view, in order to enter into truly representational combinations such as those expressed in sentences, symbolic material must achieve this independence from material action.

Comparing Combinatorial Ability in Play and Language

It is at this level of pretend play that I hypothesized children might express the capacity to use symbolic combinations in language that follow consistent patterns of order. Regularities in word order of children's two-word utterances, first termed "pivot-open" structures and later designated as "positional patterns" (Braine,1963, 1976), occur earlier than true syntactic combinations and indicate a similar level of planning to that of hierarchical pretend. The use of consistent lexical orders may be the first evidence of the child's ability to link symbolic vehicles directly, with internal schematizing underlying the total performance, rather than the child producing sequences of words or actions by virtue of their relationship to the ongoing events.

Positional patterns may facilitate the mental and motor action needed for multiword speech. The capacity for ordering rules is an essential element in syntactic development where the conventional arrangement of grammatical elements in the ambient language applies. Initial regularities are lexically based, with children developing consistent but idiosyncratic two-word ordering patterns that may or may not match the most frequent order in the ambient language. Unlike the use of single words, where each designates an entire event, words in these combinations are somewhat more delimited, often one to the entity aspect of the event, the other to the dynamic aspect (e.g., *more cookie*). Because of the structural similarity with level 5 play, I proposed that positional patterns would be observed at the same time as or following this representational play level. In the months following this transition, I predicted a spurt in mean length of utterance (MLU) due to the facilitation of language production by this new representational ability. Both of these predictions have been confirmed in small-sample longitudinal studies (e.g., McCune-Nicolich & Bruskin, 1981).

In the McCune-Nicolich & Bruskin (1981) study, we followed five girls beginning at 15 to 19 months of age, when all produced only single words, until positional patterns were observed in their language and multiword utterance types were greater in number than single-word types. The methods of data collection and coding were the same as those described in McCune (1995). It can be seen in Table 6–3 that the five girls all first produced multiword utterances after attainment of combinations in play, with lags of 0 to 3 months between these milestones. In addition, they first gave evidence of positional patterns following level 5 play with a 0- to 2-month lag. Both of these results are significant at the 0.05 level, testing that the language milestone would be observed at or after the predicted play level by the Fisher exact test. Furthermore, the children first produced greater numbers of multiword types than single-word types either in the same session or the session following the observation of positional patterns. A spurt in MLU was also observed following observation of level 5.

In McCune (1995) I undertook a partial replication of these findings with the cross-sectional ($N = 102$) and longitudinal ($N = 10$) participants described earlier (Table 6–4). Analysis for positional patterns was beyond the scope of this larger study. In order to evaluate the relationship between level 5 play and language combinations in the cross-sectional sample, I considered

Table 6–3
Age in Months at Play and Language Milestones for Study Participants

Name	Level 4	First Multi-words	Level 5	Positional Patterns	Multi >Single Words	MLU[a] Spurt Months	MLU Spurt Values
Janis	18	18	21	22	21	20/21	1.19/1.47
Meri	16	16	20	21	21	20/21	1.17/1.54
Mira	16	17	18	20	21	20/21	1.15/1.62
Shanti	15	18	21	21	21	20/21	1.09/1.49
Tracy	23	23	26	27	28	26/27	1.19/1.31

From McCune-Nicolich & Bruskin (1981), with permission.

Children's first multiword combinations were observed in the same month or after play combinations. Following observation of hierarchical combinations in play, three language changes were observed: Positional patterns (defined in the text), greater frequency of combinations than single words, and a spurt in MLU.

[a]MLU (mean length of utterances) was computed in words averaged across all language expressions in a session.

several variables that might show the effects of increased symbolic ability. One important milestone is the shift from single words as modal behavior to a predominance of multiword utterances. Of the 26 children who attained level 4 but not level 5 play, only 1 produced more multi-word types than single-word types. In contrast, 6 of the 22 children who had achieved level 5 showed this predominance. These results were significant by the one-tailed Fisher exact test ($P < 0.017$). Furthermore, children who attained level 5 showed significantly greater MLU (1.53 versus 1.31), mean number of word combinations (61 versus 25), and total intelligible utterances (249.6 versus 144.6) than those who had attained only level 4. Level 5 marks the point at which children's capacity for mental representation is first freed from a reliance on perceptually available information.

In addition to the evaluation of specific hypotheses regarding transitions by individual children, a regression analysis was conducted using level of play in conjunction with age to predict MLU for cross-sectional participants in the McCune (1995) study. The purpose of this analysis was to evaluate the joint contribution of representational development and chronological age to a general index of language maturity. Both play level and age were significant contributors ($R^2 = 0.78$), F (degrees of freedom $df = 1,99$) 173.99, $P < 0.001$. Results of analyses relating representational play level and language maturity in the longitudinal sample demonstrated a pattern consistent with the cross-sectional findings but provided additional information regarding time lags between expression of the play and language variables (Table 6–4). The children first produced language combinations following level 4 play combinations, with lags from 0 to 6 months and a modal lag of 2 months. After onset of level 5, the combinatorial ability was more fully expressed in language, as was apparent in MLU spurts observed following level 5 onset. The proportion of multiwords did not exceed single words until later than 24 months for most children. Alice, Aurie, and Rick showed this milestone at 4-, 3-, and 1-month lags, respectively, following level 5 onset. Data from Danny and Kari, who developed language many months after the play skills, support the hypothesis that the language variables will emerge either at the same time as or later than the play variables while indicating the importance of additional developments, to be considered in following chapters. (See Table 6–4 on p. 148.)

Representational Play and Mother–Infant Intersubjectivity

Thus far in the chapter we have concentrated on the gradual development of mental representation in the child without much attention to the adult partner in the process of representational and language development. However, the process of symbol formation is essentially a dyadic interpersonal quest of adult and child for the means of maintaining and enhancing their sense of intersubjectivity (Schactel, 1954; Werner & Kaplan, 1963). The goal of this

Table 6–4

Age in Months at Play and Language Milestones for Study Participants

Name	Pretend Onset Level 2/3	Context-Limited Words	Level 4 Play	Ref. Word Prod.	First Multi-words	Level 5 Play	Multi > Single Words	MLU[a] Spurt Months	MLU Spurt Values
Alice	9	10	11	14	17	15	19	17/19	1.03/1.82
Aurie	12	14	13	14	17	19	24	19/21	1.08/1.36
Rick	13	10	15	15	18	21	22	21/22	1.32/1.74
Rala	12	15	14	15	20	18	22	20/22	1.03/2.48
Jase	12	14	15	15	17	18	24	21/23	1.06/1.45
Kari	10	16	12	16/18	23	19	—	—	—
Ronny	11	11	15	16/18	18	18	—	23/24	1.09/1.22
Nenni	12	11	17	21	23	22	—	23/24	1.01/1.24
Vido	13	13	16	17/19	21	21	—	21/22	1.06/1.27
Danny	13	16	18	27	27	22	—	—	—

From McCune (1995), with permission.

[a]MLU (mean length of utterance) was computed in words averaged across all language expressions in a session.

quest is construction of a mutual representational approach to the world that can form a bridge to the child's independent mental activity and participation in the larger social world of his ambient language. Here I would like to focus on the primordial sharing situation in play, emphasizing the critical ongoing role of the dyadic relationship in the process of the infant's symbol formation. In the earliest period of object exploration, the relationship functions subtly, in the background, as the infant's sense of internal security with mother or other caregiver nearby allows him to explore freely, unconcerned by feelings of insecurity. Later, specific initiatives from both mother and child ensure their continued mutual engagement in this critical process. In fact, the child's reactions and initiations with the mother in representational play provide clues to his growing awareness of her status as an independent partner in potential interaction. The quality termed "theory of mind" is meant to designate an understanding on the part of an infant that others do not necessarily share the infant's perspective but have mental states of their own, which can be influenced by the child's actions. Young children's use of the mother in pretend play, beginning as early as 1 year of age, demonstrates an initial sense of this duality, indicating that the properties described as theory of mind do not involve a sudden attainment. Rather, the child's understanding of self and other develops gradually during the first months and years of life. The sequential levels of mental representation as they emerge display the gradual extension of this understanding and the child's compensation for the perceived discrepancy between own and maternal perspective through communication in play and language.

It is in the course of playful construction and vocal exchange that the mother or other trusted adult can offer knowledge from the foundation of his or her own representational intentions to attract the infant into an increasing capacity for representational consciousness. As the baby portrays a pretend event in action or displays an object of interest, the mother comments, providing linguistic and conceptual knowledge. The overt acts of play and the availability of correlative language [Vygotsky (1934) 1962] become the means for maintaining representational focus. It is well known that children are more likely to engage in pretending in the presence of the mother (Dunne & Wooding, 1977) and that they play for a longer period and at more advanced levels depending on mother's presence and level of participation (Slade, 1987).

Representational play as a reliable indicator of representational consciousness also becomes a vehicle for examining knowledge of self and other. On the one hand, the experience of shared consciousness with a valued caregiver, usually the mother, is considered a motivator for representation. On the other hand, the mother is credited with the role of partner in the child's gradual transition to a broad capacity for representational thought. In the developmental course of representational play, subtle but universal changes in the manner in which play acts are produced give evidence of an orderly change in accompanying internal states. Similarly, changes in the child's use of the mother in representational play gives evidence of increased understanding of maternal consciousness.

Clearly inferences concerning likely mental states underlying the observed play behavior are essential to determining the representational status of that play. By addressing the course of play development from the perspective of internal states, I intend to link each level with its precursor, demonstrating that the entire range of representational play behaviors constitutes a single domain of competence. It is of great interest that as play depends less and less on the perceptual context for support, the child concomitantly shows increasing evidence of intuitive understanding of the mental states of self and other (see Figure 6–1).

Level 1 presymbolic play offers observant parents the opportunity to note their child's dawning knowledge of objects by demonstrating their use out of context. However, the infant's consciousness seems concentrated on the enacted meaning as such, without incorporating others' interest or giving evidence of understanding the distinction between the "real" and out-of-context actions. Similarly, the mother is not alluded to as audience or invited to act, so this play gives no evidence of knowledge of self and other.

In self-pretend (level 2), the child begins to make reference to the similar past experiences underlying play acts by elaborating the simple actions of play in a manner that makes them more like the (presumably) internally represented experience that now guides them. He shows evidence of the distinction between the real and pretend contexts by attempting to compensate for absent aspects of the real context, simulating them with exaggerated gestures or actions. He also seeks shared representational understanding with the mother by displaying pretend acts to her with an inviting smile. Here is the first evidence of the child's intuitive expectation of shared representational consciousness with the mother.

In decentered pretend (level 3), the child pretends at others' activities or adapts other agents to enact his own typical self-pretend schemes. Both cases show the capacity to differentiate an action from the typical agent and hence the separation of the internal meaning symbolized from a specific typical sensorimotor action. There is evidence that the child is aware of meaningful acts as generally applicable to animates and is capable of inventing variation in agent–action events. At the same time, the play acts are still dependent upon typical objects, similar to those used in the real version of the activities portrayed. Many acts played at this level are derived from maternal behaviors, providing additional evidence as well as continued support for the integration of representation in the mother–child relationship. An infant's request that mother engage in representational play acts constitutes direct evidence of the expectation that mother's representational consciousness can be influenced to match that of the child.

In linear combinatorial pretend (level 4), play shows a sequential character as the baby strings play acts together, often alternating acts between self and mother as agent. This behavior further serves to demonstrate the infant's recognition of the potential equivalence of representational consciousness in self and other. In such sequences, one act may suggest the next. However, the ability to shift from one pairing of agent and action and from one action to another within the frame of a meaningful event indicates the differentiated (decontextualized) understanding of the event as well as the use of the event structure to provide integration for the component acts. In fact, the play sequence can be considered as contemplation of multiple potential aspects of an event, perhaps leading to more complex understanding of the event supported by multiple actions. The infant, by playing in representational sequences with the mother, presents himself itself with external, perceptually bound material that makes reference to absent reality. Alternation of activities with the mother suggests increased interest in coordinating representational perspectives. At this level, the child seems first capable of using maternal pretend suggestions when these occur in the context of ongoing play. Thus in the context of representational play there is a shared evocation of absent reality.

Hierarchical combinatorial pretend (level 5) demonstrates greatly reduced reliance on the perceptual world as a support for representational consciousness. While realistic props are still preferred, play at this level is guided by a prior internal intention rather than elicited in response to present objects. For Piaget, this prior act defines play as symbolic; other theorists have preferred the term *functional play* for the earlier levels. However, given the gradual nature of the evolution of representational play over time, it seems important to encompass the full range of acts with the term *representational*, where symbol–symbolized relationships gradually become more differentiated, culminating in the advanced behavior of hierarchical pretend. At this level, because a purely mental act, separate from perceptual reality, is now represented by the child, the motor performance can be considered symbolic, standing in for a meaning other than itself. This decontextualization is most obvious where a substitute object (e.g., block = cup) is used. The critical feature is that consciousness of representational possibility precedes the motor act. The source of the activity is mental rather than perceptual or motor, and the pretend identity of objects can shift as new meanings occur to the child. The child can accept decontextualized suggestions from the mother, recognizing shared representational consciousness more fully. In one charming example, when a child was having a pretend conversation with her father at the office, the mother's question, "What will Daddy bring you?" elicited the response, "Bagels," much to mother's enjoyment!

Conclusion

In this chapter I have described transitions in mental representation as expressed in play, the milestones in language that would be anticipated based on the structural properties of play, and how the child's changing incorporation of the mother and her initiations into play reflects development of a gradually more articulated understanding of own and other's consciousness. The structural analyses of play and language follow from the theoretical framework presented by Piaget and my own analyses of representational play and language. Mahler and colleagues (1975) and Werner and Kaplan (1963) assert that the child's developing consciousness of distinctions between self and other is the primary motive for representational development. Werner and Kaplan further propose that the articulation of the representational meanings of language is an active process on the part of the child that depends on both maternal joint understanding with the child and the child's gradual differentiation of self-consciousness from maternal consciousness. This same process of differentiation can be seen in the child's expression of representational understandings in play. In the development of language, Werner and Kaplan recognize an equipotentiality for gestural and vocal communication, with both modalities, at first, expressing presymbolic communicative messages. Language as it exists in a community offers the child a systematic means of shaping and expressing increasingly complex meanings and messages. Therefore, as the child extends the personal symbols shared only with the mother and a few others to reflect more differentiated meanings, the linguistic system of the community begins to emerge in his or her productions. Because for hearing children and parents the ambient language is vocal, the verbal tends to overcome the gestural system in expression of meanings.

7

The Vocal Story: Forming Sounds into Words

> . . . *symbol formation . . . rests on twin form-building processes, one directed towards the establishment of meaningful objects (referents), the other directed towards the articulation of patterns expressive of meaning (vehicles).*
> —Werner and Kaplan, 1963, p. 22

Language expresses meanings with words and sentences, but how do such meanings become clothed in words? This is truly the question of how the child enters language. Beyond simple maturational views, one of two explanations is often favored. The child might first develop concepts nonverbally, then seek out words to label them—a position often attributed to Piaget but one that he never espoused. Or the child might first become aware of words, then seek to determine what adults meant by the sounds they made. According to Piaget (1962) and Werner and Kaplan (1963), neither of these explanations is adequate. Rather, their theories propose an integrative alternative: that internal meanings related to objects and events in the real world are co-constructed with the words that come to refer to them. A vocal or gestural expression comes to stand as symbol to symbolized in relation to an internal meaning by coordinated and simultaneous development of both.

In this chapter I emphasize phonetic skills that serve the child in construction of form/meaning correspondences: first the production of a repertoire of well-practiced consonant sounds and second the development of individual and systematic phonological motor patterns. Vygotsky claimed that language and thought have separate roots, but he also marked their crossing at significant points in development. One such point is the onset of word learning as speech production facility and the meanings of language develop together.

The child's most noticeable vocal production from birth is cry. Precursors of later vocal control for babbling and speech can be found in cry. In particular, the respiratory timing, which includes brief inhalation followed by prolonged exhalation, is also characteristic of speech. Vihman (1996), in her detailed review of child phonological development, finds "the vocalic elements of later speech, as well as prosodic elements such as variation in intensity and pitch, rhythmic patterning, and phrasing in cry long before they enter vocal play" (p. 104). In contrast, it is in noncry vocal play that elements of breath interruption or closure, typical of later consonants, occur.

In speech, vowels (vocalic elements) occur when air is released through the open vocal tract. Consonants occur when there is an interruption of this airflow.

Vihman (1996) reports general agreement on the development of vocal behavior in the first year of life. First, noncry differentiates from cry, and by 3 or 4 months of age babies produce "comfort sounds," "coos" and "goos." These result from close contact between the back of the tongue and the soft palate typical at that age and from playful or reflexive action with the muscles of the glottis during expiration. These are the earliest preconsonantal closures. Laughter begins around the same time. It is of interest that both crying and laughter involve rhythmic cycles of alternative and repetitive very rapid breath intake and longer expiration, a pattern typical of speech. Controlled exhalation, varying in length to suit speech goals, managed and shaped by laryngeal action, is characteristic of mature language.

The grunt vocalization (discussed in the next chapter), although widely observed, was not considered a developmental contribution to the production of language prior to my initial report (McCune, 1992). Glottal sounds (the basis of grunt forms) occur from birth in cry and in relation to airway adjustments. Stark, Bernstein, and Demorest (1993) observed vocalizations of this sort in 3-month-olds held upright and engaging in social interaction. Oller (1992) distinguished vegetative grunts from later-occurring, perhaps more social vocalizations termed "quasi-vowels," omitting the former from phonetic analyses.

Glottal control is an essential aspect of speech production. Considering the mechanics of speech, the breath, controlled by inspiratory and expiratory muscles at and below the larynx, is the essential medium on which speech rides. Acoustic properties of speech are strongly influenced by forms of activation of the larynx. Therefore the primary structures for producing grunts, the lungs and larynx, are at the core of language production. Continuity in form between vegetative grunts and later communicative grunts discussed in the next chapter argues for inclusion of this form in phonetic analyses.

Between 4 and 7 months, vocal play is generally recognized by parents and professionals. According to Vihman (1996), vocalizations of this "expansion period" include squeals, growls, yells, and possibly whisper, resulting from prosodic features such as pitch level and change managed at the larynx, while friction noises including "raspberries" result from manipulation of consonantal features, partial closures involving lips and tongue, which seem vowel- and consonant-like. Some consonant-like and vowel-like vocalizations may be produced during this period.

Babbling in syllables, beginning between 6 and 10 months in almost all typically developing children, is often considered the hallmark of the child's movement toward language. Babbling involves rhythmic alternation of opening and closing the jaw, with sufficient laryngeal control to produce a vowel and relatively complete closure of the upper vocal tract yielding a consonant.

The distinct separation between phases of opening and closure of the vocal tract along with regular syllabic timing are the defining features of "canonical babbling" (Oller, 1986, 1992). Oller (1986) distinguishes an earlier phase of "marginal babbling" that "impressionistically includes slow or shaky transitions between consonant-like and vowel-like elements" and vocalizations that "do not have the mature regular-syllable timing characteristics" of canonical babbling (p. 98).

Babbling is only one sort of rhythmic behavior developing at this time. Thelen (1981) describes a phase of rhythmic alternation across the motor system, including kicking when supine and repetitive manual banging when the child is seated before a surface. These activities all follow from the ability to perform repetitive movements, perhaps because of the emergence of neurological systems termed central pattern generators. Continued execution of repetitive acts, eventually with variations, exemplifies the sensorimotor strategy Piaget described as the "circular reaction" whereby the child engages in a controlled action, experiences the results of that movement, and then repeats the cycle again. In Piaget's view, the cycle has conservative properties such that the child is able to repeat an action almost exactly; but circular reactions are also a source of learning as the child modulates the action, experiencing resultant changes in outcome. For example, in the course of a babbled sequence, a baby might rhythmically open and close his jaw during an expiration of the breath, at each closure bringing the lips together, with the nasal passage closed, producing [b]. He might, by chance, adjust the velum allowing some air to escape from the nose and thus produce [m] on the next open/close repetition. Noting the results of these differentiated experiences, the baby might learn to produce either effect "at will." *This goal-directed ability to produce a given vocalization in babble is the essential phonetic ingredient for referential production of speech.*

As children are producing sounds, perhaps at first randomly and later more "at will," they are greatly influenced by the perception of speech sounds in the environment, both the talk and vocal play of adults and the sound of their own vocalizations. The lack of this important influence is one of the reasons that children with transient hearing loss due to infection or other causes during the prelinguistic period may be seriously disadvantaged as they begin to learn language.

Vihman (1996) documents the importance of infant speech sound perception for production of the earliest words. Children vary in the consonant sounds they favor during the babbling period. Not surprisingly, their early words partake largely of the babbling repertoire. Vihman suggests that "the child may be . . . experiencing the flow of adult speech through an 'articulatory filter' which selectively enhances motoric recall of phonetically accessible words" (p. 142). Perceptual preferences for sounds in the production repertoire, constituting evidence for an articulatory filter, have been demonstrated well before the first word productions (De Paolis, 2006; Ferguson, 1978; Vihman, 1996, pp. 28–30).

Werker and Tees (1983, 1984) demonstrated that young infants (8 months or so) successfully discriminate contrasting consonant sounds of their own language as well as many contrasting consonant sounds from other languages. Adults, 12-month-olds, and many 10-month-olds continue success at native language contrasts but fail to discriminate sounds not in the native language. Werker, Lloyd, Pegg, and Polka (1996), in a review of work since the initial findings, report that not all discrimination of nonnative consonant contrasts is lost. In fact very few contrasts have been studied. Furthermore, with training, even adults can learn to discriminate nonnative contrasts. However, it is clear that children around 1 year of age are much more sensitive to the sounds of their own language than they are to those of other languages. Some of these effects may be due to attention, with more differentiated attention to notable differences between the native language sounds and more global attention to the unfamiliar nonnative sounds rather than to the differences between them.

Lalonde and Werker (1995) examined the possibility that children's shift in the ability to discriminate nonnative contrasts might be related to more general child abilities developing around 9 months of age. In an age-held-constant study of 9-month-olds, about half of whom were able to discriminate the Hindi retroflex-dental contrast that had been used in earlier studies, Lalonde and Werker examined whether success on two nonlinguistic tasks, a visual categorization task and solution of the A not B error in an object-permanence task, developed in synchrony with the shift away from the Hindi discrimination. They found that these three characteristic changes of infancy tended to occur in synchrony, suggesting a broader cognitive shift rather than an isolated linguistic one. Object permanence has significance for mental representation, while visual categorization indicates perceptual recognition of equivalence across stimuli. Children succeeding in these tasks tended to discriminate the sounds of their own language but not the Hindi sounds. The convergence of these tasks demonstrates integration of more focused speech perception with recognized cognitive processes. The relationship between these developments and phonetic production skill has not yet been studied.

Phonetic Skill at the Transition to Speech

While studies of early lexical development assume that reference entails a relationship between sound and meaning, data regarding the influence of phonetic skill on the entry into word learning remain limited. Although babbling is considered the vocal behavior that is most speech-like, prediction of the onset of speech ability by babbling characteristics has not proven highly successful. Most studies of early phonological patterning are restricted to small samples of children [case studies (e.g., Leopold, 1939; Lleó, 1990; Macken, 1978, 1979; Menn, 1971; Priestly, 1977; Vihman,

1976; Waterson, 1971) or studies of two or three children each (e.g., Ferguson & Farwell, 1975; Stoel-Gammon & Cooper, 1984; Vihman, Velleman, & McCune, 1994].

Although nonlinguists may still maintain the belief that children initially babble the sounds of the world's languages at random and then begin independent construction of a speech repertoire with their early words [a view codified by Jakobson (1968) at the dawn of the formal study of child language in the mid-twentieth century], the language acquisition research community has long been aware of continuity between babbling and speech. Vihman and coworkers (1985) presented definitive evidence that (1) the babbling repertoire is the speech repertoire and (2) that individual children draw on their own specific babbling resources in early word productions. Previous, less comprehensive studies had suggested this might be the case (e.g., Oller, Wieman, Doyle, & Ross, 1976; Stoel-Gammon & Cooper, 1984).

Consistency in the overall repertoire of babbled consonants across languages and children is a well-documented feature of early speech acquisition, but less is known about individual differences. Locke (1983) provides evidence from a variety of sources, including diary studies, that a relatively small number of consonants, [p, b, t, d, n, k, g, h] characterize the babbling repertoire of infants across a large number of the world's languages. Vihman (1992), in a careful longitudinal study of children learning English, French, Japanese, and Swedish, found that the children's earliest stable syllables incorporated these same consonants. In that work , transcribed consonants differing only in voicing were pooled, both because reliability for voicing is low and because young children are inconsistent in their production of voicing contrasts (e.g., p/b, t/d, k/g). Practiced syllables (those occurring in at least 5% of a given vocal sample, pooling voiced and unvoiced variants) included the consonants [b, d, n, g, w, h,], overlapping with the Locke group except for [w]. These consonants occurred in practiced syllables across all the languages despite the fact that adult French lacks [h]. Inclusion of a segment omitted from the ambient language implicates endogenous processes in the child's babbling activity.

In order to determine what phonetic skills an individual child brings to the language-learning task and the usefulness of the repertoire in word learning, close examination of both prespeech babbling and early words is needed. For example, Stoel-Gammon and Cooper (1984) compared the babbling consonant repertoires of 3 children in the single month prior to onset of words with the specific consonant repertoire noted in at least two of each child's first 50 words. While over half of the consonant phones appearing in babble occurred in speech, the match was not perfect, with neither the most frequent nor the earliest phones necessarily characterizing speech. Sampling a single month of preword consonant use did not allow analysis of longitudinal vocal control for consonants, and frequency of specific consonant production in words was not analyzed.

Vocal Motor Schemes

Following Werner and Kaplan (1963), I assume that the capacities for constructing referential meanings and for expressing meaning phonetically in word forms are fully integrated, together constituting the process of symbol formation. Longitudinal measures of these interdependent capacities as they interact across the early months of language development made it possible to describe the interrelationships and mutual influences of phonetic and lexical learning in 20 children at the transition to reference (McCune & Vihman, 2001). Regression analysis demonstrated the power of phonetic skill to predict that transition. The outcome of those analyses is described in the following sections.

The success of our approach relates to the critical distinction between well-practiced and longitudinally stable vocal productions as distinct from more infrequent sporadic and possibly accidental occurrences. We (McCune & Vihman, 1987) defined vocal motor schemes (VMSs) as the longitudinally stable motor capacity to produce specific speech sounds. For purposes of gauging children's vocal aptitude at a given point in development, we focused on supraglottal consonant production in this initial study, following from Vihman's earlier work (Vihman, 1986; Vihman et al., 1986). Supraglottal consonants are those that involve relatively complete closure of the vocal tract [t/d, p/b, k/g, s/z, m, n]. The rationale for choosing this measure was twofold. First, on empirical grounds, consonant use has proven to be a reliable developmental variable. Developmental change in vocal production across the babbling period is most consistently manifest as an increase in the proportion of vocalizations including a consonant (Holmgren, Lindblom, Aurelius, Jalling, & Zetterson, 1986; Koopmans-van Beinum & van der Stelt, 1986) and in the size of the consonant repertoire (Stoel-Gammon, 1988; Stoel-Gammon & Otomo, 1986). Extent of consonant use is predictive of successful language acquisition (Menyuk, Liebergott, & Schultz, 1986; Stoel-Gammon, 1989). Second, from a motor control point of view, it seemed more likely that children would gain control of the more discrete movements of consonant production in comparison with the more continuous shaping of the oral cavity for vowel production.

We devised our approach to assessing consonant development in the following manner. Subsequent to transcription and summary of the 20 children's vocalizations over approximately 8 months of data collection (9 to 16 months, as described in Chapter 3), we took an initial exploratory approach to the data. In examining the longitudinal phonetic transcripts of Alice, the most precocious early talker in our study, we saw that from the earliest months of the study she showed high proportional as well as high raw frequency production of palatal articulations—that is, raising the tongue to the palate during articulation and producing a sound that approximated that of the palatal glide [j]. (The symbol [j] is pronounced "yod." Examples of the palatal glide [j] in words are the initial sound in *yellow* and the sound initiating the second syllable of *onion*).

In the early months of the study, this was transcribed as [j], and we considered it to be a "favorite consonant" for this child. As she developed words and her vocal strings became longer, the palatal gesture continued, but as a seeming articulatory modification rather than an attempt at rendition of the specific consonant [j]. In retrospect it could be seen that she had developed motor control of a tongue movement yielding palatal articulation rather than targeting a particular favored consonant. We reasoned that having what we initially termed a "favorite consonant" helped launch this precocious talker (Alice) on her early transition to speech. Another successful early talker (Timmy) showed early and continuing preference for [b], providing further evidence for this initial "favorite consonant" hypothesis. As we pursued this line of inquiry, considering longitudinal raw frequency and proportional occurrence of consonants across all of our 20 participants, the notion of idiosyncratic favorite consonants had to be discarded. Instead, it turned out that stable control of some subset of the range of consonants found to be prominent in babble by previous investigators characterized each of our early-speaking participants as well.

Our challenge became devising a phonetic measure that might predict onset of referential language, distinguishing early- from later-talking participants, which could be easily and successfully applied to all. We assumed that learning motor control for speech is similar in many ways to other aspects of motor control in service of a goal. The Piagetian notion of an "action scheme" can be applied to production of consonant sounds. Action schemes can then provide a motor foundation for the process of creating symbolically corresponding vocal productions and word meanings.

A sensorimotor action scheme is an underlying "plan" for accomplishing a given goal. This cannot be a prespecified motor pattern because, for even the simplest of goals, such as contacting an object with the hand, movement patterns vary somewhat from one attempt to the next. Even if a 6-month-old is seated at a table with an object placed 12 inches in front of him, successive reaches will necessarily vary at least slightly, as postural adjustments occur from one reach to the next. In dynamic systems terms this is the "degrees of freedom problem," and careful studies of the dynamics of movement are documenting both the complexity of achieving a consistent motor goal and the parameters that lead to this success. Consistency in the form of a child's reach to a given target develops with age and practice. Thelen, Corbetta, and Spencer (1996) demonstrated that children's successive reaches toward an object at 6 months of age showed random variation in trajectory, while by 8 months each child showed a somewhat consistent trajectory in repeated reaches. In Piagetian terms, we would assume that this behavioral consistency is based on a consistent and repeatedly utilized "reaching motor scheme" a movement theme with variations. Analogously, any consistently occurring identifiable phonetic pattern may be attributed to an underlying "vocal motor scheme" or VMS.

A sensorimotor scheme consists in internal neurological activity in response to a behavioral goal. In reaching for an object, the goal is obviously object contact. In vocal motor control, the initial goal may be a playful one, the repetition of the identical proprioceptive and auditory experience from action to action, and perhaps the achievement of playful variation leading to slightly different auditory and proprioceptive experience. Such experience contributes to an emergent recognition of the correspondence of auditory and motor sensations (Edelman, 1987, 1992). Speech, rather than sound production for its own sake, is the eventual outcome of children's development of a phonetic repertoire. Vocal imitation of adult speech sounds in play is a well-documented aspect of production during the babbling period. Vocal imitation in service of lexical acquisition has also been demonstrated (e.g., Bloom, 1970; Bloom, Hood, & Lightbown, 1974; McCune-Nicolich & Raph, 1978). The majority of children's productions, once they have begun to use words referentially, follow from the goal of expressing some meaningful content to a hearer. In babbling the child's immediate goal may be sensory experience and perhaps a sense of achievement that accrues to producing an anticipated sound. However, the regularities observed in babbling during the prespeech period and the early period of speech production also provide critical neurological experience that serves to prepare the system for later production of speech. Across a number of mammalian species, playful activity has been shown to co-occur with periods of rapid neurological development, suggesting that such activity prepares the motor system for critical species-specific activities that may only be evident later (Fairbanks, 2000).

Rather than emphasizing "favorite sounds," we realized that we needed to estimate each child's skill in speech sound production. Assessing children's capacity for producing particular consonants, whether or not they differed by child, became our approach to detecting more specific continuities between prespeech and speech vocalizations than had previously been demonstrated and to predicting the transition to reference. Alice's initial articulatory skill with a tongue-to-palate gesture did contribute to her shift into referential language, as described further on; but this was somewhat idiosyncratic both in terms of previous literature regarding consonant use and of our own emerging findings.

Longitudinal productivity with a specific consonant provides indirect evidence of a capacity for consistent phonetic patterning. It may be the case that the child's earliest control of the consonantal movements of speech is the open-close motion of the jaw, executed while other parts of the articulatory apparatus maintain a relatively consistent position. This thesis—initiated by MacNeilage, Studdert-Kennedy, and Lindblom (1985) and further developed by MacNeilage and Davis (1987, 1990) and summarized in MacNeilage (1998)—is termed the "frame then content" theory of speech production, where the open-close action producing the consonants is considered the frame, and the intervening vowels are considered the content. These authors suggest an evolutionary basis for this initial production strategy based on similarity to the common primate communicative "lip smack," a rapid open-close movement of the jaw, where sound is produced either by "release of the lip closure or tongue contact with the roof of the mouth" (MacNeilage &

Davis, 1990, p. 56). One could also consider the open-close action to be a fundamental aspect of a range of vocal motor schemes, where varying but consistent placement and action of articulators, particularly the tongue, yields more specific vocal motor schemes identifiable with specific consonants.

Kent (1992) observed that phonetic consistency is based in motor consistency and that a child's repeated productions allow development of consistency in phonetic pattern, while providing opportunities for neurological coordination of a given sound pattern with perception of a given acoustic signal (p. 179), an earlier application of the role of play suggested by Fairbanks (2000). The VMS concept incorporates frequency and longitudinal stability, providing a new approach to evaluation of the consonant repertoire characterizing the child's prespeech and early speech vocalizations.

Vocal Motor Scheme Consonant Repertoires and Production of Words

In order to characterize the relationship between babbling and speech with more precision than had as yet been achieved, we (McCune & Vihman, 1987, 2001) first arrived at criteria for VMSs as productive, ongoing elements of the babbling repertoire. Specifically, we defined VMS consonants as those supraglottal consonants produced with a minimum frequency of 10 occurrences per session in at least three monthly vocal samples over a four-session span (whether in babble or words). By measuring consistency in production of specific kinds of speech sounds rather than consonant skill per se, we aimed not only to sharpen our own findings but also to contribute a better index of phonetic capacity in general.

The consonant repertoires of the 20 children of the Rutgers and Stanford samples were determined by applying VMS criteria, and the transition to reference was defined as the first month in which two words had been considered referential (as described in Chapter 3). Two startling findings emerged. First, the 13 children who made the transition to reference by 16 months of age exhibited VMS-level skill with at least two supraglottal consonants, specific consonants varying by child, at the time of their transition. In fact, when mean VMS, mean volubility (total number of vocalizations produced), and mean proportion of vocalizations including a consonant were evaluated by stepwise multiple regression for their ability to predict the children's level of referential language, VMS skill was the most effective predictor. Second, considering individually each of the 9 children who made the transition to reference by 15 months, more than 80% of their words produced in both of the final 2 months of observation relied on the children's own specific VMS repertoire. (Details of this analysis of "stable words" follow in a later section.)

The most common VMS consonants, as summarized in Table 7–1 (bottom row) were [t/d] (17 children) and [p/b] (10 children). Mastery of [p/b] was limited to referential children. The five most precocious children,

Table 7-1

Age in Months at First Use of Vocal Motor Scheme (VMS) Consonants

Participant	Supraglottal Consonants Meeting VMS Criteria							Total VMS[a]	Mean Frequency of Vocalization	Age at Two VMS	Age at Referential Transition	Glottals and Glides Meeting VMS Criteria		
	t/d	p/b	k/g	s	m	n	l					h	j	w
1. Alice	14	10				14		3	122	14	14	9	9	
2. Sean	9	9	12				9	4	213	9	13	9	10	
3. Molly	12	9	9	9		11		5	298	9	14	9	–	
4. Deborah	9	9	9	11	9			5	251	9	14	9	12	
5. Timmy	11	9	11					3	249	11	14	10	–	
6. Emily	11	12			13			3	125	12	14	11	–	
7. Aurie	11	14						2	125	14	14	11	13	
8. Rala	9	15		12				3	92	12	15	9	–	
9. Rick	9	13						2	137	13	15	11	–	
10. Jase	13			13			2	118	13	16	9	12		
11. Thomas	10	9	10				3	180	10	16	9	14	14	
12. Kari	11			11			2	73	11	16	11	–		
13. Ronny	11						1	85	–	16	–	11		
14. Andrew			14				1	111	–	–	9	13		

162

15. Camille	12	12	12			3	107	12	–	9	–
16. Nenni	11					0	49	–	–	10	–
17. Jonah						1	126	–	–	10	–
18. Danny						0	40	–	–	12	–
19. Susie	11	13	13	13		3	142	13	–	12	13
20. Vido	13				13	1	95	–	–	–	–
Consonant Frequency as VMS	**17**	**10**	**7**	**5**	**4**	**1**		**18**		**9**	**1**

[a]Number of supraglottal VMS consonants by participant.

those demonstrating the largest production repertoire of referential words by 16 months, were using [p/b] at VMS level by 9 or 10 months of age. Either [t/d] or [p/b] tended to be the first consonant to reach VMS level among the 10 children who exhibited both. No child who exhibited [p/b] at VMS level failed to also produce [t/d] at that level, but order of entry was not consistent across children. Only one child lacking VMS [t/d], Andrew, produced any other consonant at VMS level: his only VMS consonant was [k/g].

The precedence of [p/b, t/d] is consistent with the Davis and MacNeilage view that initial vocal motor control entails raising and lowering of the jaw. Number of VMS consonants per child ranged from 1 to 5, but no consonants other than [p/b, t/d] reached VMS level for 50% (10) of the children ([k/g], 7; [s], 5; [m], 4; [n], 3 and [l], 1). The onset ages for these VMS consonants for individual children are summarized in Table 7–1, which, for completeness, includes glottals and glides (nonsupraglottal consonants) occurring with VMS frequency. No additional consonants met VMS frequency criteria. While the VMS consonants identified here are drawn from the roster of consonants commonly found in babbling (e.g., Locke, 1983), the criteria of frequent and continued use defining VMS exposed individual differences across children affecting their transition to language.

Vocal Motor Scheme Repertoire: A Measure of Specific Consonant Skills Related to Language

When the consonant repertoire was defined by frequency, longevity, and (by implication) stability in production, only a small number of consonants was attributed to each child. The VMS repertoire provides a well-practiced and perhaps automatically accessible substrate for production in the service of expressing meaning. The VMS measure can provide criteria for degrees of consonant production skill, allowing identification of what may be the minimum competence needed for early lexical milestones in development. Consonant-based VMS skill may also be a shorthand approach to more general speech motor control ability in the prelinguistic period.

What is the minimum skill in consonant production required for the transition to reference? By the time of this transition, 92% of successfully referential participants had demonstrated VMS-level productivity for at least two supraglottal consonants. Ronny, the only participant making the transition to reference while controlling a single supraglottal consonant, also produced [k/g] at nearly VMS level (mean frequency 10.3 from 14 to 16 months) Furthermore, Ronny's transition occurred only at 16 months, and he included only two referential nominals and no dynamic-event words among his productions by that month. He thus marginally met the referential transition criterion while marginally missing the VMS criterion. It thus appears that production skill with two routinized speech production actions (ordinarily supraglottal consonants) constitutes the minimum production skill for the referential transition. Additional nonphonetic variables also contribute. This may account for the case of Susie (Stanford sample), who did not make the referential transition by 16 months despite the availability of [t/d], [m], and [n] from 13 months.

Use of Vocal Motor Scheme during the Transition to Reference

Level of VMS skill appears as an important constituent of the transition to reference in individual children. McCune and Vihman (2001) also wished to establish the predictive strength of the VMS measure in relation to children's referential repertoire assessed at the end of the study (16 months). Analysis of mean VMS across the months of the study allowed inclusion of all participants regardless of their timing of the referential transition. This measure necessarily includes VMS in words as well as in nonwords, so it is not a predictor of the referential transition, as is the measure of VMS in relation to referential onset just described. Rather, this measure of VMS use across the study speaks to the effects on the initial development of a referential repertoire of both (1) prespeech practice and (2) continued use of consonants from babble during the early speech period.

One way to gauge this relationship is to consider the children in three groups: those who made the transition to reference by 13 to 14 months (referential early); those who did so by 15 to 16 months (referential later), and those who did not exhibit referential language by 16 months (prereferential). It can be seen in Figure 7–1 that mean VMS for the early group diverged in frequency from the later and prereferential groups beginning in the first few months of observation, but variability even in the early group was at first high (range 0 to 5 VMS). The mean early group advantage increased across the months of the study, and variability was reduced (VMS range 2 to 5 in the final 2 months). One-way analysis of variance (ANOVA) of total VMS score by child across all months indicated mean differences across the three groups [$F(2, 17) = 16.125$, $P = 0.000$]. Post hoc comparison (Tukey's HSD procedure) revealed that the mean number of VMS consonants produced was greater for children meeting referential criteria by 13 to 14 months (early, $n = 7$, 3.09 ± 0.42; mean $\pm$ SE) than for those meeting criteria at 15 or 16 months (later, $n = 6$, 1.52 ± 0.48; $P < 0.007$) or those not meeting criteria at all by that age (prereferential, $n = 7$, 0.67 ± 0.25; $P = 0.000$). The difference between the latter groups was not statistically significant ($P > 0.172$).

As Figure 7–1 indicates, the later group shows VMS growth beginning between 11 and 13 months of age, at least 2 months prior to their referential transition, and sustained increased VMS scores across succeeding months. The mean for the prereferential group shows a slight peak at 13 months, reflecting VMS onset in 6 of the 7 participants in this group between 11 and

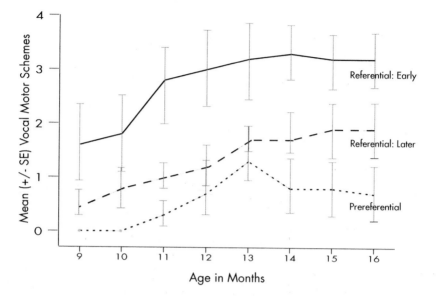

Figure 7–1. Mean number of vocal motor schemes (VMS) by month for three groups. Children who began referential word use by 14 months (Referential: Early) produced more consonants with VMS frequency (10 uses per month for three of four consecutive monthly observations) than those beginning later (Referential: Later) or those remaining prereferential at 16 months. [Adapted from McCune and Vihman (2001), Figure 1, p. 677, with permission.]

13 months (see Table 7–1). Of the 7 children, 4 in this group (participants 14 to 20 in Table 7–1) began VMS-level use of a single consonant between 11 and 13 months. Of these, 2 remained at this level throughout the study, 1 dropped back to zero at 16 months, while the other (Susie of the Stanford sample) increased to three VMS consonants at 13 months and continued these to the end of the study. Of the remaining 3 children, 1 produced three VMS consonants only at 12 and 13 months, and the other 2 produced no VMS consonants in the course of the study. In other words, although some children in the prereferential group began to use certain consonants at VMS level, this growth trend did not continue except for a single member of the group.

We again compared the groups at 16 months, when the later group had shown some VMS growth and made the transition to reference. Of the prereferential group, 4 produced no VMS-level consonants in that month. One-way analysis of variance (ANOVA) of the 16-month data, while still showing group differences [$F(2, 19) = 7.882$, $P < 0.004$], demonstrated that the early (3.14, ±0.40) and later (2.0, ±0.516) groups no longer differed by Tukey's HSD procedure ($P > 0.20$) and that the early but not the later group differed from the preferential group (0.714, ±0.42; $P < 0.003$ and < 0.161 respectively). Additional data available for the Rutgers sample allowed for follow-up analyses regarding Danny, Nenni, and Vido of the prereferential group presented in Chapters 8 and/or 9.

Predicting the Referential Repertoire

In order to determine whether the VMS measure would be an effective predictor of referential word use, we compared its influence to that of other vocal production variables known to be influential on language acquisition. Both frequency of vocalization (volubility) and proportion of vocalizations including a consonant are known predictors of subsequent lexical development (Vihman & Greenlee, 1987; Stoel-Gammon, 1992, 1998). The VMS measure differs from these in incorporating both frequency and a longitudinal dimension, which indexes stability of infant phonetic production for specific consonants. As noted above, the VMS measure incorporates both nonword and continued lexical use of specific consonants.

We analyzed three quantitative production measures: VMS, volubility, and proportion of vocalizations including a consonant. These were averaged across sessions as predictors of the total number of different referential word types produced by 16 months of age. Simple regression analysis revealed that each of these independent variables was a significant predictor of total referential word types produced by 16 months. Stepwise regression demonstrated that VMS alone was the strongest single predictor, however, accounting for 43% of the variance ($t = 6.7$, df = 19, $P < 0.001$). In fact, the partial regression coefficient for VMS was the only one significantly different from zero, implying that neither of the other measures had predictive value when VMS was partialed out. In other words, VMS alone was the best vocal predictor of referential ability at 16 months.

In the McCune and Vihman (2001) study summarized here, the transition to reference signaled onset of a sharp increase in number of different words produced in a session by the most precocious talkers. Each child making the transition at 13 to 14 months approximately doubled the number of different words produced in a session over the next 2 months [means: 15.3 ± 4.9 at 14 months versus 30.3 ± 9.3 at 16 months; $t(6) = -5.63$; $P < 0.002$, two-tailed: Figure 7–2]. The referential transition involves new linguistic production skill and enhanced motivation to communicate with language. This motivation, in turn, leads to more frequent word production with the potential for investigators to identify larger numbers of words, suggesting a "vocabulary spurt." We know from Chapter 6 that the participants of the Rutgers sample for whom representational play data were available had demonstrated mental representation in their pretend play, showing meanings related to common objects and activities by the time of the referential transition. McCune and Vihman proposed that with the transition to reference, consciousness of phonetic material and of meanings begin to arise together for the child with both mental representation and vocal production ability, facilitating the learning and production of words.

Figure 7–2. Mean number of word types produced by month for three groups. Children who began referential word use by 14 months (Early) showed a sharp increase in word use at the transition that continued across the final two months of the study, in contrast with the "later" and "Pr-Referential" children, whose word frequency remained low during the same age range. [Adapted from McCune and Vihman (2001), Figure 2, p. 678, with permission.]

Consonant Basis of Stable Words

For this hypothesis to have merit, the children must be shown to use the VMS repertoire in the words they produce. We reasoned that phonetic skill and mental representation in conjunction with referential ability should allow production of stable word forms that continue to be used over time, thus both facilitating an increase in lexical production and leading to observation of the same words across multiple sessions. We therefore chose to analyze in detail *all words* produced in both of two sessions (termed "stable words") once the referential transition had been made. Only those children who had attained referential production by 15 months of age could contribute 2 months of postreferential transition data. (Jase, although credited with the transition at 15 months, produced too few word tokens for this analysis, so data from nine participants were analyzed.) In fact, only those children who had attained referential ability by 15 months made repeated use of a number of the same words at both 15 and 16 months (4 to 11 types per child, 61 in total, as shown in Table 7–2). In contrast, in the early months, when none of the children had made the referential transition, few words recurred across sessions for any participant. All VMS consonants had been established

Table 7–2
Stable Words Observed at 15 and 16 Months for the Nine Most Advanced Participants

Child	Total Types[a]	Total Tokens, 15 & 16 Months[b]	Words[c]
1. Alice	11	57, 47	baby,* bang,* bottle,* bunny,* bye,* clean,* daddy,* elephant,* *hat*, mommy, tea*
2. Sean	7	31, 49	block,* book,* bug,* butterfly, horse, moo, *oh*
3. Molly	8	100, 58	baby,* book,* down,* grandma,* nose,* stuck,* *vroom*,* *woof*
4. Deborah	8	27, 49	baby,* ball,* bye,* down,* *hi*, kitty, three,* up
5. Timmy	5	36, 28	ball/balloon,* car,* *eyes*, light, Ruth*
6. Emily	6	32, 18	beads,* box,* open,* more,* tickle, *up*
7. Aurie	6	24, 30	apple,* hello, *hi*, stuck,* *up/out/ open*, uhoh
8. Rala	4	28, 26	baby,* ball,* spoon,* *uhoh*
9. Rick	6	16, 27	ball,* doggie,* *eye*, *hi*, no, open*

[a]Number of stable words types produced at both 15 and 16 months, regardless of status as context-limited or referential, imitations included.
[b]Number of occurrences of stable words in each of two sessions: 15 months and 16 months. Frequency of production across types (number of tokens) is shown.
[c]All occurrences of words marked with an asterisk included a VMS consonant established for that child. All occurrences of words printed in italics included a glottal consonant (h or glottal stop). Across children, 89% of word tokens included either a VMS consonant for that child, a glottal consonant, or both.

by 14 months, prior to the sessions analyzed for stable words, so no word productions analyzed contributed to establishment of measured VMS. To determine the role of specific elements of phonetic patterning, we analyzed (individually for each of the nine children) all of the word types (referential, context-limited, and imitated) produced at both 15 and 16 months for the consistent presence of any consonants in all occurrences (tokens). Total stable words for each child where all tokens included a consonant meeting VMS criteria for that child ("VMS words") was compared across children with total stable words including only non-VMS consonants (again determined by child repertoire). Children based virtually all stable words consistently including a consonant on their own specific VMS consonants (Table 7–3; on average, 92% versus 8% for other consonants (Figure 7–3, inset).

Table 7–3
Number of Stable Word Types Based on VMS and Other Consonants for the Nine Most Advanced Participants

	Total Word Types	t/d	p/b	k/g	s	m	n	j	h/?	Variable
1. Alice	11	**2**	**5**			1	1	1[c]	1	
2. Sean	7		**3**	**1**[a]	**1**[b]	1			1	1
3. Molly	8	**1**	**2**	**1**[a]		**2**[b]	1			1
4. Deborah	8	**1**	**3**		1				2	1
5. Timmy	5		**2**[b]	1					1	1
6. Emily	6		**3**[b]			1			1	1
7. Aurie	6	**1**	1						3	1
8. Rala	4		**3**						1	
9. Rick	6	**1**	**2**[b]				1		2	
Total of 9 participants Including consonant in: VMS		9	9	4	1	3	1	6	9	
Stable words		5	9	3	2	4	4	1	8	7

Note: Each column lists the number of stable word types for which all of a child's tokens included a particular consonant. For Sean, more than one consonant was included in some word types. Bold face indicate that the consonant is a VMS for that child. By definition, j, h, and ? are not VMS even if they reach frequency criteria. Variable indicates that no consistent consonant was included in all tokens of a word. Consonants occur in initial position unless otherwise noted. The last two rows indicate how many of the nine most advanced participants produced this consonant with VMS frequency and how many used it as a basis for stable words.

[a]Consonant occurs only in final position.
[b]Consonant sometimes occurs in final or medial position.
[c]Consonant consistently occurs in medial position.

Considering all consonants used by any child as a basis for one or more stable words, the bilabial stop [p/b] clearly dominated production, although all of these children also had access to VMS [t/d] (see Table 7–3 and Figure 7–3, large graph) The glottal consonant [h], involving no supraglottal gesture, also formed the basis for a number of stable words. In addition to the dominance of [p/b], it is of interest that the other consonant-based words for each child incorporated that child's own previously specified VMS repertoire (e.g., the children who exhibited VMS for [k\g] were the children who incorporated these segments in stable words). Only a relatively small proportion of stable words (those termed "variable" in Table 7–3: less than 10%) lacked either a consistent consonant, or glottal stop, across all productions. These findings reveal the developmental significance of VMS skill in general, and of bilabial production in particular from early in the babbling period through the development of stable word forms at the transition to reference.

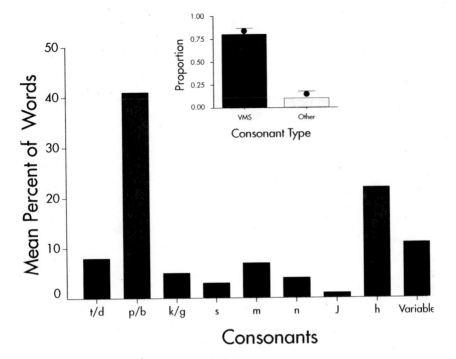

Figure 7–3 Mean Percent of stable word types with VMS versus other consonants (inset) and with each consonant for nine children. The nine children who produced the same words at both the 15 = and 16 = month sessions (Stable Words) based these words almost exclusively on consonants with VMS frequency (10 uses per month for three of four consecutive monthly observations: inset) and showed especially high use of [p/b], although all had produced [t/d] at VMS level. [Adapted with permission from McCune and Vihman (2001), Figure 3, p. 679, with permission.]

Relation of Vocal Motor Scheme to Referential Word Development

Why should a phonetic variable such as VMS contribute to a qualitative language transition? This question is at the heart of the child's process of constructing a language. If the meanings of language and its forms are co-constructed by the child, he or she must have resources available that can be shaped to the meanings and forms of the ambient language. I take VMS to be a shorthand measure for the broader range of production skills available to successful early talkers. Management of breathing in relation to speech is one critical variable, and laryngeal activity underlies all speech production. In addition to supraglottal consonant control, 12 of 13 referential children also showed VMS level control of [h]. (Ronny, marginally credited with the transition lacked [h].) Here laryngeal control is more directly implicated, as this segment involves maintaining the vocal chords slightly apart but still vibrating (Ladefoged, 1975, p. 123). Considering the stable word production data summarized in Table 7–3, 6 of the 9 children making the referential transition by 15 months, and thus offering 2 months of postreferential data for the stable-word analysis, based all stable words including a consistent consonant in all tokens on VMS consonants or [h].

Only 3 of the 9 children used one or two non-VMS consonants in stable words (bilabial [m] in two cases). Alice produced *mommy*, as she had for several previous months, and Sean produced *moo* (with [m] in first position) and *horse* with non-VMS [s] in final position, and Rick produced *no* with non-VMS [n]. Rick and Sean began producing these words in the final 2 months of the study, seeming to extend their phonetic repertoire on the basis of new lexical interests, while Alice's production of *mommy* over many months demonstrates a highly significant form, produced with bilabial articulation (similarly to [p/b]), which stretches her VMS repertoire only slightly under motivation to produce a very salient word. (We will consider the special aspects of bilabials shortly.) These exceptions demonstrate the interaction of meaning and form. While children base many early meanings on well-practiced forms, the challenge of expressing new or highly salient meanings is a motivator for stretching the repertoire.

DePaolis, Keren-Portnoy, and Vihman (2005), in a study of 12 English-learning children in the United Kingdom, have replicated the McCune and Vihman findings regarding relationships between VMS development and the productive referential lexicon. In their study, children were followed longitudinally beginning prior to VMS use, then the number of VMSs at first words and at the referential transition were examined. They report:

> Eleven of the twelve children had two VMS by the time they produced their first words (mean age, first context-limited word: 14 mos.). All children had two VMS before producing a first referential word (mean age: 15 mos.). This suggests that VMS are more critical for learning referential words than for learning context-limited words.

For individual children in this study, only 10% to 15% of words produced were based on non-VMS consonants.

Prominent Features of the Early Stable Lexicon: Bilabial and Glottal Productions

Considering all of the stable words produced by participants in the studies by McCune and Vihman during the early period of referential language production, two phonetic characteristics are most prominent: the extensive role of the bilabial [p/b] (40% of productions based consistently on a given consonant) and the extent of [h] use (20% of productions where [h] was the only closure). We will first consider the significance of the bilabial finding.

A special role for labials in the transition to language is a previously noted but as yet unexplained phenomenon. This was the first study to link bilabial production and language transitions in precocious children. Consistently higher use of labials in early words than in contemporaneous babble was previously observed in children learning each of four languages, although the languages differ in the proportion of labial consonants used in words addressed to children (Boysson-Bardies & Vihman, 1991; cf. also Locke, 1983; Vihman et al., 1985). Stoel-Gammon and Cooper (1984) found that all three children studied produced words with initial labials within their first 10 words, and words incorporating labials in their production (e.g., [m], [b]) were fairly stable throughout the study. Stoel-Gammon (1998), in analyzing order of development of target words in English on the McCarthur-Bates Communicative Development Inventory (CDI) (Fenson et al., 1994), found that 22% of words acquired between 9 and 11 months included bilabials in the adult form. Both later talkers and children recovering from tracheostomy showed a very marked bilabial bias in their early words (Bleile, Stark, & McGowan, 1993; Rescorla & Bernstein-Ratner, 1996; Thal, Oroz, & McCaw, 1995), although they began producing speech many months later than the children studied here. Roberts (1998) found that children credited with achieving a vocabulary spurt produced a greater proportion of bilabials than comparison children who had not shown a spurt, although words and nonwords were pooled in her analyses.

Both "mechanical" (motoric) factors and visual and proprioceptive cues differentiate bilabials from other consonants. Production of labial-onset syllables is motorically simple, requiring the mandibular oscillation that underlies any CV production but no shift in tongue placement for vowel production [that is, labial consonant-plus-vowel sequences constitute default syllables or "pure frames" (Davis & MacNeilage, 1995)]. In addition, the means of production is visually apparent to the infant—a highly salient source of information, given the child's early attraction to faces (Fantz, 1961) and the evidence of audiovisual matching of speech sounds to mouth movements (Kuhl & Meltzoff, 1982; Patterson & Werker, 1999) well before the onset of supraglottal consonant production.

Enhanced neurological feedback may also be an influence. Language production requires continual afferent feedback that, for most consonants, depends on the complex integration of information from the responses of muscle spindles and Golgi tendon organs, absent in the lips (Barlowe & Farley, 1989). In contrast, for bilabial consonants, afferent feedback is transmitted to the sensory cortical representation directly from cutaneous contact of the lips and spread over the entire lip area (Evarts, 1982). Thus the visual salience of bilabial productions may cue the child to attempt targeted production of sound patterns (words) that include these consonants, while the motoric simplicity and cutaneous advantage increases their likelihood of successful production.

Simultaneously maintaining internal consciousness of referential sound/ meaning correspondence while phonetic production is engaged would seem to create a neurological burden that might be eased by use of the highly accessible default bilabial gesture. For this reason the reliance on VMS consonants should not be surprising, and the ease of production for bilabials provides an obvious advantage. A well-practiced phonetic repertoire was expected to have a direct effect on the transition to reference, because as the child experiences the intention to communicate and the internal meaningful experience might find expression only through fairly routinized motor activity. The child's internal idea (or meaning) is essentially clothed with sounds and words in the process of its formation. In other words, having basic motoric potential at the ready when the communicative intention is experienced is an essential feature of communicative speech. Consider the experience of speaking to a colleague and suddenly finding that the desired word simply does not emerge from your mouth. The surprise and discomfort we experience in this situation speaks to the automaticity we expect from our speech productions. While early childhood speech may sometimes be more labored, there is nevertheless an essential automaticity requirement between sound and meaning.

Concerning production of [h], recall from Table 6–2 that the five most precocious early talkers demonstrated VMS level [h] beginning at 9 or 10 months of age, and 13 of the remaining 15 children did so by 12 months of age. Furthermore, Vihman (1992) found [h] in frequently used prespeech syllables for infants across four languages, including French, which lacks [h] in the adult language. Netsell (1981) suggested that "certain laryngeal muscles act as "an articulator" (p. 130) and noted the importance of the abduction/adduction of the vocal folds as a critical component in syllable repetition and the rhythmic aspects of speech. Ladefoged (1975) described the position of the vocal folds for certain productions of [h] (termed "voiced" or "murmured") as pulled apart, a position in which air escapes very rapidly but with the vocal folds still vibrating "as if they were waving in the breeze" (p. 123). Apparent [h] in the transcripts may demonstrate the child's development of control of vibrating abduction/adduction of these muscles. Thus it contributes to the sensorimotor foundation of vocal capability as well as to the use of this sound in words. The infrequent and later occurrence of [h] in the preword repertoire of later-talking children in the McCune and Vihman (2001) study suggests its omission is an indicator of limited laryngeal control. Laryngeal control is essential to all speech. Availability of [h] in the repertoire of the early talkers should naturally prompt its inclusion in the word production repertoire. A child who uses glottal stop or [h] as a foundation for words need control only laryngeal action rather than integrating such action with jaw movement and possible tongue deformation in the service of more complex articulations.

Consider again the adult experience of searching for a word. This search may not be silent, as the speaker fills in with sounds such as [eh] or [m] (Goffman, 1978). In adults these glottal utterances may represent the laryngeal activation required for all speech or may be pragmatic or phonetic devices to keep the conversational rhythm. Ward (2001, 2004) terms these vocal expressions "conversational grunts." He reports their broad use in English and other languages, with some correspondence between phonetic aspects of such expressions and their meaning in context. McCune and Vihman (1997) found that the mean proportion of stable word tokens including a glottal (glottal stop or [h]) increased from .33 (SD = 0.27) at 15 months to 0.53 (SD = 0.28) at 16 months (Z = –2.19, P < 0.03, Wilcoxon, signed rank sum test, two-tailed) in the nine most advanced children described here. Similar unexplained increases in glottal production early in the second year have previously been reported (Roug, Landberg, & Lundberg, 1989; Robb & Bauer, 1991) and in word production in the first period of lexical expansion (Vihman & Miller, 1988). To some extent reliance on glottals follows from the particular words produced by the children. The words *eye, hi, oh,* and *uhoh* rely on glottal action, including no supraglottal consonants in the adult model. However, the words *apple, elephant, hat, hello, open, out, up,* and even *light* were typically produced by the children with glottals or glides, with or without a supraglottal consonant. The fact that words coexist in the child's repertoire with potentially high frequency communicative grunts, as described in Chapter 8, is another reason for anticipating glottal articulation in words during this period.

"Representation" and Word Production in the Early Referential Period

In the early part of this chapter I emphasized the development of motor control of the articulatory apparatus as a critical factor in children's ability to produce language. Assessment of the number of vocal motor scheme consonants in the children's repertoire was taken as an index of such motor control. This is not to say that children acquire their language primarily by learning to pronounce consonants and vowels, then concatenating consonant and vowel segments. Rather, the child's goal is to express internal meanings by means of interpretable sound patterns for communication. To accomplish this goal, the child must shape integrated internal patterns of sound production and meaning, according to Werner and Kaplan (1963), through a process of dynamic schematizing. With multiple experiences a given meaning and phonetic pattern will arise together.

According to dynamic systems theory, each experience of hearing and/or producing a given phonetic sequence while experiencing a particular internal meaningful state of consciousness contributes to this process. The phonetic pattern thereby comes to represent the internal meaning state as symbol to symbolized. The phonetic pattern and meaning state may then arise for the child in circumstances similar to those in the past that gave rise to such sound/meaning correspondences, even if the exact circumstances have not been encountered before. (This innovation marks the transition to reference, and is described by Werner and Kaplan as arising from internal schematizing rather than a response to external context.)

Such internal schematizing might yield a temporary consistency across a child's productions of the various words in the repertoire at this time of transition because (1) the words produced draw on the same underlying and somewhat limited phonetic resources and (2) the functional task of word production entails similarity in motor activation. Specific patterns of word production by individual children would provide evidence for such a process. If children's words in the early referential period differ in form from adult productions, show similarity within repertoire, *and differ* across children, individual construction processes would be implicated.

This constructive process, both in development and individual word production, has implications for the nature of "internal phonological representations" of word forms, a subject of debate within child phonology where the cognitive metaphor of mind remains prominent (e.g., Ingram, 1974; Jaeger, 1997; Menn, 1978; Stemberger, 1992; Vihman et al., 1994). How can one accommodate child patterns differing greatly from adult phonetic shapes and maintain a meaning for phonological representation? Menn (1978) proposed two internal representations for each word, one for recognition, the other for production, while others (e.g., Stemberger, 1992) assumed that the child's internal representation correctly reflects the adult form and that production errors based on child production limitations account for deviations from the adult form in the child's word. The most common approach to characterizing deviations from adult form in children with speech difficulties is to impute "phonological processes" to the child. Such processes are assumed to be internal rules that derive an erroneous child form from a correct internal representation of the adult word. While this seems a plausible approach with older children, it is less so for the initial period of language acquisition where evidence of phonetic and phonological knowledge or their representations on the part of the child is lacking. In discussing children's reactions of comprehension to adult forms of words (e.g., *doggie*) while their own productions were onomatopoetic, Werner and Kaplan suggest that the child's underlying meaning/sound schematization could provide a unifying link.

The dual definition of the term *representation* characterizing recent psychological research and theory as well summarized by Haith (1998) and discussed in Chapter 4 provides a further clue. Consciousness of mentally represented meaning in real time (definition 1) yields access to a neurologically "represented" (definition 2) potential for the motor activities of phonetic production. While these potentials for action are based on underlying neurological history, that history need not exist in identifiable "representations" specific to particular words or sounds.

Children's Individual Production Patterns

As early as 1971, Waterson reported that many investigators were beginning to notice the rather extreme differences between child and adult productions of the same word, along with consistencies in phonetic pattern across the child's word productions. This sort of pattern is termed a "word production template." And as recently as 1997, Jaeger, in presenting the nonsegmental analysis of several critical steps in her daughter's phonological development, noted the importance of documenting such "rare" phenomena as the several production templates that her child, Alice, used.

There is increasing recognition that adopting one or more word production templates may be a typical step in the acquisition of language for most children (e.g., Velleman & Vihman, 2002). Vihman and Kunnari (2006) examined word shapes produced by 33 children representing six language groups (English/United Kingdom, English/United States, Finnish, French, Italian, Welsh), seeking to characterize word templates in a consistent way cross-linguistically. The patterns found showed both individual variation and consistent cross-language variation. For these children, who produced 25 to 50 words per session, those producing the most words in the session showed strongest evidence of template use: with later development, these individual patterns are expected to fade. Vihman and Croft (2007) propose that template organization, rather than universally learned segments, forms the transitional basis for children's initiation into the phonology of their language.

The broad range of template types found in the literature on early child words was previewed more than 30 years ago with the classic case studies of Menn (1971) and Waterson (1971). Whereas Menn's son showed strong consonant harmony constraints (repetition of the same consonant across syllables where the adult form calls for a consonant change), Waterson's son "P" made use of a variety of different "structures," each clustering around a particular articulatory feature or segment type. These included (1) <CV> or harmonizing <CVCV> structures in which the consonants are (a) stops (*biscuit, bucket, pudding, kitty, dirty*), (b) labial fricatives or glides (e.g., [wœ] for *fly,* [vœ} or {vœwœ} for *flower*), or (c) the palatal nasal ([ˆ}: *finger, window, another*); (2) <VhV> (*honey, hymn* or *angel*); and (3) <VC> for words ending in a sibilant (*fish, fetch, vest, brush, dish*). Vihman (1981) reports a similar range of unrelated patterns, characterized by a good deal of homonymy, in her son's early words.

Other studies have also revealed consonant harmony to be the basis for many children's early word patterns (Sean: Donahue, 1986; Caitlin: Donahue, 1993; Laura: Lleó, 1990; J: Macken, 1978; Daniel: Stoel-Gammon & Cooper, 1984; Virve: Vihman, 1976). However, some children show strong sequential patterns instead. For example, Macken (1979) reported an initial labial/medial coronal <CVCV> pattern (e.g., [pwœta] for Spanish *sopa,* "soup"), while Priestly (1978) identified a <CVjVC> pattern (e.g., [bajak] for *basket* and *blanket,* [tajak] for *tiger* and *turkey,* etc.). Donahue (1993) describes the phonetic and lexical development of Caitlin, who produced only context-limited words from 9 to 17 months, relying predominantly on glottal and nasal consonants and tuneful productions. Beginning at 17 months, she exhibited a routinized production pattern involving reduplicated bilabial production, and frequent disyllables, and she began to acquire new words with the single exposure strategy termed "fast-mapping."

I consider the application of a template as the vocal motor aspect of the larger underlying mental process of producing a meaningful word. A word production template automatically accessed in response to the intention to produce a word might function similarly to the default bilabial gesture of babbling and early words during the period of lexical expansion. Unlike a single VMS gesture, the production template yields differentiated forms in relation to different word meanings, showing the influence of the adult form of each word. The final motor plan for a given production would be instantiated simultaneously with the intention to express a particular meaning. Similar constraints would not apply to babbling, which globally reflects phonetically salient aspects of the adult speech to which the child is exposed (Vihman, 1996), without relation to meaning.

Template Use:
Summary of McCune and Vihman's Empirical Findings

While the earliest words may be closely matched to adult models, and do rely on children's babbling patterns (Vihman 1996, p. 141), along with the onset of referential language and sharp increases in word production, McCune and Vihamn (1997) found evidence of such individual word production strategies, or templates. When Alice first began to use words, each word type tended to have a distinct form of production. Later, following development of a template, production similarities were evident across different word types. This can be seen in Table 7–4 (McCune & Vihman, 1997).

Vihman and I (McCune & Vihman, 2000) wanted to determine the quantitative effect of an available template on children's word production. We examined the extent to which the more complex, somewhat stereotyped production routines or templates reported for some children characterized our participants' repertoires. We analyzed all word productions of the 15- and the 16-month sessions (limited to nine children who made the referential transition by 15 months as in the previous analysis of VMS use in stable words) for evidence of a consistent pattern or word template. Evidence of a template involves consistency in phonetic and/or phonotactic (sound combination) patterning across word tokens. The following criteria were applied: (1) the child forms are phonetically similar to one another, (2) words are selected from the adult model for production based on their accessibility to the template, and (3) words not fitting the template are "adapted" to suit the child's production pattern. Our analysis revealed word production patterns or templates for only the five most productive early talkers, accounting for more than 50% of tokens by 16 months (mean 73%). These were the same five children who began VMS [p/b] by 9 or 10 months of age and those with the largest total of referential word types produced in the course of the study (Chapter 3).

Table 7–4
Phonetic Relationships among Words for Alice[a]

9–10 Months		14 Months		
Adult Target	Child Form	Adult Target	Child Form	Template Schema
baby	[pɛpɛ:]	*baby*	[bebi]	\<CVCi\>
daddy	[dæ]	*bottle*	*[baḷi]	
hi	[ha:i]	*daddy*	[tæḷi]	
mommy	*[m:an:ə]	*hiya*	*[ha:ji]	
no	[njæ]	*lady*	[jɛiji]	
		mommy	[maɲi]	

[a]Alice's first spontaneous words, recorded at 9 to 10 months and listed here in full, show little similarity in phonetic form (although the adult target words show evidence of selectivity: note that three of the five are disyllables including a single repeated stop or nasal and ending in the vowel /i/). In contrast, 15 of the 19 words (0.79%) that she produced at 14 months, a sample of which are listed here, exhibit a phonetic form consistent with the template schema given above, where C = consonant and V = vowel. Child forms that distort the adult target toward the template schema are marked with an asterisk. In Alice's case the word shapes targetted at 9 to 10 months foreshadow the template schema that emerges in word-form production only at 14 months.

See Appendix A (from McCune & Vihman, 2000) for the form of each child's template and illustrative tokens of each child's stable word types.

We hypothesized that if construction of a lexicon is a dynamic schematizing process involving mutual regulation between sound and meaning, the children's stable words, produced over two sessions, were more likely to share the phonetic characteristics of a production template than were words produced in only a single session. Paired sample Student's t-tests revealed that proportionally more stable words than other words exhibited the influence of a template at both 15 months (0.79 ± 0.16 versus 0.60 ± 0.23, t (4) = 4.21, $P < 0.005$, one-tailed) and 16 months (0.78 ± 0.14 versus 0.58 ± t (4) = 2.43; $P < 0.035$, one-tailed: Figure 7–4). In fact, there were strong template influences apparent in words produced in only one or the other of the two sessions as well.

Previous longitudinal analyses have revealed the early phonetic sources of the patterns identified for Molly (Vihman & Velleman, 1989), Timmy, and Alice (Vihman, et al., 1994). Molly arrived at her full-fledged pattern after beginning with attention to final consonants in her early words. She then showed similar patterns of reorganization involving both final obstruents and nasals between 12 and 15 months. Vihman and Velleman (1989) documented this process, which culminated in the abstract structure shown in Appendix 7A, with continued targeting of final consonants in adult words, usually produced with a reduced final vowel or [i].

Timmy began word production early with a bias toward [b] yielding many homophones (homonyms) of the form \<ba\>. At 13 and 14 months

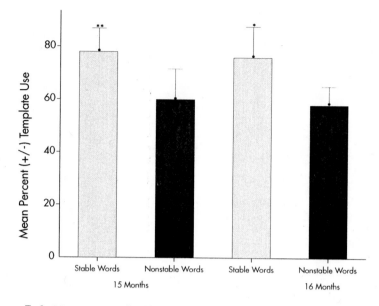

Figure 7–4. Mean Percent of stable word types based on templates at 15 and 16 months for the five children showing templates. The five participants meeting criteria for template use (see text) showed high proportional frequency of template effects across both months. Word types occurring in both sessions (stable words) were significantly more likely than those occurring in one session to show template effects.

he expanded his repertoire to include <ka> and <ja>words, respectively, with additional consonant expansion and variation at 15 months. It was only at 16 months that the complex pattern shown in the Appendix fell into place, with its various options. Timmy produced just one and then two specific consonants in initial position paired with the same vowel across early word forms, which tended to consist of a single CV syllable or reduplicated CVCV, sometimes preceded by schwa.

Alice's template may be described as a "palatal pattern," involving the articulatory gesture of raising the front of the tongue toward the hard palate. Examples of its influence are the forms [bŪ^i] (with a palatal [^] in place of the target word's alveolar /n/) for *bunny* and [ti:ni] (with its final [i] in place of the single closed syllable of the target) for *clean* (both at 16 months). In disyllables her template incorporates a high-front (palatal) vowel at the end of the word, optionally preceded by a palatalized supraglottal consonant or the front glide [j], preceded by another use of the vowel [i] or an [ê] off-glide from the nuclear vowel of the first (stressed) syllable. For monosyllables, the pattern involves only production of the vowel or off-glide [i]/ [ê] ([pāi] for *bang:* 16 months). In both cases the palatal pattern as a whole may be seen as the product of a palatal (or raising) gesture of the front of the tongue. This pattern originated in unusually strong (VMS-like) use of the glide [j] as early as 8 to 10 months, followed by a gradual integration of this palatal gesture into the more complex phonetic structures described above and illustrated in Appendix 7A.

Deborah shows the effects of an established but maximally simple template (<VCV> or <CV(CV)>, with harmony across the two consonants). Sean was only beginning to develop a template (based on monosyllables and final consonant use) by the 16-month session.

Conclusion

Both VMS development and template-based organization of the early lexicon exemplify the mutual regulation between sound and meaning hypothesized by Werner and Kaplan (1963). Once a greater capacity for mental representation has developed, this capacity prompts integrative application of phonetic capacities to potential word meanings experienced in the environment. Both VMS phonetic gestures and the phonological patterns reflected in the adult words that the child attempts contribute to this process, yielding the consistency of production recognized as a template. The template can be thought of as an underlying motoric potential that comes into play as the child produces a word. These productions arise in the interactions among child-intended meaning, vocal pattern history, and partially known adult forms, yielding a growing repertoire of phonetically related forms capable of expressing a growing array of meanings. The repertoire reflects ease of production for the individual child, resulting in the observed increase in production frequency. Mental representation capacity further renders this repertoire of words accessible to production across situations that share meaning in a way that the child can recognize. Thus the shift to reference, improvement of phonetic capacity, and increase in frequency of word production are interrelated phenomena.

Acknowledgments

Data presented in this chapter are all derived from collaboration with Marilyn Vihman in both our published and unpublished papers. Phonetic analyses, although often jointly planned, relied on her expertise. The final section of the chapter, regarding templates, is derived from a prepublication version of McCune and Vihman (2001).

Appendix 7A: Phonetic forms and Template Schemata for the Five Most Precocious Talkers

All stable word types produced are included. For each child the template schema is noted at the head of the listing of child phonetic forms fitting the template. In each case, a single typical word form (token) is provided as an exemplar of the child's somewhat varied phonetic productions. The total number of word tokens exhibiting the template is noted in the next column, over the total occurrences of each word type in the 16-month session (e.g., 5/7 means 5 tokens fitting the template out of 7 tokens produced for a particular word type). In the last column we provide an illustrative token of each type for which fewer than half the tokens fit the template. The schemata include the following symbols and conventions: C = consonant, V= vowel; parentheses bracket optional elements. Asterisks mark word forms that have been adapted or "distorted" to fit the template.

Child	Adult Word and Phonemic Transcription	Child Template and Examples of Forms Fitting Template	Tokens fitting Template/ Total Tokens	Child Word Types Not Fitting Template
1. Alice		**CV(C)i**		
	baby /ˈbeɪbi/	[beɪbi]	7/7	
	bang /bæij/	*[pãi]	1/1	
	bottle /ˈbaɾəl/	*[baji/ˈbadiç]	14/14	
	bunny /ˈbʌni/	*[bʌɲi]	3/3	
	bye /baɪ/	*[baɪ]	1/1	
	clean /klin/	*[tiːni]	1/2	
	daddy /ˈdædi/	[dadi]	2/2	
	elephant /ˈeləfənt/	*[æɪji]	2/4	
	hat /hæt/		0/2	[ʔa]
	mommy /ˈmami/	*[maːɲi]	9/10	
	tea /ti/	[tiː]	1/1	
2. Sean		**(C)VC**		
	block /blak/	[pak]	13/16	
	book /bʊk/	[bɪk]	3/4	
	bug /bʌg/	[ᵐbʌkl]	1/2	
	butterfly /ˈbʌɾəflaɪ/		0/3	[bʌjʌi]
	horse /hɔɹs/	[ʔʊʃ]	12/12	

(continued)

Appendix 7A (*continued*)

Child	Adult Word and Phonemic Transcription	Child Template and Examples of Forms Fitting Template	Tokens fitting Template/ Total Tokens	Child Word Types Not Fitting Template
	moo /mu:/		0/6	[mɔ]
	oh /oʊ/		0/6	[ʔɔː]
3. Molly		**CVC (i/ə)**		
	baby /ˈbeɪbi/	[pebi]	2/2	
	book / bʊk /	[pʊk]	7/7	
	down /daʊn/	*[taŋ:ə]	10/10	
	gran'ma/ˈgrænma/	*[ˈmeʊwə]	1/1	
	nose /noʊz/		0/1	[noː]
	stuck /stʌk/	*[kak]	2/2	
4. Deborah		**CV((C₁)i)**		
	baby /ˈbeibi/	[pebi], *[pe]	7/7	
	ball /bɔl/	*[pɔ]	7/7	
	bye /baɪ/	[paɪ]	1/1	
	down /daʊn/	*[ta]	4/4	
	hi /haɪ/	[haɪ]	15/15	
	kitty /ˈkiɾi/	[tletli], *[tli]	3/4	
	three /θri/	[si]	8/8	
	up /ʔʌp/	*[ʔa]	3/3	
5. Timmy		**(V((C))Vi(CV)**		
	balloon /bəˈlu:n/	*[bʌi]	3/5	
	car /kaɹ/	*[kʰəi]	2/2	
	eye /ʔaɪ/	[ʔæɪ]	3/5	
	light /laɪt/	[eɪzæ]	12/12	
	Ruth /ɹu:θ/	[æβwæi]	1/4	

8

Prelinguistic Communication: Grunts as a Gateway to Language

> *The earliest clear-cut expressions of reference to objects are, on the one hand, the characteristic bodily gesture of pointing and, on the other, vocal utterances such as "da" or "ta."* . . . *The first sounds uttered in the context of object-directedness are manifested as ingredients of the straining movements of the child toward objects in the environment which are beyond his immediate reach. Such sounds may be designated as "call-sounds."*
>
> —Werner and Kaplan (1963, pp. 77 and 81)

Children's earliest intentional communication often occurs in the gestural modality. This, along with the fact that the vocal apparatus of other living species of primates does not support speech, has led some to believe that the evolutionary origin of language may have been through gesture. The later shift to vocal communication is thought to have taken place as evolutionary neurological and anatomical changes suited our earliest protohuman ancestors for speech. In this view, the new vocal modality was then integrated with extant gestural communication. It is certainly also possible that simple vocal and gestural communication arose together in evolution, only later including the complex systemic quality that we identify with language. In development, gesture and speech first occur separately and synchronization of gesture with speech begins between the onset of single-word speech and the first sentences (Goldin-Meadow, 1998).

Languages comprise both signed and spoken forms. Signed languages are recognized as complete grammatical modes of communication characterizing the cultures of their use. Children show equipotentiality for learning signed or spoken languages, with outcome depending upon the form of language directed to them by parents and caregivers (Abrahamsen, 2000; Werner & Kaplan, 1963). Children deprived of language input (e.g., some deaf children of hearing parents) have been shown to invent their own gestural communicative modes. Children delayed in vocal communication have responded to enhanced gestural communication with more rapid development of both gesture and vocal language (Abrahamsen, 2000). In this chapter we consider prelinguistic communicative behavior in a subset of the Rutgers sample, the earliest and the latest talkers. These children experienced only spoken English models from their parents. Results might be different for children experiencing both signed and spoken language or those receiving enhanced gestural communication.

A particular form of prelinguistic vocal communication may be of critical importance both in development and evolution. *Communicative grunts,* simply formed vocal signals, perhaps analogous to gestures were not identified as highly relevant to children's language acquisition until the 1990s (McCune, 1992; McCune, Vihman, Roug-Hellichius, Delery, & Gogate, 1996). The developmental timing of grunt use, along with the autonomic functions associated with laryngeal activation, indicate that this simple vocalization may provide a critical link for children between their internal sense of personal meaning and the words of the ambient language. In this chapter I will describe the developmental course of grunt and gesture use, providing information regarding the precommunicative use of grunts and the physiological basis of this vocal production.

As with many scientific findings, the information reported here was discovered serendipitously; only in retrospect were earlier reports of the phenomenon and its place in the larger developmental enterprise recognized. It was in the course of investigating consonant development as described in the last chapter that we observed such a high frequency of communicative grunts across our 9- to 16-month-old children that the phenomenon cried out for study. In that analysis we also noted the prominence of laryngeal elements, [*h*], and glottal stop in the children's babble and word forms.

A grunt is defined as the vocalization that results when glottal closure (by activation of laryngeal muscles) is followed by abrupt vowel-like release (i.e., a brief egressive voiced breath) occurring with open or closed lips but no other supraglottal constriction. Grunts occur from birth, when the baby vocalizes during reflexive adjustments of the vocal tract, food ingestion, and protective closure of the airway. This vocalization constitutes a major means of communication in most nonhuman primate species and may have contributed to the evolution of language (McCune, 1999). In adult humans, a grunt may serve as a "response cry" (Goffman, 1978), accompanying effort (e.g., opening a jar lid or lifting a heavy box), or marking a reaction of interest or attention during solitary experiences such as reading. In conversation, grunt-like vocalizations (e.g., "*mm*") may serve, among other communicative functions, to signal continued attention to a speaker on the part of a listener (Schegloff, 1972) or to mark the pause when a speaker gives attention to word search (Goffman, 1978). Ward (2004) reports diverse pragmatic functions for such "nonlexical utterances," and Ward (2006) finds consistency in the use of phonetic elements comprising these utterances across speakers of American English.

In the course of summarizing children's lexical development (Vihman & McCune, 1994), we identified a small number of children who produced very few words. I undertook an exploratory investigation of these children's videotapes and transcripts in an effort to determine whether the children might be substituting some other communicative strategy for words. It was immediately apparent that Danny, the child who produced the fewest words across the months of study (he produced none prior to 16 months of age), was producing a large number of communicative grunts in situations where words might have been expected. This led to review of videotapes of the children who used words with high frequency to determine if they, too, were producing communicative grunts that might have gone unnoticed because of our focus on the search for words. They too frequently produced grunts.

The importance of the grunt vocalization was highlighted when we examined the timing of initial communicative grunt use in relation to the development of referential words. McCune (1992) found that of the 10 children of the Rutgers sample (described in Chapter 3), those who began producing referential words in the course of our observations all did so either in the same monthly observation when they began high communicative grunt use or in the following month. It was then imperative to understand the physiology of grunt production and examine its developmental history.

Why Grunts?

Physiological Basis of Grunt Vocalization

The laryngeal vocalization termed a grunt appears in the research literature as a universal feature of mammalian behavior. Peter Marler (1969) found the similarity in acoustic structure between human and chimpanzee grunts both "amusing" and "intriguing," and speculated that certain grunt forms observed in chimpanzees might be a bridge to differentiated referential expression. The grunt has occasionally been studied for its own sake, but more often the goal has been to answer a research question that turns out to involve this vocalization. Thus, the picture of its physiology and purpose emerge from a variety of sources.

When nurses in neonatal intensive care units observed grunting sounds in premature infants with hyaline membrane disease, they prevented grunting by intubating the infants—only to find that despite the increase in oxygen offered, the infants became cyanotic (significantly oxygen-deficient). Harrison, de V. Heese, and Klein (1967) investigated this phenomenon and determined that while the infants grunted during the earlier portion of the expiration phase of breathing, they maintained a higher oxygen level in the lungs at that time than in the subsequent more rapid expiration phase, where grunting ceased. They further determined that contraction of the abdominal muscles co-occurred with the grunt phase of expiration, leading to slightly elevated pressure within the lungs. They speculated that the increase in pressure allowed fuller recruitment of alveoli to the respiration process. Grunting is produced similarly to crying, and the assessments of these investigators also found elevated oxygenation during crying. They concluded that expiration against the closed glottis was a protective form of breathing aimed at raising the oxygen tension of arterial blood.

The relationship between the maintenance of lung volume during laryngeal closure and the following sudden release leading to a grunt is now well documented. England, Kent, and Stongryn (1985) provided supportive data in this regard from their research with dog pups by demonstrating the use of larynx and diaphragm muscles to maintain end-expiratory lung volume. Further, Milner, Saunders, and Hopkins (1978) observed grunting in healthy full-term babies following experimentally induced changes in thoracic gas volume. Typical modern treatment to enhance oxygenation of the lungs in newborns with respiratory challenge is positive end-expiratory pressure (PEEP), which mimics the function of laryngeal constriction (Slonim & Hamilton, 1981).

It turns out that the autonomic vocal response (here termed a grunt) has communicative significance in rats. Rat pups' ultrasonic grunt vocalizations ("isolation calls") induce retrieval to the nest by dams (Allin & Banks 1972; Hofer & Shair 1978, 1993). Blumberg and Alberts (1991) demonstrated that the isolation cry could be attributed to the increased oxygen demand brought about by thermoregulation needs when the pups experienced temperature reduction. The investigators therefore determined that the ultrasonic grunted vocalizations were the result of a laryngeal maneuver termed "laryngeal braking," which involves repeated glottal closure serving to enhance oxygenation. Nevertheless, robust findings regarding maternal response to this vocalization by rat dams demonstrate its functional communicative value. While the pups may not be "calling their mothers," mothers respond to this autonomically based signal of pup distress. Blumberg and Alberts (1990) had demonstrated the acoustic similarity of adult rats' copulation call with the infants' isolation cry, attributing both calls to metabolic strain on the animals.

The mechanism for these events is as follows (Figure 8–1). The laryngeal muscles interact with those affecting lung inflation, maintaining appropriate oxygenation of the blood in response to metabolic demand. This process involves reflexive relationships between the intercostal and laryngeal muscles mediated by the vagus, the 10th cranial nerve (De Troyer, Kelly, Macklem, & Zim 1985; Remmers 1973). Under conditions of metabolic demand, activation of the intercostal muscles during expiration sets in motion reflex contraction of laryngeal muscles, thus creating a system under pressure that lengthens the expiration phase of the breath and enhances oxygenation of the blood. Expiration against the constricted larynx produces pulses of sound, audible as grunts in humans and some larger mammals and ultrasonic in small rodents (Blumberg & Alberts 1990.)

The intercostal muscles serve the dual role of contributing to breathing patterns and stabilizing the thoracic spine. Bramble (1989) has described locomotor respiratory coupling, which ensures appropriate oxygenation in relation to the demands of locomotion in large mammals. Due to their role in spinal stabilization and rotation, the intercostal muscles are constantly active during high-speed locomotion. This leads to intercostal-laryngeal reflex activation, such that expiration occurs against an adducted (closed) larynx. In fact, the expiration phase of the breath in galloping animals is initiated when the leading foreleg lands, causing the forward displacement of the internal organs

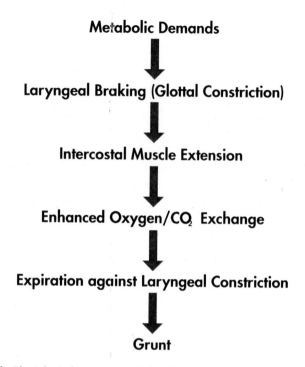

Metabolic Demands

Laryngeal Braking (Glottal Constriction)

Intercostal Muscle Extension

Enhanced Oxygen/CO$_2$ Exchange

Expiration against Laryngeal Constriction

Grunt

Figure 8–1. Physiological processes underlying autonomic grunt production. The laryngeal muscles interact with those affecting lung inflation, maintaining appropriate oxygenation of the blood in response to metabolic demand. Reflexive relationships mediated by the vagus, the 10th cranial nerve set in motion contraction of the laryngeal muscles, and engagement of the intercostal muscles, creating a system under pressure that lengthens the expiration phase of the breath and enhances oxygenation of the blood. Expiration against the constricted larynx produces pulses of sound, audible as grunts in humans and some larger mammals, and ultrasonic in small rodents.

(principally the liver). This results in sudden forced laryngeal opening and expiration (characteristic of a grunt), which can then be followed by inspiration. These varied findings demonstrate that the vocalized autonomic grunt can be seen as an epiphenomenon of the complex physiological processes of response to metabolic demand. Porges and colleagues (e.g., Porges, Doussard-Roosevelt, & Maiti, 1994) define this laryngeal mechanism as part of a larger system regulating processes of motion, emotion, and communication.

Evidence of Communicative Use

From prior informal analysis, we also knew that grunts were used communicatively and that, for children using words early, communicative grunts either closely predicted or co-occurred with the onset of referential language. Based on the common observation that grunts occur in the context of effort or physical activity, we assumed that some grunts produced by the children would occur in the context of movement or effort. We therefore undertook a detailed exploratory study of five children from the Rutgers sample to determine the developmental course from grunts of effort to communicative use.

A Plan to Study Grunt Use in Human Infants

Our initial working hypothesis (McCune, 1992) was that we would first observe grunts co-occurring with physical effort to attain some goal, perhaps followed in subsequent sessions by grunts of "mental effort," indicating that the autonomic grunt vocalization had become associated with goal-directed behavior and was now produced "voluntarily" when the children addressed means/ends tasks; we expected communicative uses to follow next. This hypothesis was attractive because of prior work linking the pragmatics of language to cognitive means/ends skills as suggested by Bates and colleagues (Bates et al., 1975, 1979; see Chapter 4).

Because our original transcription of the videotapes had emphasized words and consonants, we undertook a careful review of the videotapes from the five children's sessions, adding grunt vocalizations missed in the earlier transcription. To qualify as a grunt, a vocalization had to meet three criteria: (1) abrupt glottal onset, (2) lack of any supraglottal constriction except lip closure, and (3) short duration. Two transcribers then viewed all tapes independently, nominating specific vocalizations as grunts. They then met and reviewed all nominated utterances, strictly applying the criteria to ensure that both coders agreed that a given utterance was a grunt. When disagreements occurred, the utterance was not submitted to further analysis. This occurred most often when the infant's mouth was not in full view or the utterance was too soft to be heard by one or both coders at playback.

Mental Effort

We began the analysis of contexts of grunt use with one of the children, Aurie, who began words early and included a fair number of glottal vocalizations among her productions. This initial contextual analysis involved meetings of the entire team contributing to the eventually published report of this research (McCune et al., 1996). The earliest months of study, as anticipated, yielded frequent grunts accompanying movement or effort. We were at first gratified to identify many grunts accompanying means/ends activities, such as placing a puzzle piece that did not appear to involve physical effort. These we termed grunts of "mental effort." These three categories—physiological effort, mental effort, and communicative—encompassed virtually all of the grunts produced by this child. We then undertook analysis of a second child's repertoire, seeking the same three categories of use but leaving open the possibility of some grunts being "uncoded" because they did not match these categories. The second child studied produced few "mental effort grunts" and enough uncoded grunts for us to recognize that our three categories needed modification.

Careful study of the uncoded grunts yielded the insight that all of these grunts, as well as those attributable to mental effort, occurred in the context of focused attention on the part of the child. Because of the known relationship between focused attention and cognitive processing, this observation was of great interest. Our final coding system involved effort grunts, attention grunts, and communicative grunts. Prior to reviewing that study we will consider the physiology of focused attention, establishing a rationale for this category.

Attention and the Grunt Vocalization

Attention, characterized by moderate arousal and the affect of interest, is considered metabolically demanding (Kahneman, 1973; Porges, 1992). Cohen (1986) reviewed early research suggesting that certain motor activities are associated with all forms of attentional effort. He reports that James (1890/1950) linked tension in the glottis and activation of the respiratory muscles with effort. Similarly, Ribot (1889) found modification in respiratory rhythm accompanying intense reflection (Cohen, 1986, p. 25). Physiological changes reported in recent studies of focused attention in young children suggest that the metabolic demands of this cognitive activity have effects on the organism similar to those of physical effort (Porges, 1992; Richards & Casey, 1992). Ward (2004) found that the duration of grunt-like nonlexical utterances in adult conversation was correlated with depth of thought.

Primary accompaniments of focused attention are motor quieting, sustained lowered heart rate, lowered heart rate variability, a lengthened expiratory phase of the breath, and "either reduced respiratory amplitude or a temporary cessation of breathing" (Porges, 1992, p. 209). According to Richards and Casey (1991), the changes in heart rate are effected by "cardio-inhibitory centers in the neocortex, including the frontal cortex and the limbic system. These higher centers directly affect the vagus nerve, resulting in heart rate deceleration during orienting and attention (p. 49)." The vagus nerve, central to the Porges model, also mediates laryngeal constriction in response to intercostal action (Remmers, 1973), maintaining lung inflation during expiration.

Laryngeal constriction, the mechanical basis of the grunt vocalization, seems fully integrated in the metabolic processes surrounding focused attention. Maintenance of lung inflation by intercostal activation, in addition to promoting reflex activation of the muscles of the larynx, also stabilizes the thoracic spine and maintains the trunk upright, thus facilitating the manipulation of small objects—a frequent occasion of focused attention in 1-year-olds (Ruff, 1982). The respiratory changes during attention and the finding that bradycardia and/or arrhythmia can be induced by manual stimulation of the mucosa immediately above the larynx (Jacobs, Wetzel, & Host, 1976; Kirchner, 1987) support the integration of laryngeal function with the processes of focal attention. Pressure from laryngeal constriction affects the vagus nerve and the adjacent mucosa and may thus influence the changes in heart rate characterizing focused attention.

Thus glottal activity involved in physiological regulation of body systems may be the source of observed grunts under conditions of both effort and attention. The infant may also experience an internal conscious "sense of volition" during both effort and attention. If so, a learned association might develop between such an internal state and the accompanying grunt vocalization that at first occurs autonomically. This association might then lead to "voluntary" production of grunts when the infant experiences a similar internal conscious sense of volition, even in the absence of metabolic demand. In other words, the grunt that was an original part of the physiological process related to metabolic demand might now occur as a sign of the purely mental process.

Attention to objects is a necessary condition for the development of reference to objects and events (Werner & Kaplan, 1963), and experimental evidence has demonstrated that young children are more successful at acquiring lexical items when their attention is already focused on an object as it is named (Dunham, Dunham, & Curwin, 1993).

Having established a rationale for how grunts might come to accompany focused attention, in the following section we consider the developmental course of the grunt vocalization in relation to lexical learning and gestural development.

Analysis of the Origins of Communication

In order to more fully understand the role of grunts in communicative development, we analyzed the occurrence of all grunts as well as gestural communication for the three earliest talkers in our longitudinal sample (Alice, Aurie, and Rick; mean length of utterance at 24 months of age: 3.59, 2.17, and 2.20 respectively) and the two latest-talking and lowest-volubility children in the study (Danny, who produced too few words at 24 months to allow computation of mean length of utterance, and Nenni (mean length of utterance at 24 months: 1.24). Two girls and a boy were early talkers; a boy and a girl were later talkers. Aurie had a 3-year-old sister who was usually at preschool when the sessions occurred; the others were first-born children. At 3-year-old follow-up, all five children produced language within the normal range.

Monthly sessions described in Chapter 3 were employed for study of grunt vocalizations and gestures at the transition to speech, including the 9 to 16-month sessions for the early talkers and, for the later talkers, sessions beginning at least 2 months before the observation of spontaneously produced words (12 months for Danny and 11 months for Nenni). A total of 4,161 vocalizations were reviewed in the analysis of the five children. Once the definitions of grunt categories had been determined, we established reliability of assignment to these categories. Twelve half-hour videotapes were randomly selected from the 35 included in the study. Two judges independently coded the first third (10 minutes) of these tapes. Of 83 grunts that occurred in these segments, the two judges assigned 72 to the same categories, yielding a percentage of agreement of 0.87.

Gesture analysis had originally been undertaken in a previous study (Lennon, 1984), using the 9- to 18-month videotapes of the nine Rutgers participants (eliminating Rala). I first describe the sequential development of categories of grunts and then turn to categories and results regarding gesture.

Categories of Grunts

The categories were formally defined as follows:

Effort Grunts

For this category, the timing and intensity of the accompanying movement or effort were judged sufficient to account for the grunt observed. Examples were moving from standing to squatting, trying to lift the lid on a plastic bottle, reaching for a toy, crawling.

Attention Grunts

These occurred when the infant was engaged in visual (and often tactile) focal attention to objects or events in the environment (Ruff, 1986) without evidence of communicative intent or observable movement or effort. Examples include looking at a toy, touching the dial of a toy phone, picking up a small toy, dropping a bead in a cup, and manipulating a small jack-in-the-box.

Communicative Grunts

These were directed toward the mother and might be accompanied by infant looks at mother, extension of objects, pulling at mother or reaching toward her, or other gestures (Bates et al., 1979). Examples were grunts occurring while giving a pocketbook to the mother, patting mother's head, giving a jack-in-the-box to mother to open, taking a toy from the mother, and holding up a finger that had been pinched to the mother.

Applying the Grunt Categories

In practice, coders first considered the category of effort. If a vocalization could be attributed to effort, it was placed in that category. If the physical situation was insufficient for attributing the grunt to effort, coders next sought evidence of communicative intent. This could involve, for example, a look to the mother, placing an object in her lap, or ongoing interaction surrounding the grunt vocalization. Grunts not meeting criteria for either of these categories were then evaluated to determine whether they occurred in the context of focal attention. Given the physiological basis of grunts and the physiological responses accompanying focal attention, it is not surprising that all grunt vocalizations identified met criteria for one of these three categories.

Sequential Development of Grunts

Grunts accounted for a substantial proportion of each child's vocalization across the months studied, with mean frequency and standard deviation as follows: Alice (M = 25.5, SD = 14.3), Aurie (M = 35.6, SD = 33.7), Rick (M = 31.35, SD = 11.36), Nenni (M = 20, SD = 17.36), and Danny, who vocalized infrequently, (M = 0.98, SD = 10.6). Total grunt frequency did not show developmental trends, but developmental patterns emerged when the categories of grunts were examined.

All five children showed effort grunts from the first month of the study. Frequency of effort grunts was unstable, but they continued throughout the study, varying with infant activities session by session (Figure 8–2). Grunts associated with infant attention were distinguished from grunts of effort on the basis that the children were not engaged in metabolically demanding motor activities that might yield a grunt. Attention grunts were infrequently observed in the early sessions, and increased as the children developed. The children produced these grunts while holding and examining objects, sometimes manipulating them as well, or when gazing at objects or events at a slight distance. Attention grunts were distinguished from communicative grunts because the infants made no observable attempts to engage adults when these vocalizations were expressed. First observation of communicative use of grunts followed two or more months of observed use of attention grunts for all five children. Grunts were used both to solicit interaction and as requests from their onset. They were used for both functions without interesting variation in frequency across time or across participants.

Grunts and the Transition to Referential Words

Onset for the development of referential word use in these children had been established in earlier studies (McCune, 1992; Vihman & McCune, 1994; Chapters 3 and 7 of this volume). Lennon (1984) had identified the time when gestural evidence indicated the referential comprehension of words across a variety of contexts. For example, children responded with a point to the correct object or picture across several instances following maternal questions such as, "Where is the kitty?" Coders in the grunt analysis were unaware of the timing or possible relevance of these events.

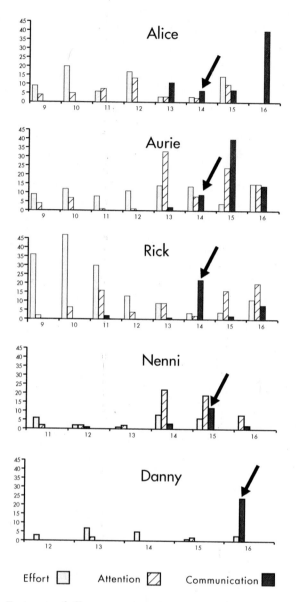

Figure 8–2. Frequency of effort grunts, attention grunts, and communicative grunts for each child by month. Each child showed a pattern of more frequent effort grunts than other types of grunts during the first month of observation. Attention grunts showed increasing frequency, followed by the onset of communicative grunts. The arrows mark the months of referential transition in production for Alice, Rick, and Aurie; in referential comprehension for for Nenni and Danny. [Adapted from McCune et al. (1996), Figure 4, p. 32 with permission.]

Two important findings linked communicative grunts with referential words (McCune et al., 1996). First, the transition to linguistic reference was linked in time to communicative grunt use. For the early talkers, referential word production, and for the later talkers, referential word comprehension, were first observed either in the same or the following monthly session as onset of communicative grunt use, as can be seen in Figure 8–2. Second, the early talkers all showed sharp increases in word production following only limited use of context-dependent words in earlier sessions. When we turned to study of the children's communicative gestures, additional relationships with grunt communication emerged.

The Role of Gesture

For analysis of communicative gestures and the occurrence of "pointing for self," we relied on Lennon's (1984) study of these same children and sessions. To accomplish this, we reviewed all videotapes and transcripts, creating a database that allowed alignment of all communicative events produced by the children (McCune, Greenwood, Lemmon, 2001). We then analyzed occurrences of gesture accompanying word, grunt, or other vocalization as well as independent use of the motor modality (gesture alone) and the vocal modality (grunt alone and word alone). By noting the timing of developments and the relationships across modalities of use, we could infer the role of these communicative forms in the developmental trajectories of the five individual children.

Gesture Categories

Lennon had analyzed gestures using communicative categories derived from Halliday (1975), who first applied them to vocal communication by his son. The categories employed were (1) point for self, (2) request, (3) interactional, (4) emotion expression, (5) heuristic, (6) imaginative, and (7) informative. Pointing for self occurs naturally in the context of examining an object, and children will sometimes point to a picture as they look at it carefully. Halliday did not include pointing for self, as this is not a communicative bid, nor does it involve vocalization, which was the focus of his work. For completeness, a study of gestural development should include point for self. Table 8–1 includes definitions of these categories. Two raters independently scored the first 10 minutes of videotape for each of 4 children randomly selected from the 9 who comprised Lennon's (1984) study at ages 10, 14, and 18 months. Interrater agreement for categorizing gestures identified by both raters was 0.83 (69/83).

Developmental Sequence for Gesture

Across the five children, the vast majority of gestures, no doubt influenced by the situation, were either pointing at an object of interest or extending

Table 8–1
Communicative Functions of Gesture

1. Point for self	Noncommunicative pointing in the context of attention. C points to book page, looking at it.
2. Request	Request for help or object. C hands closed purse to M, whining.
3. Interactive	Bid for social interaction. C points to book page, looks at M.
4. Expression of feelings	Gesture is used to express emotion. C holds up finger to M, crying, after pinching it in toolbox.
5. Heuristic: knowledge related	Request for label, reply to question, combine a gesture and a label. M says "Where's the baby?" C digs in toy bucket until she finds doll.
6. Imaginative	Request for pretend interaction. C holds baby doll and bottle toward M after feeding the doll himself.
7. Informative	Information beyond the immediate perceptual context. C points to key picture, looks at M, vocalizing, then points to key rack by front door.

Source: From Lennon (1984), following Halliday (1975), with permission.

an object to the mother. In fact, in the 9- to 16-month age range, in the play observation setting, very few other gestures were used for communication. Danny occasionally guided his mother's hand to indicate a request; Nenni and Alice each produced an "all gone" gesture. Because of the low frequency of other gestures, Lennon limited her analysis to pointing and extending the hand either toward an item of interest or to mother while holding an object. Although they rarely produced symbolic communicative gestures (Acredolo & Goodman, 1988) in the situations observed, the children were capable of symbolic actions and used them in their play. Table 8–2 shows the ages at which the children first demonstrated the various communicative functions through their gestures and the age at which they used symbolic gestures in pretend play (level 2/3, Chapter 6).

Pointing for self was first observed between 8 and 10 months of age (except for Nenni, who did not show this behavior), but only Danny continued to produce such points for several months. For the other children, pointing shifted function and became a means of engaging their mothers in joint attention and interaction. It is of interest that the shift from pointing for self to the beginning of interactional gestures tended to occur close in time to transitions in mental representation (stage 6 of object permanence and/or representational play onset (Table 8.2; Aurie produced a few interactional

Table 8–2
Month of First Occurrence for Gesture Functions, Communicative Grunts,
and Pretend Play

Functions	Alice	Aurie	Rick	Nenni	Danny
1. Point for self	10	9	8		10
2. Request	11	11	13	14	13
3. Interactional	9	9	10	9	10
4. Feeling expression	11	15		16	15
5. Heuristic	11	14	15	15	16
6. Imaginative	13	14	16		
7. Informative					16
Communicative grunt	13	14	14	15	16
Stage 6 object permanence	10	12	10	9	9
Pretend play	9	13	13	12	11

gestures in the earlier months). The interactional function (9 to 10 months) occurred earlier than request (11 to 14 months) for all five children. Request accounted for a much smaller proportion of gestures than the dominant function, the interactional. This may have been because the setting involved mother and baby on the floor with many toys in easy reach. However, the children did occasionally use gestures to request help with the toys or to request a specific toy. This difference in frequency may account for the earlier observation of the interactional function. Conveying emotion through gesture was extremely rare in the observations, occurring at most once or twice per child.

The use of the more advanced representational functions of gesture to convey or respond to information going beyond the perceptual situation, Halliday's informative, heuristic, and imaginal functions (onset between 11 and 16 months), differed across children based on kinds of interactions with their mothers. Aurie and her mother engaged in frequent pretend play, and Aurie frequently requested pretend activities (imaginative). The others used the heuristic function, requesting names and answering questions or accompanying their gestures by language. Only Danny, who used no names to label objects, showed the informative function in gesture at 16 months both by pointing outside the room in answer to questions (e.g., "where is your bear?") and by spontaneously pointing in sequence to categorically related objects or pictures.

These advanced communicative functions were observed only after the onset of pretending, an expected finding due to their symbolic nature. Children showed individual differences in the extent of their use of these functions and increasing frequency except for Danny, who began to produce them only at 16 months, the final month of analysis.

Timing of Communicative Grunt use in Relation to Gesture

Prior study of communicative grunts had shown that their use predicted the transition to referential word production and/or comprehension (McCune et al., 1996). How might consideration of the children's gestural communication affect that finding? First, communicative gestures preceded communicative grunts by several months for all five children. It can be seen in Table 8–2 that communicative grunts tended to begin around the same age as those gestures, with the most advanced communicative functions (heuristic, imaginative, and informative), and after onset of pretend play. Second, when communicative grunts began, they tended to occur in the absence of gestural support (0% to 20% accompanied by gestures). Subsequently the children varied in their tendency to accompany communicative grunts with gestures. Danny, Nenni, and Rick continued to produce communicative grunts and gestures in separate events throughout the study, while Alice and Aurie, the most advanced of these five participants, increased the proportion of communicative grunts accompanied by gestures by 15 to 16 months (Alice, 25%; Aurie, 50%). It was clear from these findings that use of communicative grunts did not depend on gestural support. However, the precedence of gestural communication in acquisition suggests that this prior communicative experience provided a foundation for subsequent grunt communication.

Overall Communicative Frequency Increases with Communicative Grunt Onset

McCune and colleagues (1996) reported that the onset of communicative grunts heralded the shift to referential word production and/or comprehension in these same five participants and a doubling of lexical production by the three children who were early talkers. An unexpected finding from the analysis of gesture was that this increase in production also extended to the gestural mode. The onset of communicative grunts was immediately followed by a sharp increase of communicative acts across all categories of communicative events, including gestures for the five children (Table 8–3 and Figures 8–3 to 8–8). Following communicative grunt onset the gestures were increasingly accompanied by vocalization. It appeared that the developmental shift accompanying the onset of grunt communication also heralds a general facilitation of communication, affecting both the gestural and the vocal modalities.

This synchrony does not necessarily imply a causal role for grunt communication; it may be that some additional variable is affecting both phenomena. However, if this effect is confirmed in larger studies, the shift to

Table 8–3
Monthly Totals of Communicative Events and Words in Relation to Communicative Grunt Onset and Play Milestones

	Alice		Aurie		Rick		Nennie		Danny	
	Total Events	Total Words	Total Events	Total Words	Total Events	Total Words	Total Events	Total Words	Total Events	Total Words
9	23	+, ++	3		6	6	5			
10	23		1		9	5	17		1	
11	32	23	7		10	8	14	2	3	+
12	32	9	5		1	1	13	+	9	
13	**25**[a]	14	**11**[a]	7 +, ++	22	11[+]	26	1	3	
14	**111**[b]	90	**62**[b]	36	**50**[a]	1	**55**[a]	6[++]	2	
15	106	80	71	26	31[b]	23[++]	45[b]	5	3	
16	143	85	87	54	65	49	27	0	**55**[a,b]	21

[a]Month of communicative grunt onset.
[b]Month of referential transition in production (Alice, Aurie, Rick) or comprehension (Nenni, Danny).
[+]Onset of play level 2/3 (pretend).
[++]Onset of play level 4 (combinations). For Danny, level 4 onset occurred at 18 months.

Note: This table shows the increase in children's frequency of communication ("Total Events" column for each child). The + and ++ marks indicate steps in representational play. The month of communicative grunt onset (marked with [a]) and the number of events in that month are shown in bold. It can be seen that total communicative events increased substantially within a session of the occurrence of this milestone. The referential transition, designated by [b], occurred in the following session (same session for Danny). The number of word tokens produced each month is indicated. This number also showed a sharp increase with communicative grunt onset for the early talkers. Figure 8–4 illustrates the word and communicative event data in the form of graphs.

communicative use of grunts might serve as a signal for communicative advance across modalities. The auditory and proprioceptive experience of the grunt vocalization naturally accompanying physically demanding activities may set in motion a developmental process leading to the insight that bodily action (ordinarily sounds) can convey an internal meaningful state. The fact that the shift to communicative grunts is followed by an increase in gestural as well as vocal communication suggests that this same process may also affect children learning signed languages.

For Alice (Figure 8–4) this increase was primarily due to increased word production, but use of the motor modality also doubled to 25 gestures, 13 of which were unaccompanied by words.

For Aurie and Rick (see Figure 8–4), the sharp increase from 11 to 62 communicative events encompassed both gestures and words. For none of these three early talkers did communicative grunts themselves contribute substantially to the increase in communicative frequency. Both Nenni and

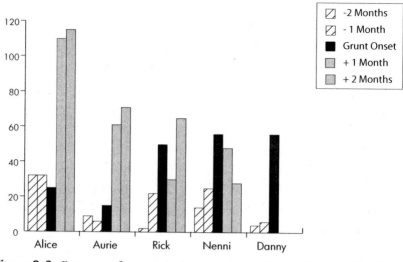

Figure 8–3. Frequency of communicative events in months preceding and following communicative grunt onset. The five participants showed sharp increases in the frequency of communicative events in the month of communicative grunt onset (black bar) or in the following month.

Danny, the later talkers, showed sharp growth in communicative frequency in the month of communicative grunt onset (14 and 16 months, respectively).

For Nenni (see Figure 8–4) the increase came in her adoption of a glottaly based and aspirated protoword (*hah*), which she used 34 times, only twice coordinated with a gesture. In contrast with previous months, where

---

Figure 8–4. → Changes in communicative frequencies for Alice, Aurie, Rick, Nenni, and Danny, due to gesture and vocalization. For each month the figure shows frequency of vocal and gestural communication and total communicative events for each child. Vocal communication includes words, grunts, and other nonwords. A single event might include both a vocalization and a gesture. Increased communicative frequency for Alice was primarily due to increased word production, but use of the motor modality also doubled to 25 gestures, 13 of which were unaccompanied by words. For Aurie, the sharp increase from 11 to 62 communicative events encompassed both gestures and words. Rick more than doubled communicative event production in the month of communicative grunt onset at 14 months but produced only one word in that session. His substantial communication increase in the next 2 months was fueled by increases to 23 and then 49 words. Nenni's increase in vocal communications resulted from her adoption of a glottaly based and aspirated protoword (hah), which she used 34 times, only twice coordinated with a gesture. In contrast with previous months, where her communication was primarily gestural, in this month she began to develop a balance across modalities. Following low communicative frequency until 16 months in both modalities, Danny began word production (using two context-limited words repeatedly) and showed substantial frequencies of both grunts and gestures.

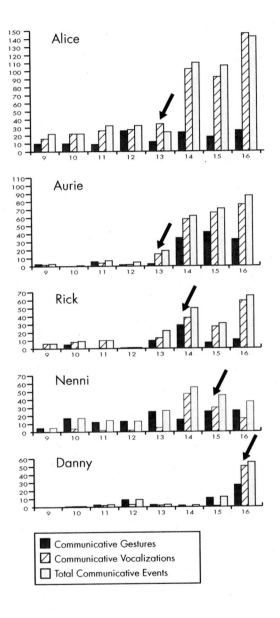

Communicative Gestures
Communicative Vocalizations
Total Communicative Events

her communication was primarily gestural, in this month she began to develop a balance across modalities.

In contrast, Danny (see Figure 8–4), who had low communicative frequency until 16 months in both modalities, began word production (using two context-limited words repeatedly) and showed substantial frequencies of both grunts and gestures and a more balanced distribution between the vocal and gestural modalities.

Previous research (Özçalişkan & Goldin-Meadow, 2005; Capirci et al., 1998) found that between 14 and 18 months children shifted from predominance of the gestural modality, as our early talking participants did, to a predominance of words over gestures. Ozcaliskan and Goldin-Meadow also report that by 18 months the children they studied had begun to use gesture to elaborate the meaning of their words rather than to reinforce that meaning as they had at 14 months. Studies have not previously included communicative grunts, so one can only wonder what their inclusion might have contributed to these studies. Future work should resolve this issue.

The Developmental Sequence: An Interpretation

The development sequence of precommunicative pointing, effort, attention, communicative grunts, and communicative gestures in relation to the referential transition can be interpreted as follows. In the context of a gradually differentiating consciousness, the infant begins to take notice of objects as separate from self and mother. This interest soon takes the form of examining, including index finger extension, and occasionally accompanied by attention grunts. Mothers and infants become more aware of each other's separate focus of attention during this period due to subliminal gaze following by both partners and the reciprocal processes of affect attunement and social referencing. The child's attention grunts may serve, like points for self, to alert mothers to infants' focus of attention. This leads, in many cases, to language expression by mothers that is suited to the infant's focus. As infants develop the capacity for representational consciousness, various intentional states (internal mental states) are accompanied by attention grunts, giving the infant a vocal accompaniment to an internal meaning.

During this transition period, the infant begins to use gestures to solicit the mother's attention. The grunt of effort and/or attention previously employed now shifts function (Werner & Kaplan, 1963, p. 18) and becomes an additional communicative strategy for attracting the mother's attention to the child's internal meaning state and/or focus of attention. This vocalization is more effective than a point because it is an aural signal that can attract visual attention. As such it can also be intensified as needed to bring about the desired goal.

Grunts became ritualized in the children's repertoires such that each child developed a characteristic grunt form similar to their dominant vocal shapes for words (see Chapter 9). This is the shaping of the first symbolic vehicle that stands as symbol to symbolized in relation to the child's intentional state at any given time of production. The glottal activation characteristic of communicative grunts is also a necessary feature of word production. Children making the transition to reference integrate glottal activation with VMS skills, increasing the capacity to produce words. The grunt form itself can also differentiate by adding a variety of upper tract modulations and often labial closure to the glottal origin, promoting the formation of words. Referential words retain the notion of "communication" and "symbolizing what is on my mind" characteristic of earlier communicative grunts, but unlike grunts these are the product of additional shifts in function as relationships are created between them and differentiated meaning states experienced by the child and coded in the ambient language.

The availability of the ritualized communicative grunt suited for differentiation provides a foundation for shaping words. It may also be possible that the directed and obvious form of this particular nonword vocalization may stimulate the parent's efforts to present and elicit language.

A Revolutionary Claim: Physiology and Mental Representation as the Roots of Linguistic Reference

Children express word meanings learned from adults. But what is the source of a child's ability to experience internal meaning and express such meaning with language? Macnamara (1982) proposed that children's private meaningful experience might form the foundation for the development of linguistic reference but found no mechanism for this transition and so assumed that referring is innate. *I propose that the occurrence of grunts in the context of meaningful internal mental states provides a vehicle for the development of vocal reference to internal meanings.* The "communicative grunt," common to both humans and nonhuman primate species, plays a significant role in children's transition to referential language, suggesting a physiological basis for intentional vocal communication. Evidence for this relationship is found both in the sequential development of the grunt vocalization from its autonomic to voluntary occurrence and from developmental relationships among gesture, grunt, and word at the transition to language.

A first step is to consider language expressions as flowing from a state of mind. McNeill (2000) sees language and gesture as means of conscious existence. "Intentional state" (Searle, 1992) is a useful concept for understanding language in relation to state of mind. Bloom, in a series of publications culminating in her 2001 monograph, has emphasized this construct. Because the term *intention* has an everyday meaning—an identified goal—Searle's use of the traditional philosophical notion of intentional state may at first confuse. In the literature of developmental psychology, *intention* usually refers to goal-directedness. In the philosophical literature, an intentional state is an internal focus of the mind on some content. This content may or may not be (as in the common usage of "intention") a plan to do something. An intentional state is roughly the same as a state of focused attention. Somewhat more formally, an intentional state is defined as a contentful conscious state that is directed at some internal or external phenomenon. Examples are thoughts of a friend, the color of a flower, the warmth of one's toes. A conscious state that is nonintentional is lacking such specified content. An example would be a mood when the mood is not about anything in particular. One might experience a sense of happiness with no particular content (a nonintentional state) and then smile at the thought of a good cup of coffee—shifting with that thought to an intentional state.

Crying accompanies a defined state of the organism, but in young infants the state marked by crying is a physiologically based feeling state without intentional content. Later, when focused on a particular meaning, such as stress or disappointment about some specific issue, crying can express an intentional state. Meaning is most often discussed as "word meaning," but Searle (1983) points out that "speakers' meanings can be defined in terms of forms of intentionality that are not intrinsically linguistic" (p. 160), recognizing the possibility that the ordinarily linguistic notion of meaning can be defined in nonlinguistic terms. In the following, I will define the child's intentional state of focused attention as "a meaningful state." The meaning of this state can neither be described nor shared because it is intrinsic to the mind of a prelinguistic child. It is this capacity for internal representational meaning, initially not definable to others, that is fertile ground for development of linguistic meaning and reference.

When a child is paying attention, engaged in effort, or saying a word, he is by definition experiencing an intentional state. Prior to the capacity for mental representation, which allows one to remember the past or imagine circumstances other than those present, the child is limited to intentional states that are perceptual in nature, such that the mind is directed to some perceived reality or some specific sensory or motor phenomenon (e.g., a pain, darkness). Grunts of effort and attention may accompany such perceptual intentional states. In the primordial sharing situation described by Werner and Kaplan, the child initially assumes (by default) that intentional focus is shared with others. Mothers and other caregivers support this illusion with their recognition of infants' needs and focus of attention and with attunements to the infant. The earliest communicative exchanges depend upon a match of intentional states that is assumed by both partners. When mother and infant both gaze at an object, the assumption is that they share intentional focus, although the mother's knowledge of the object may involve richer and more complete understanding of its meaning and associations.

According to Werner and Kaplan, reference and language learning depend upon the capacity to develop a personal system of sound-meaning symbolic relationships, which only gradually becomes socialized and systematized in relation to the ambient adult language. *I propose that the effort grunt, experi-*

enced by the child when engaged in some demanding and purposeful activity, and by definition entailing an intentional state, becomes a vocal marker recognized by the child as an aspect of the intentional state experience. The child's experience of his effortful grunt vocalizations provides auditory and proprioceptive accompaniment to the intentional state of goal-directedness. This may be the first intentional state to be vocally marked, a marking precipitated by the basic physiological aspects of effort. Initially, this experience involves physical movement or effortful activities with objects. Later, grunts accompany acts of focal attention. Mere attention may be metabolically demanding, and some attention grunts may be metabolically based. However, when adults mark interest in conversation ("mm hm") or speakers pause in search of a word ("uh"), these laryngeal vocalizations mark their intentional state of interest or cognitive search, rather than arising from physiological demand. [Recall however, that Ward (2004) found length of such nonlexical adult vocalization correlated with depth of thought.] It is plausible that infants' grunts in the context of attention become markers of an internal state, not arising directly from metabolic demand. How might the experience of effort and attention grunts lead the child to adapt this vocalization for communication?

Darwin (1872/1965) first suggested that a "useful" behavior accompanying a certain internal state might later recur under similar states, in which later case, although the behavior may have no direct use, it nonetheless expresses information about the internal state of the animal. One could consider effort grunts as useful for managing metabolic demand in cases of physical effort. Later, grunts occur when the infant experiences an internal attentional state, whether or not physiological demand is involved. Tinbergen (1952) offers numerous examples where habitual "intention movements" normally accompanying a certain motivational state might persist under similar motivation, even though they no longer serve the initial goal. Such "derived behaviors" are valuable signals regarding internal state, which might affect both the animal emitting the signal and other animals in hearing. In many primate species grunts that tend to accompany effortful movement of the animals become a signal recognized by the troop as readiness to travel (Cheyney & Seyforth, 1990; Stewart & Harcourt, 1994). The developmental processes analyzed here also characterize aspects of communicative development in some extant primate species and are implicated as contributing to the evolution of language (McCune, 1999).

In human infants, the grunt vocalization, which originally served as part of a complex physiological maneuver involved in metabolic sustenance during effort, might persist accompanying the sense of effort at attending and communicating. The effort grunt also exemplifies "natural meaning" as defined by Grice (1957): that which entails a necessary connection between some expression and a correlated situation. Peirce (1932) suggested that indexical signs (i.e., those with natural meaning) do not require cultural transmission but can be rediscovered generation by generation. Because all humans experience grunts of effort, all would be subject to the process of deriving the attention-marking and communicative uses of this vocalization, so the shift from effort grunts to those marking an internal meaningful state is virtually guaranteed. This sound comes to symbolize the general internal state of meaning experienced by the child, but not yet codified by a word.

All of the children described in this chapter used gestures to recruit their parents' attention and assistance for several months prior to communicative grunt use. Within 1 month of independent communication acts, using gestures and grunts separately, the children began to combine these communicative vehicles, suggesting that the communicative function established for gestures is now jointly carried by both gestural and vocal means. By the time communicative grunts were produced, the children also had achieved onset of mental representation as independently assessed in play observation. *I propose that the communicative grunt becomes the child's first vocal symbol, standing in representational relationship with the child's experience of an intentional state that she seeks to share with another.* Rather than symbolizing an external object or situation, this first vocal symbol represents an intentional state of focused attention directed both at some content (internal or external) and at attaining joint focus with the adult on that same content. *Unlike a word, which represents some more specific meaning, a communicative grunt has unstable meaning and represents whatever the infant has in mind at the moment.*

In Werner and Kaplan's terminology, the grunt vocalization would shift function from a response to the metabolic demand of effort to become a signal of internal attentional focus and, finally, a communicative vehicle, a "natural symbol." Once the grunt becomes communicative, it attains the state of a referential vocalization, given the child's goal of referring to an associated meaningful mental state. However, this vocalization attains neither meaning nor reference as defined linguistically because it does not specify a meaning that can be conveyed to a conversational partner. Rather, it is a transitional vocalization, termed by Werner and Kaplan a "call sound." Due to shared history and aspects of context, on some occasions mothers will correctly intuit their children's communicative goal. *I propose that the recurring expression of this personally meaningful vocalization, linked with its periodic success in conveying an intended meaning in context, prompts the child's entry into the capacity for linguistic reference, where specific words can come to refer to a more delimited range of internal meanings.*

Attention grunts are often soft and difficult to identify. Communicative grunts are often obvious and intense. How and why does the child, who has produced grunts of effort and attention for some months, come to use this vocalization for purposeful communication? By 1 year of age, children are able to follow an adult's gaze and monitor whether the child and his interests are the focus of adult attention. It may be that the vocalization that has come to mark the child's own intentional state of attention, displaced from its original integration with a full response to metabolic demand, is repeated and intensified when the child notes that maternal interest is elsewhere and therefore experiences increased motivation to recruit the mother's interest.

Tinbergen (1952) reported that derived activities tend to exhibit the first element of a fuller response (in this case glottal constriction in relation to metabolic demand). With the intensity of motivation, the signal itself is intensified and may lead to the total original activity. In this regard, it is of interest that both crying and grunting in newborns lead to high blood oxygen (Harrison, de V. Heese, & Klein, 1968). Perhaps neonatal grunting is a less intense relative of crying. In the case of communicative grunts, we observed some cases where an intense sequence of grunts that went unheeded or misunderstood terminated in a bout of crying.

Within 1 month of communicative grunt use, those children with appropriate vocal skills made the transition to referential word production. A critical difference between referential words and communicative grunts is that while the grunt vocalization is a personal symbol, referential words are conventional elements of the ambient language. The similarities between these two forms are (1) both symbolize an internal state of the organism, (2) both are vocal in form, (3) both function communicatively, and (4) both involve activation of the laryngeal muscles in their production.

An Evolutionary Role for Grunts?

I have proposed (McCune, 1999) that the same dynamic system of variables contributing to the child's transition to language contributed to the origin of language in the species. Some intriguing finding suggest that the path to grunt communication in nonhuman primate infants may follow the same trajectory as I have found in human infants: first accompanying effort, then attention, then communication. Seyfarth and Cheney (1986) observed vervet infants accompanying movement with grunts at 1 to 3 months of age, suggesting effort. By 3 or 4 months of age, 60% of their grunts predicted or noticed movement of others, suggesting attention. At 1 to 2 years they develop the acoustic properties as well as the appropriate use of the several specified communicative grunt types used by the species. While vervets are capable of producing acoustically adult-like alarm calls by 3 months of age, it is around this same age, 1 to 2 years of age, that these calls are appropriately restricted to the species, leading to alarm calls in adults. So, like human infants' sift to referential words, vervets' meaningful expression of the conspecific repertoire co-occurs with use of grunts for communication.

Plooij (1984), who studied chimpanzee infants in the wild, reported effort grunts from birth accompanying movement, followed by "uh-grunts" (p. 63) at 2 months when they observed other chimpanzees or heard them nearby (suggesting attention grunts). At 3 to 5 months, Plooij observed the uh-grunt addressed directly to adult animals. Unfortunately vocal data are sparse for the later period of chimpanzee infancy and childhood, so it is not possible to describe the path from these early roots to the full repertoire described by Goodall (1986) and others.

Falk (2004) investigated the evolutionary background preceding language by comparing mother-infant interaction in humans and chimpanzees. It would be of interest to compare the developmental trajectory of extant primate infants on the parameters studied in this volume in relation to language development. Differences between extant species in levels of mental representation favor our closer relatives (chimpanzees) over any species of monkey (McCune & Agayoff, 2001), and it is bonobos and chimpanzees who have shown success in learning human-designed communicative systems (e.g., Savage-Rumbaugh, Romsky, Hopkins & Sevcik, 1989).

Intention and Production

As a speaker intends to convey a meaning, this covert state prompts vocal expression directly. In the transition from effort grunts to attention and communication grunts, effort grunts are clearly produced in relation to physiological needs. Attention grunts might also have a physiological basis in the beginning because of the high metabolic cost of mental effort associated with attention, but communicative grunts are clearly "voluntary"—that is, expressed by the child on the basis of a meaning more conscious than the need for oxygen. The conscious state motivating communicative grunts is a sense of internal meaning including the desire to convey that meaning to mother. Under these assumption the child does not "choose" a form for any of these expressions. Rather, just as a grunt of effort follows from metabolic demand, an attention grunt will accompany focused attention, and a communicative grunt or word (if available) will mark an internal meaning. As meaning comes to mind, it is inextricably linked with form of expression (Werner & Kaplan, 1963).

By the time of transition to referential words, children have experienced a variety of representational intentional states, as can be seen in their early pretend play (Chapter 6). They are aware of the significance of various objects, such as cups, combs, baby dolls, and toothbrushes. They can operate in space and time, predicting that hidden objects can be found, that objects dropped will fall to the floor. Prior to referential word use, they lack conventional vocal symbols for expressing the specific intentional states they experience. Having achieved a single vocal symbol generalized across intentional states, the communicative grunt, I propose that the child becomes receptive to vocalizations from the ambient language that refer to more specific intentional states; that is, the child becomes receptive to learning words. Evidence for this thesis is (1) the close correspondence in time of referential function for produced and/or comprehended words following communicative grunt use and (2) production similarities between the two vocal forms, to be detailed in the next chapter. With respect to the second point, increased motor unit activity in the laryngeal muscles is observed immediately before vocalization (Buchtal & Faaborg-Anderson, 1964; Kirschner, 1987), suggesting that laryngeal activation is the result of the intention to vocalize.

When a child has achieved the capacity for referential language, three principles identified by Bloom (1993) usefully characterize the ensuing development of words: relevance, discrepancy, and elaboration (p. 15). She notes that a child's internal mental state is by definition meaningful in a way that is relevant to the child's current circumstances and attention. At the same time, the exact meaning a child is experiencing is likely to be at least partially discrepant from the immediate context. For example, a child who notices that a ball has rolled under the couch and considers its disappearance has in mind both the current absence of the ball and its prior presence, a consciousness extending beyond current perception into the recent past. A mother who says "*Allgone ball!*" may be offering a linguistic elaboration of the child's internal state. If the ball bounces against a leg of the couch and emerges, and mother says, "*Here's the ball again!*" as the child watches, she offers differentiated vocal signals that may match different elaborations of meaning experienced by the child. These maternal vocalizations offer opportunities for learning single words such as *gone, ball,* or *again.* This example is reminiscent of the words accompanying the three phases of the hiding game described by Bruner (1975) and discussed in Chapter 3.

Conclusion

In earlier chapters we considered the process of language development as emergent within a supportive emotional context. Children's activities during the first 1½ years of life lead them to understand the basics of how their physical and social worlds work. Cognitive development in the context of relationship brings about the capacity for mental representation. During this same period they vocalize, tuning the articulatory organs to production of the sounds of their language. Their own interest in phenomena in the world prompt communicative gestures aimed at engaging their caregivers. In the context of these varied developments, the metabolic physiology common to mammals takes on a special significance as children become aware of their effortful activities and attendant mental states. The link between vocalization and meaning can then unlock the door to ever expanding communication and language opportunities.

9

Dynamic Systems in Language Development and Language Production

The transition into language comes about through children's active participation in an environment of supportive interpersonal and linguistic resources. This involves self-organization of the child's system drawing on neurological and behavioral abilities, some unique to humans, that virtually guarantee the acquisition of at least one language across the broad variety of social environments experienced by children (MacWhinney, 1998). Even in the face of brain damage (Bates et al., 1994; Bates, 1999) or parental abuse and neglect (Culp et al., 1991), nearly all children are making good progress in developing a language by their third birthdays.

Earlier chapters addressed a number of critical variables developing in the first 2 years of life that can, together, predict the onset of referential language in human infants. While each individual variable has its specific effects, rather than acting independently with transitions across domains in a fixed order, these variables interact in a dynamic system, influencing one another developmentally and predicting the referential transition only when all have attained their critical level (cf. Thelen, 1993). That is, a given level for each of these variables defines a necessary (but not independently sufficient) influence on the developmental shift to linguistic reference. Following Thelen (1989; Thelen & Smith, 1994) I use the term *dynamic variables,* recognizing that each of the measured variables is the product of contributing systems at many levels.

Dynamic systems theory has more commonly been applied to the expression of motor behavior (e.g., Thelen, 1981; Thelen, Schoner, & Smith, 2001), primarily gross motor behavior but also language (e.g., Iverson & Thelen, 1999; Thall, 2003; Thelen, 1991). Thelen and Smith (1994) present dynamic systems theory as an approach to the development of embodied cognition (Johnson, 1987). More recently, Gershkoff-Stowe (2005) suggested that children's conceptual development can best be understood within this framework. Dynamic systems theory is applicable to individual language productions as well as to developmental change. In fact, it is the many individual real-time behaviors that, integrated with underlying skills and environmental supports, bring about the phase shift from prelanguage to referential words observed over the developmental time frame.

In the following sections, I (1) provide background on the dynamic systems approach to development; (2) describe the trajectory of development for 10 children studied longitudinally, demonstrating the influence of the dynamic variables under consideration; and finally (3) consider the dynamics of the child's productions in real time.

Dynamic Systems and Development: Background

The dynamic systems approach addresses problems involving complex organism–environment interactions. For example, for many years the waning of the infant stepping reflex was attributed to growing influence of the central nervous system (CNS); the relationship of early reflex stepping to later voluntary steps was unknown. In a series of studies of organic and contextual determinants of these developments, Thelen and Fisher (1982, 1983) demonstrated that, although the stepping reflex ceased to be observed when the infant was held erect, infant kicks in the supine position maintained the movement properties exhibited in reflex steps. Furthermore, stepping could be "reinstated" by immersing the infant's legs in water, thus reducing the weight load on underdeveloped muscles. Detailed study of independent locomotion at 1 year indicated that the leg movements matched those of early reflex steps and supine kicks. As a result of this work, the stepping reflex is now thought to wane because of (1) possible CNS changes; (2) infant physical maturation and growth in the first 2 months, leading to rapid deposit of fat in relation to the slower development of leg musculature; and (3) the differential effects of gravity on an organism with heavier limbs (which can be compensated for by immersion of the infant's legs in water).

Reflex steps and later independent upright locomotion may rely on preferential functional linkages among muscle groups (*coordinative structures*) (Thelen, Kelso, & Fogel, 1987, p 44). Such structures would allow integrated reaction to task demands without discrete commands to individual muscles or hierarchical CNS coordination. Additional systems that contribute to walking in the 1-year-old include muscular strength, balance, the ability to shift weight to the lead foot, and psychological readiness. Prior to independent walking, infants who are becoming motivated to walk accept help from adults and from objects to compensate for strength and balance limitations as they cruise among chairs and tables. This environmental support is no doubt an influential contributor to the differential timing of upright locomotion across individual children. It can be inferred from this example that, in dynamic systems theory, behavioral and developmental outcomes depend upon the cooperative interaction of many subsystems in the organism and/ or the environment. Dynamic stability is maintained, as the organism tends to exhibit one phase of organism-appropriate behavior until some instability, perhaps fueled by underlying developments or changes in environmental contingencies, potentiates another. These preferred phases, termed *attractor states* (Abraham & Shaw, 1982; Thelen & Smith, 1994), derive from the nature of the organism in the context in which it develops. With respect to locomotion, infants typically enjoy a stable period of creeping on all fours until the attraction of the upright posture combined with the ability to view distant goals motivates them to move while remaining upright.

With respect to speech and language, a phase of canonical babbling is potentiated by vocal tract characteristics, active oral motor experience, and, perhaps a coordinative structure for jaw open/close sequences that is influential across languages (Chen & Kent, 2005; Davis & MacNeilage, 1990, 1995). The period of rhythmic babbling occurs in the same time frame as various additional rhythmicities, such as manual banging (Thelen, 1981), suggesting that this phenomenon is related to general developmental change in motor control. The infant's own sounds and the sounds of others are contextual contributors to this process. Verbal language, as the social coin of the human community, is an attractor that is strongly influenced by context. The major question for this chapter is: "What changes motivate the infant's shift from a phase of babbling and prelinguistic communication to a phase of referential lexical acquisition?" In previous chapters, individual variables have been implicated in aspects of the transition. Here we consider the system as a whole.

Development may be continuous, as demonstrated by the common characteristics of babbling and speech (Vihman & Miller, 1988), yet exhibit *discontinuous phase shifts* leading to qualitatively different modes of functioning, which may be recognized as stages. This process is analogous to the tendency of physical systems toward certain forms of dynamic equilibrium. Data concerning human development have been similarly characterized using the concept of canalization (e.g., McCall, 1981; Sameroff, 1983; Waddington, 1966). While various subsystems may appear divergent, self-righting influences tend toward appropriate developmental outcomes (e.g., genetic unfolding within the typical environment; shifts in environmental support). The dynamic systems approach is particularly apt for describing language acquisition, a development characterized by strong individual differences in the early phase followed by greatly reduced variability within mature language groups. A sample of 10 children learning the same language, each observed at 16 months of age, may appear highly divergent in their approaches to language. By 24 months, many of them can be characterized by a similar pattern of typical linguistic performance. By 36 months, variability is further reduced, with only later talkers who may possibly be clinically affected showing obvious divergence from the dominant pattern (Thall, 2003).

Linguistic reference as a dominant mode of communicative behavior can be considered an attractor state or phase that occurs following a prior phase of prelinguistic communication and noncommunicative babbling. Individual children show differences both in the timing of development shifts and in the particular variables that appear most influential in holding back their development or launching it forward. Thelen (1989) saw the last of the contributing variables to reach its critical value prior to a phase shift as the *rate-limiting vari-*

able or *control parameter* for a given transition in the sense that, given readiness in other subsystems, a new phase may emerge only when that component or those components reach a critical value. While all of the variables discussed in the preceding chapters are equally important for the phase shift to referential language (and hence could be considered as control parameters for that shift), for each child one or more of these variables was identified as the control parameter whose attainment allowed the phase shift to occur for that child; prior to that transition, therefore, it was the rate-limiting factor.

For example, a child with a developmental disability might develop the vocal capacity for speech by 1 year but not develop appropriate mental representation for language until age 2, at which point language, in theory, becomes evident. In this case, development of mental representation is the rate-limiting control parameter. A child with a production lag caused by tracheotomy might exhibit representational play for many months before vocal development permitted a productive vocabulary. Here vocal capacity acts as the rate-limiting control parameter. In each case the shift from a less mature to a more mature (prelanguage to language) phase is initiated when the status of contributing variables leads to instability. That is, variability in the child's behavior should be evident as the newly available system is integrated. While the same variables contribute to the shift, control parameters immediate to the transition to referential language differ across individuals even when no identified condition limits a child's development, as we report later on.

Dynamic Systems in Language Development

The relationship with a caring adult provides the critical context for success in these infant developments. The abilities identified as contributing to language acquisition (described in some detail in earlier chapters) are (1) mental representation (the capacity for internal representation of meanings and sound patterns), which can be observed in certain levels of *object permanence* and *representational play;* (2) phonetic skill sufficient to produce consistent and differentiated vocalizations (*vocal motor schemes*) as well as to allow laryngeal activation in the service of language production; (3) recognition of sound/meaning correspondence, exemplified prelinguistically in communicative use of a consistent vocal form to solicit adult attention to the infant's focus (*communicative grunt*), which may also serve as the criterion for an additional needed skill, namely (4) the capacity for preverbal gestural and/or vocal communication with a social partner. Once all of these variables reach threshold levels, referential language production should commence. Details regarding development of the first three variables were provided in several reports reviewed in earlier chapters (McCune, 1992; McCune, 1995; McCune et al., 1996; McCune & Vihman, 2001; Vihman & McCune, 1994). Moreover, gestural communication precedes communicative grunts in the data reviewed here, and may independently facilitate the transition to referential language (Iverson & Thelen, 1999; McNeill, 2000). It is of particular interest that pointing, like grunt vocalization, shifts function from marking focused attention (point for self) to soliciting interaction. However, gesture use does not appear as the rate-limiting factor for any participants in this report. Only detailed study of children learning signed languages will demonstrate the importance of the parameters described here for the transition to reference in nonvocal modalities.

Referential word production or comprehension involves conscious simultaneous attention to the social, acoustic, and semantic aspects of ongoing events. Given such a conscious state, the infant will recognize meaningful vocalizations in context as integrated aspects of the social situation. Either at the same time and/or later, when reminded of the original situation, he will produce words related in form and meaning to the words spoken by the adult, but these word productions will be shaped by the parameters of his own unique phonetic organization and internal meaning state.

A general story of the transition might read as follows. The child gradually experiences the self in relation to social beings external to the self. Mental representation emerges as distinct from perceptual experience (object permanence, representational play). During this transition the child takes note of objects in the world, examining them manually and visually, and communicative gestures emerge. Phonetic skill develops through babbling and experiencing acoustic and proprioceptive aspects of the infants' own and others' vocalizations. Experience of laryngeal vocalizations (grunts) accompanying consistent psychological experiences of meaning leads to experiences of mental integration of such meaningful states with the autonomically accompanying grunt vocalization. The communicative grunt, derived from physiological experience, emerges as the child's initial personal symbol. Unlike word meanings, the meaning of this personal symbol varies with the child's conscious state at the time of each communicative grunt production. A capacity for conscious mental representation comes to support the construction of specifically meaningful delimited symbol-referent relations (words) as these are exposed in the ambient language and correlatively constructed by the child. Prior image-schematic experiences of meaning (Johnson, 1987; Mandler, 2004) contribute to this process. The integration of these developmental processes yields the capacity for the intentional acts of denotative reference (Werner & Kaplan, 1963) by which the child comes to acquire referential words accepted as part of the linguistic system of the community. The role of earlier context-limited words and imitated words in facilitating this process is not yet known.

A second transition, that to word combinations, may also be predicted, relying on further development related to the variables listed above and perhaps additional variables: (1) advanced mental representation indicated by the capacity for hierarchically organized representational play (McCune,

1995; Chapter 6 of this volume); (2) differentiated phonetic skill indicated by one or more phonetic templates applied across a variety of lexical items (e.g., Chapter 7 of this volume; McCune & Vihman, 1987; Vihman & Croft, 2007; Macken, 1995; Waterson, 1971; Matthei, 1989); (3) recognition of differentiated expressions of meaning as possible for the same event (Veneziano, 1999) (e.g., potentially referencing either the entity or relational aspect); and (4) a repertoire of referential words encoding both entity and dynamic event meanings (e.g., Barrett, 1995). The developmental timing of children's access to and reliance on syntactic sequencing and morphological "rules" is controversial. However, it seems clear that the earliest combinations do not demonstrate such general rules (Herr-Israel & McCune, 2006; Tomasello, 1992, 2003). Data regarding linguistic and nonlinguistic variables influencing the transition to sentences remain scattered across numerous studies often based on conflicting theoretical paradigms. Among interesting ideas is that of Smiley and Huttenlocher (1995) that a child's sense of self may be a prerequisite to verb use (Chapter 5 of this volume). The attempt to construct a dynamic systems model for the shift to multiword combinations would be premature.

Control Parameters and the Shift to Referential Language

In this section we will evaluate the contributions of the dynamic variables as these emerged for the 10 children of the Rutgers sample, described in Chapter 3. Rather than emerging in a fixed linear sequence, these developments vary in order of accomplishment, although some may be prerequisite to others and thus exhibit a consistent order of emergence. These behavioral skills are mutually influential; therefore varying orders of development may affect aspects of children's language at the transition.

All of these children enjoyed harmonious relationships with their mothers, who were their primary caregivers. In an analysis of their interaction patterns, we found variation, but there was consistent responsiveness across all mothers (McCune, DiPane, Fireoved, & Fleck, 1994), and all mothers provided good models of the English language. Consequently the children experienced the appropriate environmental background context for the development of their first language.

The 10 children varied widely in timing of the transition to reference and in the sequences of development of contributing variables, as can be seen in Figure 9–1. Of these children, 2, Alice and Aurie, were in the early referential group (transition at 13 to 14 months, as described in Chapter 7); 5 were in the later referential group (Rick, Rala, Jase, Kari, and Ronny: transition at 15 to 16 months); and 3 (Nenni, Danny, and Vido) were in the prereferential group, indicating that the last 3 did not make the referential transition in language production by 16 months of age.

	Name	9	10	11	12	13	14	15	16	Referential Words
Early Referential	Alice	I, P, PP	OP V[1], CW			G	**W**			27
Early Referential	Aurie	I			OP, P	PP G	V, **W**			12
Early Referential	Rick		I, OP CW			P V	G	PP **W**		11
Later Referential	Rala			Missing	OP, P V		Missing	PP G, **W**		8
Later Referential	Jase				I, P	OP V, G		PP **W**		5
Later Referential	Kari	OP	I, P (V[1])		PP	G			**W**[2]	2
Later Referential	Ronny		OP	I, P CW	PP		V[1]		G, **W**[2]	2
Prereferential	Nenni	I, OP		CW	P	PP	G	**(W)**		1
Prereferential	Danny	OP		I		P			G, **(W)**	0
Prereferential	Vido		OP		I	CW	P		PP G, **(W)**	0

Figure 9–1 Timing of dynamic variables in relation to reverential word onset and total referential words produced across sessions. This figure displays the sequence of emergence of the dynamic variables hypothesized to account for the transition to referential language for each child. For clarity, nonvocal variables are displayed in the upper portion of the row for each child. For children with all dynamic skills in place, referential words begin within 1 month. The rate limiting control parameter(s) were identified for each child as the last dynamic variable to reach criterion either before or at the same time as referential word production and/or comprehension. Examination of the figure demonstrates that VMS, use of communicative grunt, and pretend combinations were rate limiting control parameters for one or more children.

[1]In these individual analyses, VMS was examined more clinically than in McCune and Vihman (2001), where group comparison demanded strict application of criteria. Here Alice is credited with VMS at 10 months on the basis of frequent use of a palatal gesture that continued throughout the study and contributed to word learning. Ronny and Kari marginally met both VMS and referential word criteria but are more accurately considered as "in transition" at the 16=month data point. For purposes of this discussion, Ronny was credited with 2 VMS based on inclusion of [k/g] (mean frequency 10.3 from 14 to 16 months, rather than a strict frequency of 10 at each month, as exhibited by [t/d] produced continually from 11 months). Kari was credited with 2 VMS in Chapter 7 but exhibited VMS for [t/d] and [s] only from 11 to 14 months. She then reduced consonant production and vocalization rate at 15 and 16 months and did not meet VMS criteria in those months, suggesting that she was not phonetically prepared for referential language production.

[2]Kari produced no entity words and Ronnie produced no dynamic event words, additional evidence of the marginal nature of their transition.

Because 5 of the 10 children made up the sample for the study of gestures and grunts described in Chapter 8, more complete information was available for their vocal behavior than for the others, we begin with the early talkers from that study. The two children in the Rutgers sample who made the referential transition earliest, Alice and Aurie, offer a useful comparative example of how this dynamic system might work. All 10 Rutgers participants were followed across the second year and through their referential transition.

Early Referential Children

By the time of our first observation at 9 months, Alice was showing good babbling ability using a variety of consonants. She had established a vocal motor scheme (VMS; defined in Chapter 7) for [p/b] at 9 months and produced [j] at VMS level at 10 months. Although Alice did not meet the VMS criteria of two supraglottal consonants until 14 months, her use of [j] in palatal articulation of complex word targets demonstrated that this gesture was a functional contributor to her phonetic repertoire for speech, equivalent to a VMS. (Other children exhibiting frequent [j] did not tend to incorporate this segment or gesture into their early words.) At 9 months Alice was already using gesture and vocalization to attract her mother to interesting objects and events and showed onset of mental representation with both single acts and pretend play combinations in interaction with her mother. She also produced a few context-limited words. Without careful analyses of these skills, the early sessions did not appear remarkable, yet these are somewhat precocious accomplishments. Each was a minimal representative of its type, but all could be discerned with careful coding, and their continued occurrence in subsequent sessions bolstered our confidence in the original observations. At 13 months, Alice began communicative grunts; at 14 months, she produced referential words. The timing of communicative grunt onset immediately before referential language identifies this as the rate-limiting control parameter for her transition to referential words.

Aurie, in contrast, showed a few gestures soliciting interaction at her 9-month observation but none of the other hypothesized variables. At 12 months she was credited with stage 6 object permanence and pretend play, followed by pretend combinations and communicative grunts at 13 months, when her interactive gestures also increased in freqency. At 14 months, she met phonetic VMS criteria and shifted to referential language. VMS was the last variable observed in the transition to referential words, functioning as a rate-limiting control parameter. Aurie's transition exemplifies the mutual dependency of these variables, as a 2-month span (12 to 14 months) encompassed the onset of all skills included in this dynamic systems model.

Alice's early and flourishing vocal skill continued to influence her development. By 16 months, she had produced 32 different referential words (compared with Aurie's 12); by 24 months, she had produced 1,141 different multiword utterances in video sessions and showed a mean length of utterance

(MLU) of 3.59 (Aurie: 240 different multiword utterances; MLU = 2.17). By 16 months, Alice's words gave evidence of a vocalization template, a complex vocal motor pattern in which a child adapts the phonetics of words such that they more easily suit the particular child's vocal skill. The central feature of this vocal pattern for Alice, raising the tongue to the palate, was constant across the 7 months of observation.

For Rick, another early talker, communicative gestures first occurred at 10 months, but additional skills, VMS and representational play, first appeared 3 months later (at 13 months). Communicative grunt use (rate-limiting control parameter) emerged at 14 months, along with referential words in that same month. At 16 months, he had produced 8 different referential words, and at 24 months, he had produced 276 different multiword utterances (MLU = 2.20). Rick's and Aurie's later development of representational play provides an interesting contrast with Alice. While Alice exhibited the earlier levels of play by 9 months and level 5 hierarchical play at 15 months, Aurie and Rick did not begin this highest level until 19 and 21 months, respectively. To the extent that this variable indexes the capacity for mental representation, or more advanced internal mental processing, Rick and Aurie had less advanced development in this cognitive area during the early months of language acquisition than did Alice.

Alice experienced optimal development across all areas and the most advanced language at 24 months. Her vocal skill began establishment early, as did mental representation; by 16 months, she was already producing words reflecting a phonetic template. The joint availability of vocal and representational capacity facilitated development of this individualized production pattern. When hierarchical mental representational ability began at 15 months, Alice's vocal skill and lexical production had grown substantially, offering a system primed to utilize the new hierarchical representational ability to address production of increasingly complex multiword utterances: hence her extraordinarily large repertoire and high MLU at 24 months. Aurie and Rick were slower to develop mental representation than Alice, perhaps limiting their ability to integrate elements of the vocal repertoire with meaning for differentiated lexical production.

Prereferential Children

In contrast with those children, Nenni and Danny began referential language production substantially later (at 19 and 27 months, respectively). They exhibited communicative ability first in gesture (9 and 11 months, respectively) and then representational play (at 12 and 13 months). Thereafter came communicative grunts (14 and 16 months) and referential language comprehension (15 and 16 months). Thus, in both cases, sound/meaning correspondence demonstrated in communicative grunt use served as a rate-limiting control parameter for the achievement of *referential word comprehension*. Neither child showed VMS ability by 16 months, making this a rate-limiting control parameter for referential word *production* in these cases. Phonetic analyses from later sessions are not available, but when referential words began, appropriate speech sound production was evident. All critical variables other then VMS were in place by 16 months. Thelen (1989) reflected on this possible outcome, suggesting:

> Although, for example, the onset of verbal language appears to reflect a major cognitive reorganization, it is at least an open possibility that what in fact delimits the appearance of words is articulatory control over the vocal apparatus. (p. 93)

The absence of both referential language production and VMS at 16 months and the emergence of referential language later, where informal observation demonstrated appropriate vocal ability, suggest that phonetic ability limited these children in referential word production, although phonetic advance was not obvious (and was not the subject of formal investigation) prior to appropriate phonetic production of words. Further research is needed regarding details of phonetic development in later talkers.

Nenni achieved hierarchical representation in play at 22 months, and her MLU at 24 months (her first session including combinations, total: 27 types) was estimated at 1.24 based on 145 utterances. Danny produced few consonants through 24 months of age. He showed symbolic combinations in play at 18 months and initial hierarchical pretend play at 25 months. He began both referential words and combinations between 27 and 31 months of age. By 36 months, all of the children were producing language appropriate to their age.

Use of gesture by Danny and Nenni was comparable to that of the other children by 16 months, and Nenni showed a gestural communication preference in 6 of the 8 months analyzed in Chapter 8. It seems possible that these children would have benefited from enhanced gestural input (Abrahamsen, 2000). In fact, since their gestural development was not studied beyond 16 months, it is possible that more advanced communication occurred in that mode. We return to these five later to discuss the interaction of word and grunt forms.

Vido, the other Rutgers participant in the prereferential group, was credited only with context-limited words at 16 months and produced only [t/d] at VMS level. He produced communicative grunts and combinatorial play in that month, and more than 30% of his words were imitations. He reached referential comprehension by gestural evidence at 16 months. His referential transition in production occurred over the period of 17 to 19 months as his vocal repertoire grew and he reduced reliance on imitation.

Later Referential Children

The other children who made the transition to referential production also show patterns of development compatible with a dynamic systems analysis.

They demonstrated rate-limiting control parameters as follows: Rala first object permanence, pretend play, and VMS all at 12 months, with communicative grunts (rate-limiting) and referential words first observed at 15 months. (Data were not collected at 14 months and gesture data are not available for Rala.) Jase showed pretend onset and interactive gestures at 12 months; object permanence, VMS, and communicative grunts at 13 months; pretend combinations (rate-limiting control parameter) and referential words at 15 months.

The referential transition implies a qualitatively different use of language in contrast with the preceding phase of prelinguistic communication. This may not be an abrupt transition. Two participants included in the later referential group in Chapter 7, Kari and Ronnie, performed marginally for both VMS (a predictor variable) and referential word onset (outcome variable) at 16 months. Detailed examination of their data suggests that they were still in transition at that time. Although all predictive variables were in place by definition at 13 months, Kari exhibited VMS for [t/d] and [s] only from 11 to 14 months. She then reduced consonant production and vocalization rate at 15 and 16 months, using communicative grunts and gestures instead of words until 16 months, when she applied glottal articulation to produce two words *up* and *uh oh*, neither of which used her previous VMS consonants. In the following months her word production remained low, while she often communicated with tuneful phrases including her earlier VMS, [s].

In contrast, Ronny produced only [t/d] at VMS level, with marginally frequent use of [k/g] (mean frequency 10.3 from 14 to 16 months). His two referential words [*baby*] and [*football*], utilized neither consonant sound. He used no dynamic event words at 16 months, but by 18 months his productivity had increased and his repertoire included dynamic-event words. Depending how marginal performances are counted, his rate-limiting control parameter is communicative grunt (16 months, when referential words were attained marginally) or VMS (later than 16 months). Neither of these children seems to have consolidated the referential transition by 16 months.

In summary, all hypothesized skills were in place for children who made the transition to reference, but this was not a lockstep process. Analysis of the sequences of emergence within and across variables provides a deeper view of underlying developmental processes.

Mental Representation and the Other Dynamic Variables

The role of mental representation in the transition to reference is of critical importance. Consider the order of emergence of stage 6 of object permanence and the representational play levels in relation to the vocalization variables and gestural communication. Both stage 6 object permanence and pretend onset were observed either before or in the same session as VMS and communicative grunts. Regarding VMS, consistency in vocal production, even aside from meaning, may rely on early mental representation. Canonical babbling was observed before children met VMS criteria (McCune & Vihman, 2001), while the consistency of VMS production occurred later, never preceding stage 6 object permanence and pretend onset. Lalonde and Werker (1995) found that 9-month-olds who showed adult-like processing of nonnative consonant contrasts also passed a stage 5 object permanence task. Phonological perception and production skills may be influenced by development of underlying cognitive processes. The articulatory filter proposed by Vihman (e.g., 1992, 1996) may utilize processes underlying mental representation to recognize and attend to adult words accessible to the child's particular phonetic abilities. Similarly, communicative grunts, although derived from an autonomic vocalization, use a vocal signal to "represent" an internal meaning and were observed only after representational play onset. Interactive gestures were first observed close in time to stage 6 object permanence and pretend onset for 8 of 9 children. Only Aurie produced a few such gestures earlier, between 9 and 12 months, but it was not until 13 months, when stage 6 and pretend play were established that she used gestures regularly to engage her mother.

Stage 6 of object permanence preceded or co-occurred with context-limited words for all 10 children, for 8 within 2 months. Pretend onset not only preceded referential words but developed closer in time to context-limited words than to referential words. The closest mental representation transition to referential words, rather than pretend onset, was that to play combinations, level 4.

My original prediction (McCune-Nicolich, 1981), based on the surface equivalence of "single" elements, was that the level of mental representation required for single pretend acts also formed the representational basis for single words. However, Werner and Kaplan (1963), in their diagram of relationships among components in the communicative situation, depict a reciprocal link between object/event and word (symbolic vehicle), suggesting a combinatorial relationship between the symbolic vehicle and meaning even at the single-word level (depicted by two concentric circles at opposite sides of Figure 2–2). I had not considered the nature of words as referential or context-limited in my 1981 hypotheses. Both Werner and Kaplan (1963) and Piaget (1962) considered these sorts of words as verbal schemes, intermediary between sensorimotor schemes and conceptual schemes. Each context-limited word "participates" with the event rather than referring to the object or event.

In McCune (1995), I formally evaluated the level 2/3 (single pretend) relationship with single words, recognizing the sometimes extensive delays between attainment of play and language milestones. When the distinction between context-limited and referential words is made, it becomes evident that single pretend acts occur early, for many children prior even to context-limited words, VMS, and communicative grunts. It seems the onset of pretend may be linked to initiating the process of transition to referential language rather than occurring at the culmination of this transition. And it seems that combinatorial mental representation, rather than onset of single pretend acts, tends to occur close to the shift to linguistic reference. This level may be more relevant as a control parameter for single referential words, predicting their development more closely than single pretend acts. Glick (1992) emphasizes Werner's view of the importance of discriminating behaviors that appear similar yet are not developmentally equivalent. This may be the case with context-limited versus referential words.

Considering the underlying cognitive basis of single pretend acts (levels 2 and 3; Figure 6–1), there is substantial overlap between the motor behavior and its meaning. Pretending to drink or give someone a drink requires grasping a vessel and moving the arm toward a target (one's own or another's mouth) and possibly vocalizing a sound characteristic of drinking. The embodied sense of the real and pretend acts is certainly similar. In contrast, play combinations additionally require immediate reorganization of the motor system to enact a second movement related to the first act, either through the meaning of the act itself (e.g., feed self, feed mother) or through a unifying theme (e.g., scrape plate to load spoon, feed doll). This motor reorganization demonstrates some independence of meaning from its motor expression even within a given context. Similarly, a single referential word by its potential for varied use across situations is qualitatively distinct from the varying contexts in which it is used. Use of more than one different referential word in a session (my criterion for the transition) requires different underlying vocal motor organization for each word. Organization for meaning and for production consitute two integrated components. By this analysis a single referential word would have underlying structure analogous to a play combination, but organized simultaneously rather than sequentially. This contrast is diagramed in Figure 9–2.

Mills, Conboy, and Paton (2005) analyzed event-related potential (ERP) responses to situations where known words were presented with matched versus mismatched pictures. They predicted that the emergence of the "N400" ERP response, known to index mismatch of meaning in older children and adults, might be linked to the "representational status of early words" in the period when children are gaining referential ability (p. 129). (N400 refers to a negative point in the ERP value occurring 400 milliseconds after a stimulus is presented.) They report that when 13- and 20-month-olds, 3-year-olds, and adults were presented with known words that either matched or did not match an accompanying picture, the N400 was universally observed at all ages. In a follow-up with 13- and 20-month-olds, they compared a condition where the picture remained to be observed while the word was presented with a condition where the picture was presented, then removed before the word was presented. In the latter case, where the children needed to keep the picture in mind in order to experience the mismatch with the word, only 20-month-olds showed the N400 while 13-month-olds did not. Where the picture remained available, both groups showed the N400. The

Context Limited Words

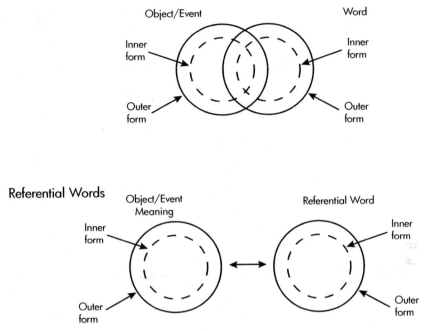

Referential Words

Referential word - equivalent to level 4 Play

Figure 9–2. Diagram of the symbolic basis of context-limited versus referential words. Context-limited words are only partially differentiated from the events where they occur and can be diagrammed in the same way as single pretend acts (levels 2 and 3 in Figure 6–1). Referential words show greater differentiation between symbolic vehicle (word) and the object/event to which it refers and are better described by the diagram for Level 4.1 in Figure 6–1 here and in Figure 2–2 from Werner and Kaplan (1963).

authors attribute this difference to "working memory." Interestingly, the two ages tested span the period between the beginning of pretend activity and the transition between levels 4 and 5, the culmination of representational play, suggesting that children's differential development of mental representation might be an influence. These group data are noted as preliminary. It would be interesting to examine individual or group data where children's representational status in play was also evaluated.

Production of Context-Limited and Referential Words in Real Time

The same variables contributing to the shift into referential language are proposed as affecting individual productions of communicative vocalizations in real time. Every production of a word draws on the underlying capacities that a child has attained, but the performance itself is "softly assembled" (Gershkoff-Stowe & Thelen, 2004, p.16). The particular word a child says as well as its exact phonetic shape is dependent upon the moment-to-moment status of aspects of both the child and the environment. For example, if a child encounters a Ping-Pong ball among the toys in our set and it is sitting near a toy pot, the child may say *egg* rather than *ball* (as one of our children did). Analogously, vocal form as well as lexical choice can be influenced by words a child has recently heard or said. The specific phonetic shape of a production can also show effects of surrounding productions by the child, as demonstrated by the synergies we found between word and communicative grunt forms detailed below.

The VMS measure is an index of vocal motor control for speech. How might this motor ability interact with the other identified skills (representational ability, recognition of sound/meaning correspondence) at the transition to speech to "explain" babies' abilities to produce typical early words?

The simplest early words involve one or two CV syllables, where the child's several productions of a given word may vary in phonetic shape. These productions involve management of motor components in relation to the intention to say "X." Dynamic systems theory suggests placing a minimum of motor information in that intention. Rather, we are free to consider potential coordinative structures unifying the movement variables as largely "explanatory" of the apparently organized character of the phonetic realizations.

Suppose the intention to say "X" arises as a meaning springs to mind in a manner analogous to the recurrence of foot kicks to a mobile in the setting where the behavior was learned (Rovee-Collier, 1995). If training involves a single mobile, only that mobile will elicit foot kicks on a subsequent visit. However, if multiple mobiles are used across 3 days of training, on the fourth day the infant will kick robustly in response to a fourth novel mobile. The single-mobile training and learning is analogous to acquisition of context-limited words.

Vihman's (1996) articulatory filter refers to children's enhanced attention to sounds in the ambient language that match their production capability. Context-dependent early words may utilize early VMS vocal patterns as part of a frequently occurring situation (analogous to the same mobile used repeatedly). At 9 months, Vihman's Timmy produced [b] initial one-syllable words in response to "What's this?" if the object was a block, a ball, or a box (Vihman et al, 1994). Asked to name a key, he was interested but silent. This behavior may reflect his previous experience of seeing [b] objects while he and/or his mother produced [b] vocalizations. It may be that such parent–child interaction constitutes "training" of context-limited words (cf. Chapter 3) before the children are capable of linguistic reference.

Context-limited words could then be learned as the baby's babbling resources are shaped to match an adult vocalization repeatedly heard in the same situation. Without the resources contributing to the referential transition, words heard incidentally across a variety of situations would not be learned, while those emphasized in recurring situations would. The difference between the Rutgers and Stanford samples described in Chapter 3 exemplifies this. Children in the Stanford Sample, who were visited weekly and whose mothers were encouraged to expose their children's words in the sessions, showed greater frequency of context-limited and imitated words than those in the Rutgers sample, visited monthly, where mothers were not instructed regarding child language. Referential word frequency was the same across the two samples.

Two lines of research are of interest in this regard. First, Rovee-Collier (1995) implicates the distribution of training experiences over time, based on the "time window" for remembering a trained response at a given age. With repeated trials occurring within the time window, the response will continue even when not reinforced. Parents who encourage specific vocalizations in given contexts take advantage of this aspect of learning and memory to keep the context-limited words active. Parents who engage in less of this type of interaction may miss the time window for effectively keeping the link between characteristic vocalization and context active. Second, the likelihood of "primed" words (those said recently) to recur across perceptually similar circumstances (Gershkoff-Stowe et al., 2006) is a further contributor to the longevity of words children practice with their parents. Mothers in the Stanford sample brought familiar objects into the weekly sessions to encourage the children to display the words they knew, contributing data to the analyses reported in Chapter 3.

When the child has made the referential transition, phonetic and representational resources should allow him or her to benefit from multiple occurrences of words across varied situations, even totally new circumstances and even when adults are not attempting to conduct a language lesson. When situations analogous to those previously accompanied by the word occur, the word may spring to mind in much the same way as an infant begins kicking in response to a novel mobile after training with a variety of novel mobiles. A critical difference between "mobile" and "word" situations is that in the former case a single response (foot kick) is learned and recurs, while in the latter referential words of varied phonetic shape proliferate in response to varied but related meaningful situations. The ability to extend word meanings in this way is dependent on changes in the child's endogenous capacity to process and produce language rather than only on parental behavior. It is interesting to speculate that the greater likelihood of context-limited words evolving to referential status in longitudinal diary studies rather than cross-sectional corpus studies (Chapter 3) may be attributable to diary-keeping parents' substantial interest in child words and their efforts to elicit words, thus keeping them in the repertoire once they occur. When the children became capable of reference, they would tend to extend these words on their own, leading to referential status for the words.

Phonetic variability across productions of the same word reflects variety in the child's motor instantiation of meaning. Edelman's (1987) principle of degeneracy, the idea that exactly the same neurological pattern is unlikely to characterize repeated behavioral actions, would indicate that neurological patterns underlying motor production of a given word would vary from instance to instance. Early word productions may depend upon well-practiced sensorimotor schemes instantiated in relation to the intention to produce a given word. Vihman (1996, pp. 142–145) reports that early context-limited words are more accurate and hence more stable in production form than referential words, suggesting more of an online constructive process for referential words. The referential intention arises based on events that remind the child of a similar prior situation, bringing aspects of that prior event to consciousness in the present. The present perceived situation and the sensorimotor production (VMS-based word) serve to maintain the child's representational consciousness of a meaning to be shared, just as replicating the sounds of eating serves to maintain representational consciousness for meaning expression in pretend play.

From Kent's (1992) description, both lingual movements and shaping of the vocal tract for speech involve necessarily continuous rather than discrete movement, while jaw opening and closure and onset of airflow for phonation are more discrete. It may be that the form of VMS development is influenced by individual maturational trajectories. Earlier differentiation of lingual from jaw movements may potentiate a broader range of VMS consonants and promote the development of a word-production template (Chapter 7). In particular, Alice's early use of [j] required flexible tongue movement in relation to jaw movement, a gesture also characteristic of her template.

The earliest talkers studied by McCune and Vihman (2001) all showed VMS for both [t/d] and [p/b]. Only those children who showed VMS [p/b] made the referential transition by 16 months of age. Davis, MacNeilage, and Matyear (2002) propose that production of labials (e.g., [p/b]) is easier than production of coronals (e.g., [t/d]) because labials require only an open/close gesture of the jaw while coronals may additionally require fronting of the tongue. (Recall also the visual and neurological support suggested for [p/b] in Chapter 7.) Davis and associates found that coronals were more frequent in babbling while labials were more frequent in words and especially frequent in initial position in both monosyllabic and disyllabic words. They refer to specific problems of initiating a motor sequence (e.g., Kornhuber, 1987), such that ease of initial gesture provides a significant advantage. When the complex goal is expressing a meaning by vocalization rather than vocalization per se, as in babbling, this advantage may be critical. In multisyllabic words where consonants varied across syllables Davis and coworkers found that the sequence labial/coronal was significantly more frequent than coronal/labial, suggesting that tongue movement was more likely to occur in the second syllable rather than in the initiating syllable. These observations provide a further rationale for the McCune and Vihman (2001) finding that only those children who showed VMS [p/b] made the transition to referential words by 16 months of age. If preexisting coordinative structures affect early vocalization, the existence of such structures should influence any proposal for the initial production units of infancy.

Any time a human produces a consonant sound, a vowel sound of some sort is necessarily included, making the syllable, rather than the individual segment, the smallest production unit. Vihman (1996) and Davis and MacNeilage (1990, 1995) have proposed likely default production syllabic patterns based on vocal motor constraints. Vihman (1992) found clearest association in a cross-linguistic study of association in "practiced" syllables between both [h] and labial consonants ([m], [p/b]) and neutral vowels. These vowels occur when the tongue rests centrally in the mouth. This was observed for almost every child and was characterized by Vihman (1992) as the "path of least resistance" in motor organization (p. 413). While other vowel-consonant synergies were found, these were either highly language-specific or found only in the repertoires of individual children. Chen and Kent (2005) examined consonant/vowel synergies in 24 Mandarin-learning infants between 7- and 18-months of age. They replicated earlier synergies but found that some were observed only in the early period, some throughout, and some only in the most advanced children. Taken together, these findings suggest that initial production biases are rapidly influenced by both linguistic context and the individual child's vocal experience.

Sensorimotor schemes (including VMS) are inferred to exist on the basis of regularity and systematic variation in behavior. The concept of VMS is compatible with the position of Browman and Goldstein (1989), suggesting that articulatory actions can be considered as specifiable gestures capable of organization into a score. The intention to produce a given word might prompt activation of such a score instantiated by neurological cell assemblies. The specific physiological and neurological basis of VMS or word scores can be addressed theoretically, but not in explicit detail based on current neurological knowledge, as "the underlying mechanisms for neuromuscular control in speech development are unknown" (Chen & Kent, 2005).

Considering Neurological Aspects of Word Knowledge

Once a child has learned to produce words, every such production (and comprehension) involves broad activation of a number of brain areas. Pulvermuller (2002, p. 69) characterizes this underlying neurological activation as a "word web" and assumes that each word learned develops its own unique and stable web of associations among neuronal groups such that, in production, all are activated, while in comprehension a more limited set of brain processes is activated. Although some form of coherence over time in neurological activation related to a given word would be expected, current knowledge does not allow assessment of the extent of stability in activation across word productions. Both Edelman's theoretical notion of degeneracy, or variability across neurological instantiations of a given behavior and the observed variability across phonetic productions of the same word point to some neurological variability. Neurons in the prefrontal, premotor, and primary motor cortices are required for articulation, while acoustic properties of the ambient language input activate the neurons in the superior temporal lobe stimulated by features of speech sounds and word semantics.

Mills and colleagues (2005) provide evidence of differential neurological linguistic activity prior to and following the referential transition. They tested high language producers (more likely to have made the referential transition) in comparison with low language producers (less likely to have made the referential transition) at 17 to 20 months of age, assessed by the MacArthur-Bates Communicative Development Inventory. Both groups of children first listened to familiar and unfamiliar (nonsense) words, while their neurological responses were monitored by electroencephalography (EEG). They then received training on two of the four nonsense words, where each word was paired with an object to establish a sound/meaning link. The words not paired with objects were repeated to provide an equal frequency of exposure but without any link to an object. Results demonstrated that when speech sounds become meaningful by association with objects, they are processed differently by the brain. In particular, high language producers likely to have made the referential transition showed more focused processing, concentrated in the left lateral brain region associated with language processing in adults.

Form/Meaning Synergies

Developmental and real time co-construction of form and meaning as proposed by Werner and Kaplan (1963) means that interaction of form and meaning should be evident in children's productions during the period of single-word development. The influence of phonological templates across word types is one example of this effect. Three additional examples follow. First, glottal activation contributing to both communicative grunts and words leads to interesting interactions across these forms of communication, varying by child. Second, careful longitudinal case studies have demonstrated this gradually differentiation, sometimes encompassing the range of a child's productions, sometimes focusing in more detail on a few forms. Third, individual children have shown phonetic/semantic interaction in dynamic event word production.

Interaction of Grunt and Word Form Production

If communicative grunts convey internal meaning states as words do, it may be that such grunts (in contrast with physiologically based effort grunts) come to share phonetic similarity with children's words. Roug-Hellichius (1998), who replicated the timing relationship between communicative-grunt onset and the beginning of referential words,, included acoustical analyses of communicative and noncommunicative grunt forms in her study of a child learning Swedish. Her analyses of vocal productions from 14 to 19 months of age demonstrated that the onset of communicative grunts was characterized by shifts in fundamental frequency, first-and second-formant frequency, and utterance duration, yielding forms more typical of words than of the physiological effort-grunt form. Communicative grunts in the child studied tended to be longer, to make greater use of front vowels, and to show a rising intonation in comparison with noncommunicative grunts occurring previously as well as those observed in the same sessions as communicative grunts.

In another example of production synergy, the five English-learning children whose grunts and words at the transition to language are reviewed in this volume demonstrated changes in vocal production such that each child's words became similar in form to their grunts (or vice-versa!) during the period when communicative grunts and referential words began. As would be expected in dynamically developing individual systems, variability in vocal behavior was observed at critical transitions and the relationships across vocal forms occurred in different ways for individual children. Alice and Rick are discussed first because both produced context-limited words prior to communicative grunt onset.

Alice

Developmental patterns of glottal and vowel use across words and grunts by Alice offer insight into the relationships among these sorts of vocalizations and suggest a rationale for the increase in glottal production observed across participants as word production was being consolidated (Chapter 7; see also Roug et al., 1989). The most productive of the early talkers, Alice produced context-limited words from her first session at 9 months and at 14 months began referential word use, showing sharp increases in word production frequency across the last 3 months of analysis (14 to 16 months).

Alice's word frequency per session increased from 5 to 23 (context-limited) word tokens between 9 and 11 months with 20% to 30% glottal onset and approximately 50% neutral vowels typical of effort grunts also used in words. At 10 and 11 months, she began to produce front vowels in words (0.33, and 0.51, respectively). Front vowels came to predominate in words throughout the study from 13 months.

A turning point occurred at 12 months, when word tokens were sharply reduced while grunts accompanying effort and attention doubled in frequency. Her small number of words showed high vowel variability in this session (one or two of each segment used), as would be predicted from a dynamic systems view, at a major turning point. Grunts were also sharply differentiated from words relying almost exclusively on the default form, glottal stop and neutral vowel.

Communicative grunts began at 13 months when there was also a sharp and temporary increase in glottal onset for words (0.42; returning to low levels of 0.12 and 0.04 at 14 and 15 months). Vowel use for communicative grunts temporarily varied from the neutral vowels typical of attention and effort grunts (0.42 other vowels), returning to above 0.80 neutral vowels at 14 and 15 months). Her referential word transition was at 14 months. At 16 months Alice produced no effort or attention grunts. Communicative grunts suddenly shifted to resemble words, reflecting a front vowel preference (0.60); of these, 0.28 included the sound [eI], also prominent in words (0.18). Words also shifted to resemble grunts, exhibiting 0.39 glottal articulation. Words seem to increase in proportion of glottal use at turning points in communicative grunt use: at communicative grunt onset, and at the point when communicative grunts began sharing vowel shapes with words. This, along with the use of similar vowels in communicative grunts and words indicates the interaction of the same production tendencies in word and communicative grunt production.

Rick

Rick produced a few word tokens (total 6 to 11) of four different context-limited words prior to the 14-month onset of communicative grunts. Unlike Alice's, Rick's words were not a prominent aspect of his repertoire prior to communicative grunt use. Vowel shapes in effort grunts maintained 70% to 100% use of neutral vowels. For Rick, attention grunts showed more use of nonneutral vowels than for Alice, with a mixture of front and back vowels varying by month.

Communicative grunts began at 14 months (0.33 neutral, 0.08 back vowel, 0.58 front vowel), a month when Rick produced no words. Communicative grunts did not occur at 15 months, his month of transition to referential words. Again, this variability in behavior is characteristic of a dynamic system at transition points. By 16 months both words and communicative grunts emphasized back vowels (0.74 and 0.60, respectively) with the remaining words relying on front vowels and remaining communicative grunts on neutral vowels. Attention grunts at 16 months showed vowel characteristics typical of both communicative grunts and words (0.19 front, 0.29 back, 0.52 neutral). Rick included glottal stop in very few early word productions. After producing no words at 14 months, his first month of communicative grunt use, in the following month 0.30 of his words began with glottal stop, reduced to 0.11 at 16 months. This suggests a temporary influence of grunt form on word form, as with Alice, at communicative grunt onset.

Aurie

Aurie produced no words prior to communicative grunt onset at 13 months, so a preestablished vowel preference for words could not influence the vowels used in communicative grunts. Higher than expected glottal use in words, particularly at 15 months: 0.71 (14 and 16 months 0.28 and 0.26, respectively) may have been influenced by prior and contemporaneous glottal use in grunts. Her effort grunts were distributed across the neutral and front vowel categories, including front vowels to a greater extent than the other children from 9 to 14 months. At 15 and 16 months, effort grunts were distinguished from words by their restriction to neutral vowels, while attention and communicative grunts were more similar to words, showing a high proportion of front vowel use.

Danny

The two additional children for whom both grunt and word data are available were both later talkers, with few words even at 16 months. Danny, who maintained neutral vowels for both effort and attention grunts, began both words and communicative grunts at 16 months. Communicative grunts matched the most prominent vowel sound in words (0.53 and 0.58, respectively), suggesting that the intention to mean included a characteristic oral configuration for vowel production at this point in time. His consonants in words were restricted to [h] and [d].

Nenni

Nenni began communicative grunts at 14 months, having produced very few words in previous months, with no consistent pattern of vowel use. Almost all of her grunts used neutral vowels prior to 14 months, and those that exhibited other vowels from 14 to 16 months tended to be communicative but were too few to be definitive.

Differentiation of Forms

Emergence of several different word forms with more specific meaning from a more globally used expression provides another example of synergistic development expected from a dynamic systems view. Werner and Kaplan (1963) (see Chapter 8) provide several examples from prior literature showing how vocal forms may begin with rather general onomatopoetic reference and gradually become delimited in reference and differentiated in form. Following Lewis (1936) they trace one child's lexical productions beginning at about 12 months, when she used only *mammam* to refer to her sister, bread, cakes, and cooked dishes. At 16 months, she added *deda,* referring to her aunt. By 17 months, *mammam* was extended to include milk. At 19 months, *mammam* was becoming restricted to cooked foods and drinks, and 1 month later, the sister was designated *desi* and the mother as *momi.* At 22 months, the end of the study period, eight distinct words were reported: *tanden* (Tande: aunt), *Mama* (mama: mother) *desi* (Daisy: sister's name), *brodi* (Brod: bread or cakes), *demis* (Gemuse: cooked dishes), *mimi* (Milch: milk), *bi* (Bier: beer and other drinks).
Carter (1975) provides an interesting example in her early case study of the development of the morphemes *more* and *mine* over a period of months

from production of [m] initial vocalizations beginning at 12 ½ to 13 months. Some of these vocalizations would meet criteria for communicative grunts (those consisting in syllabic [m] with no following vowel). The others seem to follow from a vocal motor scheme-like emphasis on the consonant [m] paired with a variety of vowels.

Semantic and Phonetic Interaction in Developing Dynamic-Event Words

Cases where children blend or generalize word meanings across categories demonstrate the process of mutual shaping of meaning and symbolic vehicle (word). Gradually children learning any language(s) shape their words to conform to ambient models in phonetic shape and meaning (McCune & Vihman, 1997).

Auri, for example, used varied but related forms derived from adult *up, out,* and *open* in a range of contexts that, when closely examined, suggested the single overall meaning "unstuck," a salient figure/ground notion expressed by no common conventional English word and thus infrequent in English single-word lexicons but typical of young children learning Korean, *an nawa* [see also Estonian, *lahti,* "free" (from attachment)]. This phonetic variability in form, characteristic of much of single-word speech, suggests the type of form/meaning shaping proposed by Werner and Kaplan. Similarly, at 18 months, Hildegarde Leopold used a word [ʔau], later [ʔaux], mixed in form between German *auf,* English *off,* and German *aus,* and English *out* for a range of meanings including removing clothing (cf. German *ausziehen*) and getting a tin box opened (Leopold, 1939). At 20 months she added English *open* with the same range of meanings, resulting in a semantic grouping much like that reflected by Aurie's "unstuck" usage.

These uses by both children indicate attachment/separation as a common figure/ground meaning and demonstrate the fluid basis for children's use of metaphorical processes (Johnson, 1987) in the development of dynamic-event words. The expression of such words, blended in form and meaning from several words in the linguistic input, draws a relationship between an aspect of the child's internal experience in a given situation and vocalizations previously heard/and or spoken that come to mind in relation to the present experience. A word meaning emerges for the child and develops some phonetic and semantic stability as a result of many such experiences.

Conclusion

In this chapter and in this volume, I have described the coming together of prior skills interacting in a dynamic system at the transition to referential language. Three features of my approach to studying child language were critical to the success of the endeavor. First is the emphasis on longitudinal study with the individual child as a unit of analysis. While the children all utilized similar skills in entering language, both timing and interaction of variables varied across children allowing a rich interpretation of developmental theory. Second, I sought to determine what variables made empirical sense within the theoretical framework I had chosen. Phonetic ability to produce word forms is an obvious component of learning, implicated by Werner and Kaplan (1963) in the shaping of child vocal production to sound/meaning correspondences in the ambient language. The VMS measure emerged on empirical grounds as a useful assessment of individual differences in sound production ability. The fact that the specific consonant sounds identified turned out to be those used in the children's words supported both the usefulness of the measure and the theoretical premise regarding the shaping of words from child phonetic repertoire to adult meanings.

Distinguishing context-limited from referential words was essential to discovering the role of the dynamic variables in the transition as was recognizing the category of dynamic-event words. If all words had been considered equal, the major transition of interest, the transition to referential language, could not have been predicted. In Chapter 3 I reviewed findings regarding the "vocabulary spurt." This phenomenon is defined with great variability across studies yet is being used as a major milestone defining a "stage" of language acquisition. Language acquisition research emphasizes vocabulary milestones, such as parental report of a lexicon of 50 words. Does such a lexicon exist within the child, or is word production a probabilistic function of referential development, phonetic resources and contextual opportunities? The field would be better served by establishing criteria for referential word use as a more direct milestone. Following the referential transition in production children tend to produce words with much greater frequency. This increase in productivity allows appearance of a "spurt" of new words, although change in true rate of development is rarely involved (Ganger & Brent, 2004).

Third, I assumed that all naturalistic child behavior occurring with relative frequency might be important and should be systematically evaluated. This assumption led to the discovery of communicative grunts. While this phenomenon had been mentioned in language literature in the past, it was not recognized as a cornerstone of communicative and lexical development. Individual children's trajectories demonstrated the importance of each variable as well as the fact that, rather than a specified order of entry, there is variability in which skills come first. Finally, the underlying bases of these same skills implicated in the transition to referential language also form the basis for each production of a word, and each production contributes to the continuing spiral of development, supporting the value of a dynamic systems approach to analyzing both development and production of language.

References

Abraham, R. H., & Shaw, C. D. (1982). *Dynamics—The geometry of behavior.* Santa Cruz, CA: Aerial Press.

Abrahamsen, A. (2000). Exploration of enhanced gestural input to children in the bimodal period. In K. Emmorey & H. Lane (Eds.), *The signs of language revisited: An anthology in honor of Ursula Bellogi and Edward Klima* (pp. 357–89). Mahwah, NJ: Erlbaum.

Acredolo, L., & Goodwyn, S. (1988). Symbolic gesturing in normal infants. *Child Development, 59,* 420–29.

Ainsworth, M. D. (1964). Patterns of attachment shown by the infant in interaction with his mother. *Merril Palmer Quarterly, 10,* 51–58.

Ainsworth, M. D. S., Blehar, M. C., Waters, E., & Wall, S. (1978). *Patterns of attachment.* Hillsdale, NJ: Erlbaum.

Akhtar, N., Carpenter, M., & Tomasello, M. (1996?). *Child Development, 69,* 94–104.

Allin, J. T., & Banks, E. M. (1972). Functional aspects of ultrasound production by infant albino rats (*Rattus norvegicus*). *Animal Behaviour, 20,* 175–78.

Baillargeon, R. (1993). The object concept revisited: New directions in the investigation of infants' physical knowledge. In C. E. Granrud (Ed.), *Visual perception and cognition in infancy.* Hillsdale, NJ: Erlbaum.

Baillargeon, R., Spelke, E. S., & Wasserman, S. (1985). Object permanence in five-month-olds. *Cognition, 201,* 191–208.

Baldwin, D. (1991). Infants' contribution to the achievement of joint reference. *Child Development, 62,* 875–90.

Baldwin, D. A., & Markman, E. M. (1989). Establishing word-object relations: A first step. *Child Development, 60,* 381–89.

Barlowe, S. M., & Farley, W. H. (1989). Neurophysiology of speech. In D. P. Kuehn, M. L. Lemme, & J. M. Baumgartner (Eds.), *Neural bases of speech, hearing. and language* (pp. 146–200). Boston: College Hill.

Barrett, M. (1995). Early lexical development. In P. Fletcher & B. MacWhinney (Eds.), *Handbook of child language* (pp. 362–92). Cambridge, MA: Blackwell.

Barsalou, L. W. (1999). Perceptual symbol systems. *The Behavioral and Brain Sciences, 22,* 577–660.

Barsalou, L. W. (2005). Abstraction as dynamic interpretation in perceptual symbol systems. In L. Gershkoff-Stowe & D. Rakison (Eds.), *Building object categories in developmental time* (pp. 389–431). Mahwah, NJ: Erlbaum.

Bartrip, J., Morton, J., & de Schonen, J. (2001). Responses to mother's face in 3-week- to 5-month-old infants. *British Journal of Developmental Psychology, 19,* 219–32.

Bates, E. (1999). Language and the infant brain. *Journal of Communicative Disorders, 32,* 195–205.

Bates, E., Camaioni, L., & Volterra, V. (1975). The acquisition of performatives prior to speech. *Merril Palmer Quarterly, 21,* 205–66.

Bates, E., Camaioni, L., & Volterra, V. (1976). Sensorimotor performatives. In E. Bates (Ed.), *Language and context* (pp. 49–69). New York: Academic Press.

Bates, E., Thal, D., & Janowsky, J. S. (1992). Early Language Development and its neural correlates. *Handbook of Neuropsychology, 7,* 69–110.

Bates, E., Benigni, OL., Bretherton, I., Camaioni, L., & Volterra, V. (Eds.). (1979). *The emergence of symbols: Cognition and communication in infancy.* New York: Wiley.

Bates, E., Thal, D., Trauner, D., Fenson, J., Aram, D., Eisele, J., & Nass, R. (1994). From first words to grammar in children with focal brain injury. *Developmental Neuropsychology,* 2–35.

Bertenthal, B. I. (1977). The importance of task analysis: A re-examination of early rep- resentation. In C. P. Shaver (Ed.), *Sequence and synchrony in cognitive development: A symposium.* San Francisco: American Psychological Association.

Bertenthal, I. (1996). Origins and early development of perception, action, and repre- sentation. *Annual Review of Psychology, 47,* 431–59.

Blake, J., McConnell, S., Horton, G., & Benson, N. (1992). The gestural repertoire and its evolution over the second year. *Early Development and Parenting, 1,* 127–36.

Bleile, K. M., Stark, R. E., & McGowan, J. S. (1993). Speech development in a child after decannulation: Further evidence that babbling facilitates later speech development. *Clinical Linguistics & Phonetics, 7,* 319–37.

Bloom, L. (1970). *Form and function in emerging grammars.* Cambridge, MA: MIT Press.

Bloom, L. (1973). *One word at a time.* The Hague: Mouton.

Bloom, L. (1993). *The transition from infancy to language.* New York: Cambridge Univer- sity Press.

Bloom, L., & Lahey, M. (1978). *Language development and language disorders.* New York: Wiley.

Bloom, L., & Tinker, E. (2001). The Intentionality Model and Language Acquisition. *Monographs of the Society for Research in Child Development, 66,* 4, Serial No. 267.

Bloom, L., Hood, L., & Lightbown, L. (1974). Imitation in language development: If, when, and why. *Cognitive Psychology, 6,* 380–420.

Blumberg, M. S., & Alberts, J. R. (1990). Ultrasonic vocalizations of rat pups in the cold: An acoustic by-product of laryngeal braking? *Behavioral Neuroscience, 104,* 808–17.

Blumberg, M., & Alberts, J. (1991). On the significance of similarities between ultra- sonic vocalizations of infant and adult rats. *Neuroscience & Biobehavioral Reviews, 15,* 383–90.

Bornstein, M., Tal, J., Rahn, C., Galperin, C. Z., Pecheux, M., Lamour, M., Toda, S., Azuma, H., Ogino, M., & Tamis-Lemonda, C. S. (1992). Functional analysis of the contents of maternal speech to infants of 5 and 13 months in four cultures: Argentina, France, Japan, and the United States. *Developmental Psychology, 28,* 593–603.

Bornstein, M. H., Cote, L. R., Linda, R., Maital, S., Painter, K., Park, S., Pascual, L., Pecheux, M., Ruel, J., Venuti, P. and Vyt, A. (2004). Cross-linguistic analysis of vocabulary in young children: Spanish, Dutch, French, Hebrew, Italian, Korean, and American English. *Child Development, 75,* 1–25.

Bowerman, M. (1975). Comment on Structure and strategy in child language.
In L. Bloom & L. Hood (Eds.), *Monographs of the Society for Research in Child
Development, 40,* (2, Serial No. 160).

Bowerman, M. (1978). Systematizing semantic Knowledge: Changes over time in the
child's organization of word meaning. *Child Development, 49,* 977–87.

Bowerman, M. (1989). Learning a semantic system: What role do cognitive predispositions
play? In M. L. Rice & R. L. Schiefelbusch (Eds.), *The teachability of language*
(pp. 133–69). Baltimore: Paul Brooks.

Bowerman, M. (1994). Learning how to structure space for language: A cross-linguistic
perspective. In P. Bloom, M. A. Peterson, L. Nadel, & M. Garrett (Eds.),
Language and space (pp. 385–436). Cambridge, MA: MIT Press.

Bowerman, M., & Choi, S. (2000). Shaping meanings for language: Universal
and language-specific in the acquisition of spatial semantic categories.
In M. Bowerman & S. C. Levinson (Eds.), *Language acquisition and conceptual
development* (pp. 475–511). Cambridge, UK: Cambridge University Press.

Bowlby, J. (1969). *Attachment.* New York: Basic Books.

Boysson-Bardies, B. de, & Vihman, M. M. (1991). Adaptation to language: Evidence
from babbling and first words in four languages. *Language, 67,* 297–319.

Braine, M. (1963). The ontogeny of English phrase structure. *Language, 39,* 1–14.

Braine, M. (1976). *Monographs of the Society for Research in Child Development. Children's
first word combinations, 41.* Chicago: University of Chicago Press.

Braine, M. (1994). Is nativism sufficient? *Journal of Child Language, 21,* 9–32.

Bramble, D. M. (1989). Axial-appendicular dynamics and the integration of breathing
and gait in mammals. *American Zoologist, 29,* 171–86.

Browman, C. P., & Goldstein, L. (1989). Articulatory gestures as phonological units.
Phonology, 6, 201–51.

Bruner, J. S. (1975). The ontogenisis of speech acts. *Journal of Child Language, 1,*
1–19.

Bruner, J. (1981). The social context of language. *Language and Communication, 1,*
155–78.

Bruner, J. S. (1983). *Child's talk: Learning to use language.* New York: Norton.

Buchtal, F., & Faaborg-Anderson, K. L. (1964). Electromyography of laryngeal and
respiratory muscles. *Annals of Otology, Rhinology and Laryngology, 73,* 118–21.

Burling, R. (2000). Comprehension, production and conventionalization in the origins
of language. In C. Knight, M. Studdert-Kennedy, & J. R. Hurford (Eds.), *The
evolutionary emergence of language: Social function and the origins of linguistic form*
(pp. 27–39). Cambridge, UK: Cambridge University Press.

Butterworth, G., & Jarrett, N. (1991). What minds have in common is space: Spatial
mechanisms serving joint visual attention in infancy. *British Journal of Developmental Psychology, 9,* 55–72.

Butterworth, G., & Morrissette, P. (1996). Onset of pointing and the acquisition of
language in infancy. *Journal of Reproductive and Infant Psychology, 14,* 219–31.

Campos, J. J., & Stenberg, C. (1981). Perception, appraisal and emotion: The onset
of social referencing. In *Infant social cognition: Empirical and theoretical considerations.* Hillsdale NJ: Erlbaum.

Campos, J., Anderson, D. I., Barbu-Roth, M. A., Hubbard, E. M., Hertenstein, M. J.,
& Witherington, D. (2000). Travel broadens the mind. *Infancy, 1,* 149–220.

Capirci, O., Ontanari, S, & Volterra, V. (1998). The development of gesture and speech
as an integrated system. *New Directions for Child Development, 79,* 11–27.

Carpenter, M., Nagel, K., & Tomasello, M. (1998). Social cognition, joint attention and communicative competence from 9 to 15 months of age. *Monographs of the Society for Research in Child Development, 63,* 1–142.

Carter, A. (1975) The transformation of sensorimotor morphemes into words: A case study of the development of "more" and "mine." *Journal of Child Language, 2,* 233–50.

Chen, L. & Kent, R. (2005). Consonant-vowel co-occurrence patterns in Mandarin-learning infants. *Journal of Child Language, 32,* 507–34.

Cheney, D., & Seyfarth, R. M. (1990). *How monkeys see the world.* Chicago: University of Chicago Press.

Choi, S. (1997). Language-specific input and early semantic development: Evidence from children learning Korean. In D. I. Slobin (Ed.), *The cross-linguistic study of language acquisition, 5:* Expanding the context. Mahwah, NJ: Earlbaum.

Choi, S., & Bowerman, M. (1991). Learning to express motion events in English and Korean: The influence of language-specific lexical patterns. *Cognition, 41,* 83–121.

Choi, S., & Gopnik, A. (1995). Early acquisition of verbs in Korean: A cross-linguistic study. *Journal of Child Language, 22.*

Choi, S., McDonough, L., Bowerman, M., & Mandler, J. (1999). Early sensitivity to language-specific spatial categories in English and Korean. *Cognitive Development, 14,* 242–68.

Clark, E. (1978). Strategies for communicating. *Child Development, 59,* 953–59.

Clifton, R. K., Litovsky, R. Y., & Perris, E. E. (1991). Object representation guides infants' reaching in the dark. *Journal of Experimental Psychology: Human Perception and Performance, 17,* 323–29.

Cohen, B. H. (1986). The motor theory of voluntary thinking. In R. J. Davidson, G. E. Schwartz, & D. Shapiro (Eds.), *Consciousness and self-regulation: Advances in research and theory* (pp. 19–54). New York: Plenum Press.

Connolly, K., & Dalgleish, M. (1989). The emergence of a tool-using skill in infancy. *Developmental Psychology, 28,* 894–912.

Corman, H., & Escalona, S. (1969). Stages of sensorimotor development: A replication study. *Merril Palmer Quarterly, 15,* 351–61.

Corrigan, R. (1978). Language development as related to stage 6 object permanence development. *Journal of Child Language, 5,* 173–89.

Corrigan, R. (1979). Language development as related to stage 6 of object permanence development. *Journal of Child Language, 5,* 173–89.

Culicover, P. W., & Jackendoff, R. (2005). *Simpler syntax.* New York: Oxford University Press.

Culp, R. E., Watkins, R. V., Lawrence, H., & Letts, D. (1991). Maltreated children's use of language and speech development: Abused, neglected, and abused and neglected. *First Language, 11,* 377–89.

Damasio, A. R. (1989). Timelocked multi-regional retroactivation: A systems-level proposal for the neural substrate of recall and recognition. *Cognition, 33,* 25–62.

Darwin, C. (1872/1965). *The expression of the emotions in man and animals.* Chicago: University of Chicago Press.

Davis, B. L., & MacNeilage, P. F. (1995). The Articulatory basis of babbling. *Journal of Speech and Hearing Research, 38,* 1199–211.

Davis, B. L., MacNeilage, P. F., & Matyear, C. (2002). Acquisition of serial complexity in speech production: A comparison of phonetic and phonological approaches to first word production. *Phonetica, 59,* 75–107.

DeLoache, J. S., Sugarman, S., & Brown, A. L. (1985). The development of error correction strategies in young children's manipulative play. *Child Development, 56,* 928–39.

DePaolis, R., Keren-Portnoy, T., & Vihman, M. (2005). Input as output. Berlin: IASCL, 2005.

De Troyer, A., Kelly, S., Macklem, P. T., & Zin, W. A. (1985). Mechanics of intercostal space and actions of internal and external intercostal muscles. *Journal of Clinical Investigation, 75,* 850–57.

Donahue, M. (1986). Phonological constraints on the emergence of two-word utterances. *Journal of Child Language, 13,* 209–18.

Donahue, M. L. (1993). Early phonological and lexical development and otitis media: A diary study. *Journal of Child Language, 20,* 489–501.

Dore, J. (1985). Holophrases revisited: Their natural development from dialog. In M. Barrett (Ed.), *Children's single word speech.* New York: Wiley.

Dore, J., Franklin, M., Miller, R. T., & Ramer, A.L.H. (1976). Transitional phenomena in early language acquisition. *Journal of Child Language, 3,* 12–28.

Dunham, P., Dunham, F., & Curwin, W. (1993). Joint attentional states and lexical acquisition at 18 months. *Developmental Psychology, 29,* 827–31.

Dunn, J., & Wooding, C. (1977). Play in the home and its implications for learning. In B. Tizard & D. Harvey (Eds.), *The biology of play* (pp. 45–58). Philadelphia: Lippincott.

Earle, D. C. (1987). On the difference between cognitive and noncognitive systems. *The Behavioral and Brain Sciences, 10,* 177–78.

Echols, C. H. (1993). A perceptually based model of children's earliest productions. Cognition, 46, 245–96.

Edelman, G. M. (1987). *Neural Darwinism: The theory of neuronal group selection.* New York: Basic Books.

Edelman, G. M. (1992). *Bright Air, Brilliant Fire.* New York: Basic Books.

Edelman, G. M., & Tononi, G. (2000). *A universe of consciousness: How matter becomes imagination.* New York: Basic Books.

Efron, D. (1941). *Gesture and environment.* NY: King's Crown Press.

England, S. J., Kent, G., & Stogryn, H. A. (1985). Laryngeal muscle and diaphragmatic activities in conscious dog pups. *Respiration Physiology, 60,* 95–108.

Evarts, E. V. (1982). Analogies between central motor programs for speech and for limb movements. In S. Grillner, B. Lindblom, J. Lubker, & A. Persson (Eds.), *Speech motor control* (pp. 19–41). Oxford: Pergamon Press.

Fairbanks, L. A. (2000). The developmental timing of primate play: A neural selection model. In S. T. Parker, J. Langer, & M. L. McKinney (Eds.), *Biology, brains, and behavior* (pp. 131–58). Santa Fe: School of American Research Press.

Falk, D. (2003). Prelinguistic evolution in early hominins: Whence motherese. *The Behavioral and Brain Sciences, 27,* 401–541.

Fantz, R. L. (1961). The origin of form perception. *Scientific American, 204,* 66–72.

Feldman, H., Dale, P. S., Cambell, T. F., Colborn, D. K., Kurs-Lasky, M., Rockette, H. E., & Paradise, J. L. (2005). Concurrent and predictive validity of parent reports of child language at ages 2 and 3 years. *Child Development, 76,* 856–68.

Fenson, L., Dale, P. S., Reznick, J. S., Thal, D. J., & Pethick, S. J. (1994). Variability in early communicative development. *Monographs of the Society for Research in Child Development, 59* (5, Serial No. 242).

Ferguson, C. A. (1978). Learning to pronounce: The earliest stages of phonological development. In F. D. Minifie & L. L. LLoyd (Eds.), *Communicative and cognitive abilities: Early Behavioral assessment.* Baltimore, MD: University Park Press.

Ferguson, C. A., & Farwell, C. B. (1975). Words and sounds in early language acquisition. *Language, 51,* 419–39.

Ferguson, C. A., Menn, L., & Stoel-Gammon, C. (Eds.). (1992). *Phonological development: Models, research, implications.* Timonium, MD: York Press.

Fernald, A. (1992). Human maternal vocalizations to infants as biologically relevant signals: An evolutionary perspective. In J. Barkow, L. Cosmides, & J. Tooby (Eds.), *The adapted mind* (pp. 329–427). New York: Oxford University Press.

Fernald, A., & Morikawa, H. (1993). Common themes and cultural variation in Japanese and American mothers' speech to infants. *Child Development, 64,* 637–56.

Feyeriesen, P., & de Lannoy, J. (1991). *Gestures and speech: Psychological investigations.* Cambridge, UK: Cambridge Universtiy Press.

Fogel, A., & Thelen, E. (1987). Development of early expressive and communicative action: Reinterpreting the evidence from a dynamic systems perspective. *Developmental Psychology, 23,* 747–61.

Folven, R. J., & Bonvillian, J. (1991). The transition from nonreferential to referential language in children acquiring American Sign Language. *Developmental Psychology, 27,* 806–16.

Freeman, W. J. (1991). The physiology of perception. *Scientific American, 264,* 78–95.

Freeman, W. J., & Skarda, C. A. (1990). Representations: Who needs them? In J. L. McGaugh, N. M. Weinberger, & G. Lynch (Eds.), *Brain organization and memory: Cells, systems, and circuits.* New York: Oxford University Press.

Frick, J. E., Colombo, J., & Saxon, T. F. (1999). Individual and developmental differences in disengagement of fixation in early infancy. *Developmental Psychology, 70,* 537–48.

Ganger, J., & Brent, M. R. (2004). Reexamining the vocabulary spurt. *Developmental Psychology, 40,* 621–32.

Gentner, D. (1978). On relational meaning: The acquisition of verb meaning. *Child Development, 49,* 988–98.

Gentner, D. (1982). Why nouns are learned before verbs: Linguistic relativity versus natural partitioning. In S. Kuczaj (Ed.), *Language development. Vol. 2* (pp. 301–32). Hillsdale, NJ: Erlbaum.

Gershkoff-Stowe, L. (2003). The joint study of real time processes and development in naming. Biennial Meeting of the Society for Research in Child Development.

Gershkoff-Stowe, L. (2005). Imposing equivalence on things in the world: A dynamic systems perspective. In L. Gershkoff-Stowe & D. H. Rakison (Eds.), *Building object categories in developmental time* (pp. 175–208). Mahwah, NJ: Earlbaum.

Gershkoff-Stowe, L., & Smith, L. (2004). Shape and the first hundred nouns. *Child Development, 75,* 1098–114.

Gershkoff-Stowe, L., & Thelen, E. (2004). U-shaped changes in behavior: A dynamic systems perspective. *Journal of Cognition and Development, 68,* 11–36.

Gershkoff-Stowe, L., Connell, B., & Smith, L. (2006). Priming overgeneralizations in two- and four-year-old children. *Journal of Child Language, 33,* 461–86.

Gershkoff-Stowe, L., Thal, D., Smith, L. B., & Namy, L. L. (1997). Categorization and its developmental relation to early language. *Child Development, 68,* 843–59.

Gibson, E. J. (1969). *Principles of perceptual learning and development.* New York: Appleton-Century-Crofts.

Glick, J. A. (1992). Werner's relevance for contemporary developmental psychology. *Developmental Psychology, 28,* 558–65.

Goffman, E. (1978). Response cries. *Language, 54,* 787–815.

Goldberg, A. (2004). Learning argument structure generalizations. *Cognitive Linguistics, 14,* 289–316.

Goldfield, B. A., & Reznick, J. S. (1990). Early lexical acquisition: Rate, content, and the vocabulary spurt. *Journal of Child Language, 17,* 171–83.

Goldin-Meadow, S. (1998). The development of gesture and speech as an integrated system. *New Directions for Child Development, 79,* 29–42.

Goldin-Meadow, S., & Butcher, C. (2003). Pointing toward two-word speech. In S. Kita (Ed.), *Pointing: Where language, culture and cognition meet* (pp. 85–107). Mahwah, NJ: Erlbaum.

Goldman-Rakic, P. (1994). Specification of higher cortical functions. In S. H. Broman & J. Grafman (Eds.), *Atypical cognitive deficits in developmental disorders* (pp. 3–23). Hillsdale, NJ: Earlbaum.

Golinkoff, R., Mervis, C., & Hirsch-Pasek, J. (1994). Early object labels: The case for a developmental lexical principles framework. *Journal of Child Language, 21,* 125–56.

Goodwyn, S. W., & Acredolo, L. P. (1998). The development of gesture and speech as an integrated system. *New Directions for Child Development, 79,* 61–73.

Goodwyn, S. W., Acredolo, L. P., & Brown, C. A. (2000). Impact of symbolic gesturing on early language development. *Journal of Nonverbal Behavior, 24,* 81–103.

Gopnik, A. (1984). The acquisition of gone and the development of the object concept. *Journal of Child Language, 11,* 273–92.

Gopnik, A., & Choi, S. (1990). Do linguistic differences lead to cognitive differences? A cross-linguistic study of semantic and cognitive development. *First Language, 10,* 199–215.

Gopnik, A., & Meltzoff, A. (1984). Semantic and cognitive development in 15- to 21-month-old children. *Journal of Child Language, 11,* 495–513.

Gopnik, A., & Meltzoff, A. (1986). Relations between semantic and cognitive development in the one-word stage: the specificity hypothesis. *Child Development, 57,* 1040–53.

Gopnik, A., & Meltzoff, A. (1987). The development of categorization in the second year and its relation to other cognitive and linguistic developments. *Child Development, 58,* 1523–31.

Gopnik, A., & Meltzoff, A. N. (1992). Categorization and naming: Basic level sorting in eighteen-month-olds and its relation to language. *Child Development, 63,* 1091–103.

Gottfried, A., Rose, S. A., & Bridger, W. H. (1977). Cross-modal transfer in human infants. *Child Development, 48,* 118–23.

Grice, H. P. (1957). Meaning. *Philosophical Review, 66,* 377–88.

Guidetti, M. (2000). Pragmatic study of agreement and refusal messages in young French children. *Journal of Pragmatics, 32,* 569–82.

Gunnar, M. R., & Thelen, E. (Eds.). (1989). *Systems and development: The Minnesota symposium on child psychology. Vol. 22.* Hillsdale, NJ: Earlbaum.

Haith, M. M. (1998). Who put the cog in infant cognition? Is rich interpretation too costly? *Infant Behavior and Development, 21,* 167–79.

Hakke, R. J., & Somerville, S. J. (1985). Development of logical search skills in infancy. *Developmental Psychology, 21,* 176–86.

Halliday, M. (1975). *Learning how to mean: Explorations in the development of language.* New York: Elsevier-North Holland.

Harmon, C., Rothbart, M. K., & Posner, M. (1997). Distress and attention interactions in early infancy. *Motivation and Emotion, 21,* 27–43.

Harris, M., Barrett, M., Jones, D., & Brookes, S. (1988). Linguistic input and early word meaning. *Journal of Child Language, 15,* 77–94.

Harrison, V., de V. Heese, H., & Klein, M. (1968). The significance of grunting in hyaline membrane disease. *Pediatrics, 41,* 549–59.

Herr-Israel, E. (2006). *Single words to combinations: Longitudinal analysis reveals constructive processes integrating lexical and pragmatic development within a conversational context.* Unpublished Doctoral Dissertation. Rutgers University, New Brunswick, NJ.

Herr-Israel, E., & McCune, L. (2006). Dynamic event expression of motion events and the transition to verb meanings. In N. Gagarina & I. Gulgzow (Eds.), *Language specificity in the discovery of verb meaning.* The Hague, The Netherlands: Kluwer Academic Publishers.

Hirsh-Pasek, K., Tucker, M., & Golinkoff, R. M. (1996). Dynamic systems theory: Reinterpreting "Prosodic Bootstrapping" and its role in language acquisition. In J. L. Morgan & K. Demuth (Eds.), *Signal to syntax: Bootsrapping from speech to grammar in early acquisition* (pp. 449–66). Mahwah, NJ: Erlbaum.

Hofer, M. A., & Shair, H. N. (1978). Ultrasonic vocalizations during social interaction and isolation in 2-week-old rats. *Developmental Psychobiology, 11,* 495–504.

Hofer, M. A, & Shair, H. N. (1993). Ultrasonic vocalization, laryngeal braking and thermogenisis in rat pups: A reappraisal. *Behavioral Neuroscience, 107,* 354–62.

Hollich, J. H., Hirsch-Pasek, K., & Golinkoff, R. M. (2000). Breaking the language barrier: An emergentist coalition model for the origins of word learning. *Monographs of the Society for Research in Child Development., 65* (1, Serial No. 123).

Holmgren, K., Lindblom, B., Aurelius, G., Jalling, B., & Zetterstrom, R. (1986). On the phonetics of infant vocalization. In J. S. Perkell & D. H. Klatt (Eds.), *Precursors of early speech.* Basingstroke, Hampshire, UK: Macmillan.

Hood, B., & Willatts, P. (1986). Reaching in the dark to an object's remembered position: Evidence for object permanence in 5-month-old infants. *British Journal of Developmental Psychology, 4,* 57–65.

Hopper, P. J., & Thompson, S. A. (1980). Transitivity in grammar and discourse. *Language, 56,* 251–99.

Hornik, R., Risenhoover, N., & Gunnar, M. (1987). The effects of maternal positive, neutral, and negative affective communication on infant responses to new toys. *Child Development, 58,* 937–44.

Huttenlocher, J., Smiley, P., & Charney, R. (1983). Emergence of action categories in the child: Evidence from verb meanings. *Psychological Review, 90,* 72–93.

Iacoboni, M., Woods, R. P., Brass, M., Bekkering, H., Mazziotta, J. C., & Rizolatti, G. (1999). Cortical mechanisms of human imitation. *Science, 286,* 2526–28.

Ingram, D. (1974). Phonological rules in young children. *Journal of Child Language, 1,* 49–64.

Iverson, J. A., & Thelen, E. (1999). Hand, mouth and brain: The dynamic emergence of speech and gesture. *Journal of Consciousness Studies, 6,* 11–12.

Jackowitz, E., & Watson, M. (1980). Development of object transformations in early pretend play. *Developmental Psychology, 16,* 543–49.

Jacobs, J. R., Wetzel, A. B., & Hast, M. H. (1976). Laryngeal aortic baroreceptor pathways and cardiac arrhythmia. *Archives Artolaryngolica, 102,* 77–79.

Jaeger, J. J. (1997). How to say "Grandma": The problem of developing phonological representations. *First Language, 17,* 1–029.

Jakobson, R. (1941/1986). *Child language, aphasia, and language universals.* The Hague, The Netherlands: Mouton.

James, W. (1890*). The principles of psychology (Reprinted: New York: Dover, 1950).* New York: Holt.

Johnson, M. (1987). *The body in the mind.* Chicago: University of Chicago.

Johnson, M. H. (1997). *Developmental cognitive neuroscience.* Cambridge, MA: Blackwell.

Johnson, M. H., Posner, M. I., & Rothbart, M. K. (1991). Components of visual learning in early infancy: Contingency, anticipatory looking, and disengaging. *Journal of Cognitive Neuroscience, 3,* 335–44.

Johnson, S. P. (2004). Theories of development of the object concept. In G. Brenner & A. Slater (Eds.), *Theories of infant development* (pp. 174–204). Malden, MA: Blackwell.

Kahneman, D. (1973). *Attention and Effort.* Englewood Cliffs, NJ: Prentice Hall.

Kamhi, A. G. (1986). The elusive first word: The importance of the naming insight for the development of referential speech. *Journal of Child Language, 13,* 155–61.

Kaulfers, W. V. (1931). Curiosities of colloquial gesture. *Hispanica, 14,* 249–64.

Kellman, P. (1993). Kinematic foundations of infant visual perception. In C. Granrud (Ed.), *Visual Perception and Cognition in Infancy.* Hillsdale, NJ: Erlbaum.

Kellman, P. J., Spelke, E., & Short, K. R. (1986). Infant perception of object unity from translatory motion in depth and vertical translation. *Child Development, 57,* 72–76.

Kelly, C. A., & Dale, P. S. (1989). Cognitive skills associated with the onset of multi-word utterances. *Journal of Speech and Hearing Research, 32,* 645–56.

Kendon, A. (1986). Current issues in studying gesture. In J. Nespoulous, P. Perron, & A. R. Lecours (Eds.), *The biological foundations of gesture* (pp. 23–50). Hillsdale, NJ: Erlbaum.

Kent, R. D. (1992). The biology of phonological development. In C. A. Ferguson, L. Menn, & C. Stoel-Gammon (Eds.), *Phonological development: Models, research, implications.* Timmonium, MD: York Press.

Kirchner, J. A. (1987). Laryngeal reflex systems. In T. Baer, C. Sasaki, & K. Harris (Eds.), *Laryngeal function in phonation and respiration* (pp. 65–70). Boston: Little, Brown.

Koopmans-van Beinum, F. J., & van der Stelt, J. M. (1986). Early stages in the development of speech movements. In B. Linblom & R. Zetterstrom (Eds.), *Precursors of early speech* (pp. 37–50). New York: Stockton Press.

Kornhuber, H. H. (1987). Voluntary activity, readiness potential and motor program. In G. Adelman (Ed.), *Encyclopedia of neuroscience* (pp. 1302–3). Boston: Birkhauser.

Kuhl, P. K., & Meltzoff, A. N. (1982). The bimodal perception of speech in infancy. *Science, 218,* 1138–41.

Ladefoged, P. (1975). *A course in phonetics.* New York: Harcourt Brace Javonovich.

Lakoff, G. (1987). *Women, fire, and dangerous things.* Chicago: University of Chicago Press.

Lakoff, G. (1994). Reflections on metaphor and grammar. In M. Shibatani & S. Thompson (Eds.), *Essays in semantics and pragmatics* (pp. 133–43). Amsterdam/ Philadelphia: John Benjamins.

Lalonde, C. E., & Werker, J. F. (1995). Cognitive influences on cross-language speech perception in infancy. *Infant Behavior and Development, 18,* 459–76.

Lasink, J. M., & Richards, J. E. (1997). Heart rate and behavioral measures of attention in 6-, 9-, and 12-month-old infants during object exploration. *Child Development, 68,* 610–20.

LeCompte, G. K., & Gratch, G. (1972). Violation of a rule as a method of diagnosing infants' level of the object concept. *Child Development, 43,* 385–96.

Lennon, E. M. (1984). *Exploration, communication, and symbolization : Gestural development in infancy.* Unpublished master's thesis. Rutgers University: New Brunswick, NJ.

Leopold, W. F. (1939). *Speech development of a bilingual child* (Vol. I: Vocabulary growth in the first two years.). Evanston, IL: Northwestern University Press.

Leslie, A. M. (1987). Pretense and representation: The origins of "theory of mind." *Psychological Review, 4,* 412–26.

Leung, E. H. L., & Rheingold, H. L. (1981). Development of pointing as a social gesture. *Developmental Psychology, 17,* 215–20.

Lewis, M. M. (1936). *Infant speech.* New York: Harcourt Brace.

Lieven, E. V. M. (1994). Cross-linguistic and cross-cultural aspects of language addressed to children. In C. Gallaway & B. J. Richards (Eds.), *Input and interaction in language acquisition* (pp. 56–72). Cambridge, UK: Cambridge University Press.

Lieven, E. V. M., Pine, J. M., & Baldwin, G. (1997). Lexically based learning and early grammatical development. *Journal of Child Language, 24,* 187–219.

Lleo, C. (1990). Homonomy and reduplication: On the extended availabiliy of two strategies in phonological acquisition. *Journal of Child Language, 17,* 267–78.

Locke, J. L. (1983). *Phonological acquisition and change.* New York: Academic Press.

Lyons, J. (1968). *Introduction to theoretical linguistics.* Cambridge, UK: Cambridge University Press.

Macken, M. A. (1978). Permitted complexity in phonological development: One child's acquisition of Spanish consonants. *Lingua, 44,* 219–53.

Macken, M. A. (1979). Developmental reorganization of phonology: A hierarchy of basic units of acquisition. *Lingua, 49,* 11–49.

Macken, M. A. (1995). Phonological acquisition. In J. Goldsmith (Ed.), *Handbook of phonological theory.* Cambridge, MA: Blackwell.

Macnamara. (1972). Cognitive basis of language learning. *Psychological Review, 79,* 1–13.

Macnamara, J. (1982). *Names for things.* Cambridge, MA: MIT Press.

MacNeilage, P. F. (1987). Speech, motor control. In G. Adelman (Ed.), *Encyclopedia of neuroscience* (Vol. 2). Boston: Birkhauser.

MacNeilage, P. F. (1998). The frame/content theory of evolution of speech production. *The Behavioral and Brain Sciences, 21,* 499–511.

MacNeilage, P. F., & Davis, B. L. (1990). Acquisition of speech production: The acquisition of segmental independence. In W. J. Hardcastle & A. Marchal (Eds.), *NATO ASI Series: D. Speech Production and Speech Modeling* (pp. 55–68). Boston: Kluwer Academic Publishers.

MacNeilage, P. F., Studdert-Kennedy, M. G., & Lindblom, B. (1985). Planning and production of speech: An overview. In J. Lauter (Ed.), *Planning and production of speech in normally hearing and deaf people. ASHA Reports* (pp. 15–21).

MacWhinney, B. (1998). Models of the emergence of language. *Annual Review of Psychology, 49,* 199–227.

Mahler, M., Pine, F., & Bergman, E. (1975). *The psychological birth of the human infant.* New York: Basic Books.

Malt, B. C., Sloman, S. A., & Gennari, S. P. (2003). Speaking versus thinking about objects and actions. In D. Gentner & S. Goldin-Meadow (Eds.), *Language in mind: Advances in the study of language and thought* (pp. 81–112). Cambridge, MA: MIT Press.

Mandler, J. (1988). How to build a baby: On the development of an accessible representational system. *Cognitive Development, 3,* 113–36.

Mandler, J. (1992). How to build a baby: II. Conceptual primitives. *Psychological Review, 99,* 587–604.

Mandler, J. (1998). Chapter 6 representation. In D. Kuhn, & R. Siegler (Eds.), *Handbook of Child Psychology: Vol. 2. Cognition, perception, and language* (5th ed., pp. 255–308). New York: John Wiley & Sons.

Mandler, J. M. (2004). *The foundations of mind.* New York: Oxford University Press.

Mandler, J. M. (2007). Actions organize the infant's world. In K. Hirsh-Pasek & R. M. Golinkoff (Eds.), *Action meets word: How children learn verbs.* New York: Oxford University Press.

Mandler, J. M., & Bauer, P. J. (1988). The cradle of categorization: Is the basic level basic? *Cognitive Development, 3,* 247–64.

Mandler, J. M., & McDonoough, L. (1996). Drinking and driving don't mix: Inductive generalization in infancy. *Cognition, 59,* 307–35.

Mandler, J. M., & McDonough, L. (1993). Concept formation in infancy. *Cognitive Development, 8,* 291–318.

Maratsos, M. (1998). Commentary: relations of lexical specificity to general categories. *Linguistics, 36,* 831–46.

Margolis, E. (1994). A reassessment of the shift from the classical theory of concepts to protorype theory. *Cognition, 51,* 73–89.

Marler, P. (1969). Vocalizations of wild chimpanzees. In C. R. Carpenter (Ed.), *Proceedings of the Second International Conference on Primatology. Vol. 1* (pp. 94–100). Switzerland: Karger.

Matthei, E. H. (1989). Crossing boundaries: More evidence for word-level phonological constraints on early multi-word utterances. *Journal of Child Language, 16,* 41–54.

McCall, R. B. (1981). Nature-nurture and the two realms of development: A proposed integration with respect to mental development. *Child Development, 52,* 1–12.

McCune, L. (1992). First words: A dynamic systems view. In C. A. Ferguson, L. Menn, & C. Stoel-Gammon (Eds.), *Phonological development: Models, research, implications* (pp. 313–36). Parkton, MD: York Press.

McCune, L. (1993). The development of play as the development of consciousness. In M. Bornstein & A. O'Reilly (Eds.), *New directions in child development. The role of play in the development of thought.* San Francisco CA: Jossey-Bass.

McCune, L. (1995). A normative study of representational play at the transition to language. *Developmental Psychology, 31,* 198–206.

McCune, L. (1999). Children's transition to language: A human model for development of the vocal repertoire in extant and ancestral primate species? In B. J. King (Ed.), *Origins of language: What can nonhuman primates tell us?* Santa Fe, NM: SAR Press.

McCune, L. (2002). Mirror neurons registration of biological motion: A resource for evolution of communication and cognitive/linguistic meaning. In M. I. Staminov & V. Gallese (Eds.), *Mirror neurons and the evolution of language and brain.* Amsterdam, NE: John Benjamins.

McCune, L. (2006). Dynamic event words: From common cognition to varied linguistic expression. *First Language, 26,* 233–55.

McCune, L., DiPane, D., Fireoved, R., & Fleck, M. (1994). Play: A context for mutual regulation within mother-child interaction. In A. Slade & D. P. Wolf (Eds.), *Children at play: Clinical and developmental approaches to meaning and representation* (pp. 148–66). New York: Oxford University Press.

McCune-Nicolich, L., & Raph, J. (1978). Imitative language and symbolic maturity. *Journal of Psycholinguyistic Research, 7,* 401–17.

McCune, L., Veneziano, E., & Herr-Israel, E. (2004). Analysis of motion-event semantics in the transition from single words to combinatorial speech: Evidence from English and French. *Second Lisbon meeting on language acquisition with special reference to Romance languages.*

McCune, L., & Vihman, M. (1987). Vocal motor schemes. *Papers and Reports in Child Language Development, 26,* 72–79.

McCune, L., & Vihman, M. M. (1997). The transition to reference in infancy. Unpublished manuscript.

McCune, L., & Vihman, M. M. (1999). *Relational words + motion events: A universal bootstrap to syntax?* Poster presentation at the biennial meeting of the Society for Research in Child Development, Albuquerque, NM.

McCune, L., & Vihman, M. M. (2000). *Early phonetic and lexical development: A productivity approach.* Unpublished prepublication draft.

McCune, L., & Vihman, M. M. (2001). Early phonetic and lexical development: A productivity approach. *Journal of Speech, Language, and Hearing Research.*

McCune, L., Vihman, M. M., Roug-Hellichius, L., Delery, D. B., & Gogate, L. (1996). Grunt communication in human infants. *Journal of Comparative Psychology, 110,* 27–37.

McCune-Nicolich, L. (1981a). The cognitive basis of relational words. *Journal of Child Language, 8,* 15–36.

McCune-Nicolich, L. (1981b). Toward symbolic functioning: Structure of early pretend games and potential parallels with language. *Child Development, 52,* 785–97.

McCune-Nicolich, L., & Bruskin, C. (1981). Combinatorial competency in symbolic play and language. In K. Rubin (Ed.), *The play of children: Current theory and research.* Basel, Switzerland: Karger.

McDonough, L., Choi, S., & Mandler, J. (2003). Understanding spatial relations: Flexible infants, lexical adults. *Cognitive Psychology, 46,* 229–59.

McNeill, D. (1998). The development of gesture and speech as an integrated system. *New Directions for Child Development, 79,* 11–27.

McNeill, D. (Ed.). (2000). *Language and gesture.* Cambridge, UK: Cambridge University Press.

McNeill, D., & Duncan, S. D. (2000). Growth points in thinking for speaking. In D. McNeill (Ed.), *Language and gesture* (pp. 141–61). Cambridge, UK: Cambridge University Press.

Menn, L. (1971). Phonotactic rules at the beginning of speech. *Lingua, 26,* 225–51.

Menn, L. (1978). *Pattern, control, and contrast in beginning speech: A case study in the development of word form and word function. Doctoral Dissertation.* University of Illinois, Urbana.

Menn, L. (1983). Development of articulatory, phonetic, and phonological capabilities. In B. Butterworth (Ed.), *Language production* (Vol. 2). London: Academic Press.

Menyuk, P., Lieberglott, J., & Shultz, M. (1986). Predicting phonological development. In B. Lindblom & R. Zetterstrom (Eds.), *Precursors of early speech.* New York: Stockton Press.

Mervis, C. B., & Bertrand, J. (1995). Early lexical acquisition and the vocabulary spurt: A response to Goldfield & Reznick. *Journal of Child Language, 22,* 461–68.

Mills, D. L., Coffey-Corina, S., & Neville, H. J. (1994). Variability in cerebral organization during primary language acquisition. In G. Dawson & K. W. Fischer (Eds.), *Human behavior and the developing brain.* New York: Guilford Press.

Mills, D. L., Coffey-Corina, S., & Neville, H. J. (1997). Language comprehension and cerebral specialization from 13 to 20 months. *Developmental Neuropsychology, 13,* 397–445.

Mills, D. L., Conboy, B. T., & Paton, C. (2005). Do changes in brain organization reflect shifts in symbolic functioning? In L. A. Namy (Ed.), *Symbol use and symbolic representation: Developmental and comparative perspectives* (pp. 123–53). Mawah, NJ: Earlbaum.

Mills, D. L., & Neville, H. J. (1997). Electrophysiological studies of language and language impairment. *Seminars in Pediatric Neurology, 4,* 125–34.

Mills, D. L., Plunkett, K., Prat, C., & Schafer, G. (2005). Watching the infant brain learn words: Effects of vocabulary size and experience. *Cognitive Development, 20,* 19–31. *Unknown.*

Milner, A. D., Saunders, R. A., & Hopkins, I. E. (1978). Is air trapping important in the maintenance of functional residual capacity in the hours after birth? *Early Human Development, 2,* 97–105.

Moore, C., & Dunham, P. J. (Eds.). (1995). *Joint attention: Its origin and development.* Hillsdale, NJ: Earlbaum.

Morissette, P., Ricard, M., & Gouin-Decarie, T. (1992). Comprehension of pointing and joint visual attention: A longitudinal study [abstract]. *Infant Behavior and Development, 15,* 591.

Munakata, Y., McClelland, J. L., & Johnson, M. H. (1997). Rethinking infant knowledge: Toward an adaptive process account of successes and failures in object permanence tasks. *Psychological Review, 104,* 686–713.

Nader, K., & Schafe, G. & Le Doux, J. E. (2000). Fear memories require protein synthesis in the amygdala for reconsolidation after retrieval. *Nature, 406,* 722–26.

Nelson, K. (1973). *Structure and strategy in learning to talk* (Monographs of the Society for Research in Child Development, 38 (1–2, Serial No. 149).

Nelson, K. (1985). *Making sense: The acquisition of shared meaning.* New York: Academic Press.

Nelson, K., Hampson, J., & Shaw, L. K. (1993). Nouns in early lexicons: Evidence, explanations, and implications. *Journal of Child Language, 20,* 61–84.

Netsell, R. (1981). The acquisition of speech motor control: A perspective with directions for research. In R. Stark (Ed.), *Language behavior in infancy and early childhood* (pp. 127–56). New York: Elsevier Science.

Neville, H. J., Kutas, M., & Schmidt, A. L. (1982a). Event-related potential studies of cerebral specialization during reading: I. Studies of normal adults. *Brain and Language, 16,* 300–15.

Neville, H. J., Kutas, M., & Schmidt, A. L. (1982b). Event-related potential studies of cerebral specialization during reading: II Studies of congenitally deaf adults. *Brain and Language, 16,* 316–37.

Nicolich, L. McC. (1975). *A longitudinal study of representational play in relation to spontaneous imitation and the development of multiword language.* Unpublished doctoral dissertation. Rutgers University, New Brunswick, NJ.

Nicolich, L. McC. (1977). Beyond sensorimotor intelligence: Assessment of symbolic maturity through analyais of pretend play. *Merrill Palmer Quarterly, 23,* 89–101.

Ninio, A. (1993). Is early speech situational? An examination of some current theories about the relations of early utterances to context. In D. J. Messer & G. J. Turner (Eds.), *Critical influences on child language acquisition and development* (pp. 23–39). New York: St. Martin's Press.

Ninio, A. (1995). Expression of communicative intents in the single word period and the vocabulary spurt. In K. E. Nelson & Z. Reger (Eds.), *Children's language* (Vol. 8). Hillsdale, NJ: Earlbaum.

Ninio, A. (1999a). Model learning in syntactic development: Intransitive verbs. *International Journal of Bilingualism, 3,* 111–31.

Ninio, A. (1999b). pathbreaking verbs in syntactic development and the question of pro-typical transitivity. *Journal of Child Language, 26,* 619–53.

Oakes, L. M., & Madole, K. L. (2003). Principles of developmental change in infants' category formation. In D. H. Rakison & L. M. Oakes (Eds.), *Early category and concept development: Making sense of the blooming buzzing confusion* (pp. 132–58). New York: Oxford University Press.

Oakes, L. M., Plumert, J. M., Lasink, J. M., & Merryman, J. D. (1996). Evidence for task-dependent categorization in infancy. *Infant Behavior and Development, 19,* 425–40.

Oakes, L. M., & Rakison, D. H. (2003). Issues in the early development of concepts and categories. In D. H. Rakison & L. M. Oakes (Eds.), *Early Category and concept development* (pp. 3–23). New York: Oxford University Press.

Ogura, T. (1990). A longitudinal study of the relationship between early language development and play development. *Journal of Child Language, 18,* 273–94.

Oller, D. K. (1986). Metaphonology and infant vocalizations. In B. Lindblom & R. Zetterstrom (Eds.), *Precursors of early speech.* Basingstoke, Hampshire, UK: Macmillan.

Oller, K. (1980). The emergence of speech sounds in infancy. In G. H. Yeni-komshian, J. F. Kavanagh, & C. A. Ferguson (Eds.), *Child phonology. Vol. 1: Production* (pp. 93–112). New York: Academic Press.

Oller, K., & Lynch, M. (1992). Infant vocalizations and innovations in infraphonology: Toward a broader theory of developmental disorders. In C. A. Ferguson, L. Menn, & C. Stoel-Gammon (Eds.), *Phonological Development: Models, Research, Implications.* Timonium, MD: York Press.

Oller, K., Weiman, L. A., Doyle, W. J., & Ross, C. (1992). Infant babbling and speech. *Journal of Child Language, 3,* 1–11.

Oviatt, S. L. (1980). The emerging ability to comprehend language: An experimental approach. *Child Development, 51,* 97–106.

Ozcaliskan, S., & Goldin-Meadow, S. (2005). Do parents lead their children by the hand? *Journal of Child Language 32, 3* (pp 481–505).

Pan, B. A., Rowe, M. L., Singr, J. D., & Snow, C. E. (2005). Maternal correlates of growth in toddler vocabulary production from low income families. *Child Development, 76,* 763–82.

Pattterson, A., & Werker, J. (1999). Matching phonetic information in lips and voice is robust in 4-month-old infants. *Infant Behavior and Development, 22,* 237–47.

Peirce, C. S. (1932). In C. Jaetshorne & P. Weiss (Eds.). *Collected Papers.* Cambridge, MA.: Harvard University Press.

Piaget, J. (1962). *Play, Dreams and Imitation.* New York: Norton.

Piaget, J. (1952). *The origins of intelligence in children.* New York: International Universities Press.

Piaget, J. (1954). *The construction of reality in the child.* New York: Basic Books.

Piaget, J., & Inhelder, B. (1969). *The psychology of the child.* New York: Basic Books.

Plooij, F. X. (1984). *The behavior of free-living chimpanzee babies and infants.* Norwood, NJ: Ablex.

Porges, S. (1992). Autonomic regulation and attention. In B. A. Campbell, H. Hayne, & K. Richardson (Eds.), *Attention and information processing in infants and adults.* Hillsdale, NJ: Earlbaum.

Porges, S. W., Doussard-Roosevelt, J. A., & Maiti, A. K. (1994). Vagal tone and the physiological regulation of attention. In N. A. Fox (Ed.), *Development of emotion regulation: Biological and behavioral considerations 59* (2–3, Serial No. 240, pp. 167–86): Monographs of the Society for Research in Child Development.

Posner, M. I., & Rothbart, M. K. (1994). Attentional regulation: From mechanism to culture. In P. Bertelson, P. Elen, & G. d'Ydewalle (Eds.), *International perspectives on psychological science. Vol. I: Leading themes* (pp. 41–55). Hillsdale, NJ: Erlbaum.

Premack, D., & Woodruff, G. (1978). Does the chimpanzee have a theory of mind? *The Behavioral and Brain Sciences, 4,* 515–26.

Priestly, T. M. S. (1977). One idiosyncratic strategy in the aquisition of phonology. *Journal of Child Language, 4,* 45–66.

Pulvermuller, F. (2002). *The neuroscience of language.* Cambridge, UK: Cambridge.

Quinn, P. C. (2003). Concepts are not just for objects: Categorization of spatial relational information by infants. In D. I. Rakison & L. M. Oakes (Eds.), *Early category and concept development: Making sense of the blooming, buzzing confusion* (pp. 50–76). New York: Oxford University Press.

Quinn, P. C. (2005). Young infants' categorization of human versus nonhuman animals: Roles for knowledge access and perceptual process. In L. Gershkoff-Stowe & D. H. Rakison (Eds.), *Building object categories in developmental time* (pp. 107–30). Mahwah, NJ: Erlbaum.

Ramsay, D., & Campos, J. (1978). The onset of representation and entry into stage 6 of object permanence development. *Developmental Psychology, 52,* 785–97.

Remmers, J. E. (1973). Extra-segmental reflexes derived from intercostal afferents: Phrenic and laryngeal responses. *Journal of Physiology, London, 233,* 45–62.

Reppas, J. B., Niyogi, S., Dale, A. M., Sereno, M. I., & Tootell, R. B. H. (1997). Representation of motion boundaries in retinotopic human visual cortical areas. *Nature, 388,* 175–79.

Rescorla, I, & Bernstein-Ratner, N. A. (1996). Phonetic profiles of toddlers with specific expressive language impairment (SLI-E). *Journal of Speech and Hearing Research, 39,* 153–65.

Ribot, T. A. (1889). *The Psychology of Attention.* New York: Humboldt.

Ricciuti, H. N. (1965). Object grouping and selective ordering behavior in infants. *Merrill-Palmer Quarterly, 11,* 129–48.

Richards, J. E. (1987). Infant visual sustained atttention and respiratory sinus arrhythmia. *Child Development, 58,* 488–96.

Richards, J. E. (1997). Peripheral stimulus location by infants: Attention, age, and individual differences in heart rate variability. *Journal of Experimental Psychology: Human Perception and Performance, 23,* 667–80.

Richards, J. E., & Casey, B. J. (1991). Heart rate variability during attention phases in young infants. *Psychophysiology, 28,* 43–53.

Richards, J. E., & Casey, B. J. (1992). Development of sustained visual attention in the human infant. In H. Campbell, H. Hayne, & K. Richardson (Eds.), *Attention and information processing in infants and adults*. Hillsdale, NJ: Erlbaum.

Richards, J. E., & Gibson, T. L. (1997). Extended visual fixation in young infants: Look distribution, heart-rate changes, and attention. *Child Development, 68,* 1041–56.

Richman, A. L., Miller, P. M., & LeVine, R. A. (1992). Cultural and educational variation in maternal responsiveness. *Developmental Psychology, 28,* 614–21.

Robb, M. P., & Bauer, H. R. (1991). The ethologic model of phonetic development: The closant curve. *Clinical Linguistics & Phonetics, 5,* 339–53.

Roberts, J. A. (1998). *Cognitive and lingusitic development before and after the vocabulary spurt*. Unpublished doctoral dissertation, Boston University, Boston, MA.

Rochat, P., & Hespos, S. J. (1997). Differential rooting response by neonates: Evidence for an early sense of self. *Early Development and Parenting, 6,* 105–12.

Rocissano, L., & Yatchmink, Y. (1983). language skill and interaction patterns in prematurely born toddlers. *Child Development, 54,* 1229–41.

Rogoff, B., Mistray, J., Goncu, A., & Mosier, C. (1993). *Guided particpation in cultural activity by toddlers and caregivers*: Monographs of the Society for Research in Child Development, *58* (8, Serial No. 236).

Rosch, E. (1978). Principles of categorization. In E. Rosch & B. Lloyd (Eds.), *Cognition and categorization*. Hillsdale, NJ: Erlbaum.

Rosch, E. (1999). Reclaiming concepts. *Journal of Consciousness Studies, 6,* 61–77.

Roug, L., Landberg, I., & Lundberg, L. (1989). Phonetic development in early infancy: A study of four Swedish children during the first 18 months of life. *Journal of Child Language, 16,* 19–40.

Roug-Hellichius, L. (1998). *Babble, grunts, and words: A study of phonetic shape and functional use in the beginnings of language*. Dissertation. Department of Linguistics, Stockholm University, Stockholm.

Rovee-Collier, C. (1995). Time windows in cognitive development. *Developmental Psychology, 31,* 147–69.

Ruff, H. A. (1982). Role of manipulation in infants' responses to the invariant properties of objects. *Developmental Psychology, 18,* 682–91.

Ruff, H. A. (1984). Infant's manipulative exploration of objects: Effects of early age and object characteristics. *Developmental Psychology, 20,* 9–20.

Ruff, H. A. (1986). Components of attention during infants manipulative exploration. *Child Development, 57,* 105–14.

Ruff, H. A., & Rothbart, M. (1996). *Development of attention in infants and children*. New York: Oxford University Press.

Sameroff, A. J. (1983). Developmental systems: contexts and evolution. In P. H. S. E. Mussen & W. V. E. Kessen (Eds.), *Handbook of Child Psychology (Vol. 1. History, theory and methods (4th ed.,* pp. 237–94). New York: John Wiley & Sons.

Sameroff, A. J. (1989). Commentary: General systems and the regulation of development. In M. r Gunnar & E. Thelen (Eds.), *Systems and development* (pp. 219–35). Hillsdale, NJ: Erlbaum.

Sameroff, A., & Fiese, B. (1990). Transactional regulation and early intervention. In S. J. Meisels & J. P. Shonkoff (Eds.), *Handbook of early childhood intervention* (pp. 119–49). New York: Press Syndicate of the University of Cambridge.

Samuelson, A. K., & Smith, L. B. (1998). Memory and attention make smart word learning: An alternative account of Akhtar, Carpenter and Tomasello. *Child Development, 69,* 94–104.

Sartre, J. (1948/1962). *The psychology of imagination.* New York: Philosophical Library.

Savage-Rumbaugh, E. S., Romsky, M., Hopkins, W. & Sevcik, R. (1989). Symbol acquisition and use by *Pan troglodytes I, Pan paniscus, Homo sapiens.* In P. Heltne & L. A. Marquardt (Eds.), *Understanding chimpanzees* (pp. 266–95). Cambridge, MA: Harvard University Press.

Schachtel, E. G. (1954). The development of focal attention and the emergence of reality. *Psychiatry, 17,* 309–24.

Schegloff, E. (1972). Sequencing in conversational openings. In J. Gumperz & D. Hymes (Eds.), *Directions in sociolinguistics* (p. 3). New York: Holt, Rinehart & Winston.

Schieffelin, B. B. (1990). *The give and take of everyday life: Language socialization of Kaluli children.* New York: Cambridge University Press.

Schieffelin, B. B., & Ochs, E. (1998). A cultural perspective on the transition from prelinguistic to linguistic communication. In D. Woodhead F & K. Littleton (Eds.), *Cultural worlds of early childhood* (pp. 48–63). New York: Open University.

Schlesinger, I. M. (1971). Production of utterances and language acquisition. In D. I. Slobing (Ed.), *The ontogenisis of grammar* (pp. 63–101). New York: Academic Press.

Searle, J. (1983). *Intentionality.* Cambridge, UK: Cambridge University Press.

Searle, J. (1992). *The rediscovery of the mind.* Cambridge, MA: MIT Press.

Seyfarth, R., & Cheney, D. (1986). Vocal development in vervet monkeys. *Animal Behaviour, 34,* 1640–58.

Shepard, R. (1994). Perceptual-cognitive universals as reflections of the world. *Psychonomic Bulleting and Review, 1,* 2–28.

Simmonds, R. J., & Schiebel, A. B. (1989). The post natal development of the motor speech area: A preliminary study. *Brain and* Language, 37, 42–53.

Sinclair, H., Stambak, M., Lezine, I., Rayna, S., & Verba, M. (1989). *Infants and objects: The creativity of cognitive development.* New York: Academic Press.

Sinclair, M. (1970). The transition from sensorimotor to symbolic activity. *Interchange, 1,* 119–26.

Slade, A. (1987). A longitudinal study of maternal involvement and symbolic play during the toddler period. *Child Development, 58,* 367–75.

Slonim, N. B., & Hamilton, L. H. (1981). *Respiratory physiology.* St. Louis, MO: Mosbey.

Smiley, P., & Huttenlocher, J. (1995). Conceptual development and children's early words for events, objects and persons. In M. Tomasello & W. E. Merriman (Eds.), *Beyond names for things* (pp. 21–62). Hillsdale, NJ: Erlbaum.

Smith, E. E. (1995). Concepts and categorization. In E. E. Smith & Osherson (Eds.), *Thinking: An invitation to cognitive science. Vol. 3* (2nd ed., pp. 3–33). Cambridge, MA: MIT Press.

Smith, L. (2005). Emerging ideas about categories. In *Building object categories in developmental time* (pp. 159–74). Mahwah, NJ: Erlbaum.

Snyder, L. S., Bates, E., & Bretherton, I. (1981). Content and context in early lexical development. *Journal of Child Language, 6,* 565–82.

Sorce, J. F., Emde, R. N., Campos, J., & Klinnert, M. D. (1985). Maternal emotional signalling: Its effect on the visual cliff behavior of one-year-olds. *Developmental Psychology, 21,* 195–200.

Spelke, E. S., Katz, G., Purcell, S. E., Ehrlich, S. M., & Breinleiner, K. (1994). Early knowledge of object motion: continuity and inertia. *Cognition, 51,* 131–76.

Spelke, E. S., & Van de Wall, G. A. (1993) Perceiving and reasoning about objects: Insights from infants. In E. Naomi, R. McCarthy, B. Brewer (Eds.) Spatial representation: problems in philosophy and psychology (pp. 297–330). Cambridge, MA: MIT Press.

Stark, R. E., Bernstein, L. E., & Demorest, M. E. (1993). Vocal communication in the first 18 months of life. *Journal of Speech and Hearing Resarch, 36,* 548–58.

Stemberger, J. P. (1992). A connectionist view of child phonology. In C. A. Ferguson, L. Menn, & C. Stoel-Gammon (Eds.), *Phonological development: Models, research, implications* (pp. 165–90). Timonium, MD: York Press.

Stern, D. (1985). *The interpersonal world of the infant: A view from psychoanalysis and developmental psychology.* New York: Basic Books.

Stewart, K. J., & Harcourt, A. H. (1994). Gorillas' vocalizations during rest periods: Signals of impending departure? *Behaviour, 130,* 29–40.

Stoel-Gammon, C. (1988). Prelinguistic vocalizations of hearing-impaired and normally hearing subjects: A comparison of consonantal inventories. *Journal of Speech and Hearing Disorders, 53,* 302–15.

Stoel-Gammon, C. (1989). Prespeech and early speech development of two late talkers. *First Language, 9,* 207–24.

Stoel-Gammon, C. (1992). Prelinguistic vocal development and predictions. In C. A. Ferguson, L. Menn, & C. Stoel-Gammon (Eds.), *Phonological development: Models, research, implications* (pp. 439–56). Timonium, MD: York Press.

Stoel-Gammon, C. (1998). Sounds and words in early language acquisition: The relationship between lexical and phonological development. In R. Paul (Ed.), The Speech-language connection (pp. 25–52). Baltimore, MD: Paul H. Brookes.

Stoel-Gammon, C., & Cooper, J. A. (1984). Patterns of early lexical and phonological development. *Journal of Child Language, 11,* 247–71.

Stoel-Gammon, C., & Otomo, K. (1986). Babbling development of hearing-impaired and normally hearing subjects. *Journal of Speech and Hearing Disorders, 51,* 33–41.

Sugarman, S. (1982). Developmental change in early representational intelligence: Evidence from spatial classification strategies and related verbal expressions. *Cognitive Psychology, 14,* 410–49.

Sugarman, S. (1983). *Children's early thought.* Cambridge, UK: Cambridge University Press.

Talmy, L. (1975). The semantics and syntax of motion. In J. P. Kimball (Ed.), *Semantics and syntax* (pp. 181–238). New York: Academic.

Talmy, L. (1983). How language structures space. In H. Pick & L. Acredolo (Eds.), *Spatial orientation: Theory, research, application* (pp. 225–82). New York: Plenum Press.

Talmy, L. (1985). Lexicalization patterns: Semantic structure in lexical forms. In T. Shopen (Ed.), *Language typology and syntactic description* (Vol. III: Grammatical categories and the lexicon). Cambridge, UK: Cambridge University Press.

Talmy, L. (1988). Force dynamics in language and cognition. *Cognitive Science, 12,* 49–100.

Talmy, L. (1996). Fictive motion in language and "ception." In P. Bloom, M. A. Peterson, L. Nadel, M. F. Garrett (Eds.), *Language and space: Language, speech, and communication* (pp. 211–76). Cambridge, MA: MIT Press.

Talmy, L. (2000). *Toward a cognitive semantics* (Vol. I: Concept Structuring Systems). Cambridge, MA: MIT Press.

Tanis-LeMonda, C. S., Bornstein, M. H., & Baumwell, L. (2001). Maternal responsiveness and children's achievement of language milestones. *Child Development, 72,* 748–67.

Thal, D. J., Oroz, M., & McCaw, V. (1995). Phonological and lexical development in normal and late-talking toddlers. *Appplied Psycholinguistics, 16,* 407–24.

Thelen. (1989). Self-organization in developmental processes: Can systems approaches work? In M. R. Gunnar & E. Thelen (Eds.), *The Minnesota symposia on child psychology: Vol. 22. Systems and development* (pp. 77–117). Hillsdale, NJ: Erlbaum.

Thelen, E. (1981). Rythmical behavior in infancy: An ethological perspective. *Developmental Psychology, 17,* 237–57.

Thelen, E. (1991). Motor aspects of emergent speech. In N. A. Krasnegor, D. M. Rumbaugh, R. L. Schiefelbusch, & M. Studdert-Kennedy (Eds.), *Biological and behavioral determinants of language development.* Hillsdale, NJ: Erlbaum.

Thelen, E. (1993). Timing and developmental dynamics in the acquisition of early motor skills. In G. Turkewitz & D. A. Devenny (Eds.), *Developmental Time and Timing* (pp. 85–104). Hillsdale, NJ: Erlbaum.

Thelen, E., Corbetta, D., & Spencer, P. (1996). The development of reaching during the first year: The role of movement speed. *Journal of Experimental Psychology: Human perception and performance, 22,* 1059–76.

Thelen, E., & Fisher, D. M. (1982). Newborn stepping: An explanation for a "disappearing reflex." *Developmental Psychology, 18,* 760–77.

Thelen, E., & Fisher, D. M. (1983). From spontaneous to instrumental behavior: Kinematic analysis of movement changes during very early learning. *Child Development, 54,* 129–40.

Thelen, E., Kelso, J., & Fogel, A. (1987). Self organizing systems and infant motor development. *Developmental Review, 7,* 39–65.

Thelen, E., Schoner, C., & Smith, L. B. (2001). The dynamics of embodiment: A field theory of infant perseverative reaching. *The Behavioral and Brain Sciences, 24,* 1–86.

Thelen, E., & Smith, L. B. (1994). *A dynamic systems approach to the development of cognition and action.* Cambridge, MA: MIT Press.

Thelen, E., & Smith, L. B. (2006). Dynamic systems theories. In R. M. Lerner & W. Damon (Eds.), *Handbook of child psychology* (6th ed., Vol. 1 Theoretical models of human development, pp. 258–312). Hoboken, NJ: John Wiley & Sons.

Thomas, D. G., Campos, J. J., Shucard, D. W., & Ramsay, D. S. (1981). Semantic competency in infancy: A signal detection approach. *Child Development, 52,* 798–803.

Tinbergen, N. (1952). "Derived" activities: Their origin, causation, biological significance, origin, and emancipation during evolution. *Quarterly Review of Biology, 27,* 1–32.

Tomasello, M. (1992). *First verbs: A case study of early grammatical development.* New York: Cambridge University Press.

Tomasello, M. (2003). *Constructing a language: A usage-based theory of language acquisition.* Cambridge, MA: Harvard University Press.

Tomasello, M., & Farrar, J. (1984). Cognitive bases of lexical development: Object permanence and relational words. *Journal of Child Language, 11,* 477–93.

Tononi, G., & Edelman, G. (1998). Consciousness and complxity. *Science, 282,* 1846–51.

Tronick, E. Z., Morelli, G. A., & Ivey, P. K. (1992). The Efe forager infant and toddler's pattern of social relationships: Multiple and simultaneous. *Developmental Psychology, 28,* 568–77.

Tucker, D. M. (2002). Embodied meaning. In T. Givon & B. M. Malle (Eds.), *The evolution of language out of pre-language* (pp. 51–81). Amsterdam: John Benjamins.

Uzgiris, I., & Hunt, J. (1975). *Assessment in infancy: Ordinal scales of psychological development.* Champaign: University of Illinois Press.

Varela, F. J., Thompson, E., & Rosch, E. (1991). Cambridge MA: MIT Press.

Vatikiotis-Bateson, E., & Yehia, H. (1997). Unified physiological model of audible-visible speech production. *ESCA Eurospeech 97,* 2031–34.

Velleman, S. L., & Vihman, M. M. (2002). Whole-word phonology and templates: Trap, bootstrap or some of each? *Language, Speech, and Hearing in Services Schools, 33,* 9–23.

Veneziano, E. (1981). Early language and nonverbal representation: A reassessment. *Journal of Child Language, 8,* 541–63.

Veneziano, E. (1999). Early lexical, morphological and syntactic development in French: Some complex relations. *International Journal of Bilingualism, 3,* 183.

Vihman, M. M. (1976). From prespeech to speech: On early phonology. *Stanford Papers and Reports on Child Language Development, 12,* 230–44.

Vihman, M. M. (1985). Language differentiation by the bilingual infant. *Journal of Child Language, 12,* 297–324.

Vihman, M. M. (1992). Early syllables and the construction of phonology. In C. A. Ferguson, L. Menn, & C. Stoel-Gammon (Eds.), *Phonological Development: Models, Research, Implications.* Parkton, MD: York Press.

Vihman, M. M. (1996). *Phonological development: The origin of language in the child.* Oxford, UK: Blackwell.

Vihman, M. M. (1999). The transition to grammar in a bilingual child: Positional patterns, model learning, and relational words. *The International Journal of Bilingualism, 3,* 267–301.

Vihman, M., & Croft, W. (2007). Phonological development: Toward a radical template phonology. *Linguistics, 45,* 683–725.

Vihman, M. M., Ferguson, C. A., & Elbert, M. (1986). Phonological development from babbling to speech: Common tendencies and individual differences. *Applied Psycholinguistics, 7,* 3–40.

Vihman, M. M., & Greenlee, M. (1987). Individual differences in phonological development: Ages one and three years. *Journal of Speech and Hearing Research, 30,* 503–21.

Vihman, M. M., & Kunnari, S. (2006). The sources of phonological knowledge: A cross-linguistic perspective. *Recherches Linguistiqes de Vincennes, 45,* 683–725.

Vihman, M. M., Macken, M. A., Miller, R., Simmons, H., & Miller, J. (1985). From babbling to speech: A reassessment of the continuity issue. *Language, 61,* 395–443.

Vihman, M. M., & McCune, L. (1994). When is a word a word? *Journal of Child Language, 21,* 517–42.

Vihman, M. M., & Miller, R. (1988). Words and babble at the threshold of language acquisition. In M. D. Smith & J. Locke (Eds.), *The emergent lexicon: The child's development of a linguistic vocabulary* (pp. 151–84). New York: Academic Press.

Vihman, M. M., & Velleman, S. (1989). Phonological reorganization: A case study. *Language and Speech, 32,* 149–70.

Vihman, M. M., & Velleman, S. (2000). Phonetics and the origins of phonology. In N. Burton-Jones, P. Carr, & G. Docherty (Eds.), *Conceptual and empirical foundations of phonology* (pp. 305–39). Oxford, UK: Oxford University Press.

Vihman, M. M., Velleman, S., & McCune, L. (1994). How abstract is child phonology? In M. Yavas (Ed.), *First and second language phonology* (pp. 9–44). San Diego, CA: Singular Publishing Group.

Vygotsky, L. (1934/1962). *Thought and Language.* Cambridge, MA: MIT Press.

Vygotsky, L. S. (1935/1978). Interaction between learning and development. In M. Cole, V. John-Steiner, S. Scribner, & E. Souberman (Eds.), *Mind in Society* (pp. 79–91). Cambridge, MA: Harvard University Press.

Waddington, C. H. (1966). *Principles of development and differentiation.* New York: Macmillan.

Walden, T. A., & Ogan, T. A. (1988). The development of social referencing. *Child Development, 59,* 1230–40.

Ward, N. (2001). *Sound symbolism in "uh-hu," "uh-hn," "mm," "uh" and the like.* : Annual Meeting of the Linguistic Society of America, Washington, DC.

Ward, N. (2004). Pragmatic functions of prosodic features in nonlexical utterances. *Speech Prosody,* 325–28.

Ward, N. (2006). Non-lexidal conversational sounds in American English. *Pragmatics and Cognition, 14 (1):* 113–84.

Waterson, N. (1971). Child phonology: A prosodic view. *Journal of Linguistics, 7,* 179–211.

Werker, J., Cohen, L., Lloyd, V. L., Casasola, M., & Stager, C. L. (1998). Acquisition of word-object associations by 14-month-old infants. *Developmental Psychology, 34,* 1289–309.

Werker, J. F., Lloyd, V. L., Pegg, J. E., & Polka, L. (1996). Putting the baby in the bootstraps: Toward a more complete understanding of the role of input in infant speech processing. In J. L. Morgan & K. Demuth (Eds.), *Signal to syntax: Boot-strapping from speech to grammar in early acquisition* (pp. 427–48). Mahwah, NJ: Erlbaum.

Werner, H., & Kaplan, B. (1948/1963). *Symbol formation.* New York: John Wiley & Sons.

Winnicott, D. W. (1966/1987). The ordinary devoted mother. In *Babies and their mothers.* New York: Addison Wesley.

Xu, F. (2005). Categories, kinds, and object individuation in infancy. In L. Gershkoff-Stowe & D. H. Rakison (Eds.), *Building object categories in developmental time* (pp. 63–90). Mahwah,NJ: Erlbaum.

Xu, F., & Carey, S. (1996). Infants' metaphysics: The case of numerical identity. *Cognitive Psychology, 30,* 111–53.

Xu, F., Carey, S., & Quint, N. (2004). The emergence of kind-based object individuation in infancy. *Cognitive Psychology, 49,* 155–90.

Zachry, W. (1978). Ordinality and interdependence of representation and language development in infancy. *Child Development, 49,* 681–87.

Zang, R., & Mills, D. L. (2007). Increased brain activity to infant-directed speech in 6- and 13-month-old infants. *Infancy, 11,* 31–62.

Zheng, M., & Goldin-Meadow, S. (2002). Thought before language: How deaf and hearing children express motion events across cultures. *Cognition, 85,* 145–70.

Author Index

Subject Index

Note: Page numbers followed by f and t indicate figures and tables, respectively.